Jubilee Celebration Comittee

Account of the Celebration of the Jubilee of Uniform Inland Penny Postage

At the Venetian Chamber, Holborn Restaurant, at the Guildhall, at the Museum of Science and Art, South Kensington

Jubilee Celebration Comittee

Account of the Celebration of the Jubilee of Uniform Inland Penny Postage
At the Venetian Chamber, Holborn Restaurant, at the Guildhall, at the Museum of Science and Art, South Kensington

ISBN/EAN: 9783337169978

Printed in Europe, USA, Canada, Australia, Japan

Cover: Foto ©ninafisch / pixelio.de

More available books at **www.hansebooks.com**

ACCOUNT OF THE

CELEBRATION OF THE JUBILEE

OF

Uniform Inland

PENNY POSTAGE

AT THE

VENETIAN CHAMBER, HOLBORN RESTAURANT

AT THE GUILDHALL

AT THE

MUSEUM OF SCIENCE AND ART, SOUTH KENSINGTON

AND AT

Various Towns and Villages throughout the
United Kingdom

1840—1890

RICHARD CLAY AND SONS, LIMITED,
LONDON AND BUNGAY.

1890.

Postmaster-General.
The Right Hon. HENRY CECIL RAIKES, M.P.

Secretary of the Post-Office.
SIR ARTHUR BLACKWOOD, K.C.B.

Financial Secretary.
ALGERNON TURNOR, Esq., C.B.

Third Secretary.
HENRY JOYCE, Esq., C.B.

Assistant Secretaries.
F. E. BAINES, Esq., C.B. | E. H. REA, Esq., C.M.G.
J. C. LAMB, Esq., C.M.G.

Committee of Management.
F. E. BAINES, Esq., C.B., *Chairman*.

Colonel J. J. CARDIN. | Colonel S. RAFFLES THOMPSON
W. H. PREECE, Esq., F.R.S. | R. C. TOMBS, Esq.

W. G. GATES, Esq.
SYDNEY BECKLEY, Esq.   *Honorary*
G. A. AITKEN, Esq.   *Secretaries.*
S. WILSON, Esq.

SUB-COMMITTEES TO ARRANGE
FOR THE
POST-OFFICE JUBILEE CONVERSAZIONE
AT THE
SOUTH KENSINGTON MUSEUM,
ON THE 2ND OF JULY, 1890.

CLOAK ROOM:—
- ANGELL, T. W.
- ARDRON, J.
- BADCOCK, J. C.
- BUNDY, C. H.

G. A. AITKEN,
Secretary.

ENTERTAINMENTS:—
- CHAMBRE, A. E.
- HILL, PEARSON.
- NOPS, E.
- PAMPHILON, A.

W. G. GATES,
Secretary.

MUSIC:—
- BECKLEY, SYDNEY
- HALL, C. S.
- SEALY, A.
- WINTER, E.

SYDNEY BECKLEY,
Secretary.

REFRESHMENTS:
- BADCOCK, H.
- LANG, C. D.
- WIGHT, J. F.
- YELD, E.

S. WILSON,
Secretary.

LADIES' COMMITTEE:—
- BROWN, MISS
- SAUL, MISS
- SMITH, MISS

MISS GUNSTON
Secretary.

CONTENTS.

INTRODUCTION.
	PAGE
THE JUBILEE YEAR	1
A BRIEF ACCOUNT OF THE POST-OFFICE	10
SOME REMINISCENCES	33
THE JUBILEE OF THE PENNY POST, FROM "PUNCH"	42
TO THE HONOURED MEMORY OF SIR ROWLAND HILL (Poem)	44

THE PENNY POSTAGE JUBILEE DINNER
47

THE CONVERSAZIONE AT THE GUILDHALL.
CATALOGUE OF ARTICLES EXHIBITED AT GUILDHALL	53
INSTRUCTIONS FOR POSTAL DUTY AT GUILDHALL	115
REPORT OF THE CONTROLLER OF THE LONDON POSTAL SERVICE	122
REPORT OF THE ELECTRICIAN	130
EXTRACTS FROM REPORT OF PENNY POST JUBILEE COMMITTEE APPOINTED BY THE CORPORATION	135
ACCOUNT OF GUILDHALL CONVERSAZIONE, FROM "CITY PRESS"	146
COLLECTION OF HISTORICAL EXHIBITS AT THE CONVERSAZIONE	165
THE GUILDHALL CONVERSAZIONE, FROM "PUNCH"	188

THE CONVERSAZIONE AT THE SOUTH KENSINGTON MUSEUM.
PROGRAMME OF THE CONVERSAZIONE AT SOUTH KENSINGTON	191
INSTRUCTIONS FOR POSTAL DUTY AT SOUTH KENSINGTON	198
REPORT OF THE CONTROLLER OF THE LONDON POSTAL SERVICE	209
REPORT OF THE ENTERTAINMENTS COMMITTEE	219
ACCOUNT OF SOUTH KENSINGTON CONVERSAZIONE, FROM THE "TIMES" AND THE "DAILY TELEGRAPH"	221
TELEGRAMS FROM FOREIGN COUNTRIES AND COLONIES RECEIVED AT SOUTH KENSINGTON	230

CELEBRATIONS OF THE JUBILEE IN THE PROVINCES.

	PAGE
ABSTRACT OF REPORTS FROM PROVINCIAL AND LONDON OFFICES .	235
EXTRACTS FROM TYPICAL REPORTS FROM LONDON OFFICES	244
,, ,, ,, ,, PROVINCIAL OFFICES .	247
,, ,, ,, ,, SCOTLAND . . .	274
,, ,, ,, ,, IRELAND	279

THE POSTMASTERS' BREAKFAST . .   285

ROWLAND HILL MEMORIAL AND BENEVOLENT FUND.

MEETING AT THE MANSION HOUSE	291
LIST OF SUBSCRIPTIONS TO THE FUND . . .	308

APPENDIX.

CHRISTMAS, 1890   319

LIST OF ILLUSTRATIONS.

	PAGE
Sir Rowland Hill, K.C.B.	*Frontispiece*
Sir Rowland Hill's Birthplace, Kidderminster	12
A Travelling Post-Office	17
The Brighton Parcel Coach	25
Loading the Brighton Parcel Coach	37
Frederic Hill, Esq.	41
Postmen's Uniforms during the last Fifty Years	87
The Mulready Envelope, 1840	104
The Guildhall Jubilee Post-Card	124
Telegraphs at Guildhall	131
The "City Press" Wire at Guildhall	160
A Post-Office in 1790	168
The South Kensington Jubilee Envelope	211
The South Kensington Jubilee Correspondence Card	213
Facsimile of Manuscript by Sir Rowland Hill	to face 14
The Right Hon. Henry Cecil Raikes, M.P. (Postmaster-General)	,, 47

Ex-Postmasters-General:

His Grace The Duke of Argyll, K.G., K.T.	to face	50
The Right Hon. The Marquis of Hartington, M.P.	,,	52
The Right Hon. Sir Lyon Playfair, K.C.B., M.P.	,,	56
His Grace The Duke of Rutland, K.G.		60
The Late Right Hon. Henry Fawcett, M.P.		70
The Right Hon. G. J. Shaw Lefevre, M.P.	,,	74
The Late Lord Wolverton	,,	80

LIST OF ILLUSTRATIONS.

		PAGE
SIR JAMES WHITEHEAD, BART.	to face	83
SIR ARTHUR BLACKWOOD, K.C.B. (Secretary of the Post Office)	,,	147
THE POST-OFFICE COMMITTEE	.,	191

    F. E. BAINES, ESQ., C.B. (Chairman).
    S. RAFFLES THOMPSON, ESQ.
    JAMES J. CARDIN, ESQ.
    R. C. TOMBS, ESQ.
    W. H. PREECE, ESQ., F.R.S.

HON. SECRETARIES TO COMMITTEE	to face	192

    WALTER G. GATES, ESQ.
    SYDNEY BECKLEY, ESQ.
    G. A. AITKEN, ESQ.
    S. WILSON, ESQ.

FREDERIC HILL, ESQ.	to face	288
DATE STAMPS USED AT GUILDHALL AND AT SOUTH KENSINGTON		218

INTRODUCTION.

CELEBRATION OF THE JUBILEE

OF

INLAND UNIFORM PENNY POSTAGE.

THE JUBILEE YEAR, 1890.

In 1889 a general feeling was expressed that the fiftieth anniversary of the introduction of Uniform Penny Postage in this country ought not to be allowed to pass without some indication of the feelings which must actuate all who look back to the great reform introduced in 1840, and consider what has since been done. A committee was accordingly formed to make the necessary arrangements, and it was resolved that, in the first place, officers of the Post-Office should meet together at dinner at the Holborn Restaurant.

The Penny Postage Jubilee Dinner on January 15 was most successful. Nearly 300 gentlemen were present, including Mr. Raikes, the Postmaster-General, and all the higher officials of the Department, as well as Sir Lyon Playfair and Mr. Shaw-Lefevre, who have held the office of Postmaster-General, Sir John Tilley, late Secretary of the Post-Office, Mr. Pearson Hill, son of Sir Rowland Hill, and others no longer in the service. A full report of the interesting speeches will be found below.

But still greater things were to come. The Corporation of the City of London, anxious to celebrate in a fitting manner the Jubilee of Penny Postage, asked the Post-Office to co-operate in arranging for an important conversazione at the

Guildhall. The invitation met with a ready response, and by the 16th of May, the date of the conversazione, the Guildhall and its approaches had undergone the strangest of metamorphoses. The great hall contained a fully-equipped post-office of to-day, and the representation of a post-office of 1790, while in an enclosure visitors were able to see how letters, papers, and parcels are sorted and made up into despatches in the Post-Office. At the other end of the room telegraphic apparatus of all descriptions was exhibited, and communication was established with cities as distant as Paris and Berlin. The Art Galleries were used for the exhibition of models of travelling post-offices, mail steamers, &c., and of a large and valuable exhibition of pictures, books, stamps, letters, State papers, and every description of curiosity illustrating the history of the Post-Office. Excellent musical arrangements were made, and Mr. Sydney Beckley, who conducted, has found in the choir gathered together for this temporary purpose the nucleus of what promises to be a successful Post-Office Musical Society. The Lord Mayor and the members of the Corporation were, it is needless to say, excellent hosts, and all the visitors, including the Prince of Wales, who honoured the occasion with his presence, were much interested in the numerous attractions provided. The Exhibition was kept open on the 17th and 19th of May, and musical entertainments were given on each day. Full accounts of the proceedings, from various points of view, are given below. If it had been practicable to keep the collections together for a month, the rooms would no doubt have been crowded to the end. Some of the objects of interest were sent on to the Exhibition of the London Philatelic Society, held in the Portman Rooms later in the month, while many of the valuable stamps shown there had been forwarded from the International Postage Stamp Exhibition, held in Vienna in April.

The proceedings connected with the celebration promoted by the Corporation were brought to a pleasant conclusion by a dinner at the Albion Tavern, under the presidency of Alderman Sir James Whitehead, Bart., at which the Postmaster-

General and the principal officers of the Department were present.

The official celebration of the Jubilee of Penny Postage took the form of a grand conversazione at the South Kensington Museum, when a gathering of nearly 4,000 persons filled the courts and galleries of the beautiful building. The Committee, in arranging for this gathering, had a double object in view, for they wished not only to mark in a fitting manner the Jubilee of a great reform, but to increase, so far as might be, the Rowland Hill Memorial and Benevolent Fund, which has for its object the giving of relief to Post-Office servants, before or after retirement, who, through no fault of their own, have fallen into necessitous circumstances, or to their widows and orphans. Her Majesty the Queen, having graciously consented to become the Patron of the Rowland Hill Benevolent Fund, extended her patronage to the conversazione, and His Royal Highness the Duke of Edinburgh consented to be President. The Lords of the Committee of the Privy Council kindly lent the Museum for the occasion, and the Postmaster-General having agreed that, as far as possible, the 2nd of July should be a general holiday in the Post-Office, application was made to the railway companies, who generously issued tickets to Post-Office servants and their families, available for a week, at charges for the double journey, which in no case exceeded the single fare. The result was that officers from the most distant parts of the kingdom attended the conversazione, and the number of persons present was considerably greater than had been generally expected.

A special Jubilee Post Card had been issued for sale at the Guildhall conversazione for the benefit of the Rowland Hill Benevolent Fund, and it was so popular that the entire issue of 10,000 was bought up in less than three hours. In view of this success it was resolved to issue a limited number of a special Jubilee Envelope, impressed with a postage stamp of the value of one penny, and containing an appropriate correspondence card, for sale at South Kensington and at all Post-Offices throughout the United Kingdom, on the 2nd of July, at one shilling each. The result of this experiment was most satisfactory, and the proceeds, after deducting the value of the paper and postage stamp, were devoted to the Benevolent Fund.

The conversazione is fully described in another part of this volume; it is enough here to say that it was in every way a great success. Postal and telegraph work was carried on as at the Guildhall, and the visitors had the benefit of seeing not only post-offices of 1790 and 1890, but also a forecast of what science would enable us to do in 1990. Models of travelling post-offices and collections of stamps, including those lent by the Board of Inland Revenue and the Government of New South Wales, were on view; and excellent concerts, at which Madame Valleria, Mr. Sims Reeves, Madame Frickenhaus, and other eminent artistes gave their aid, were arranged by Mr. Sydney Beckley. The Postmaster-General and the Secretary of the Post-Office received the guests until the arrival of the Duke and Duchess of Edinburgh, when addresses were presented to their Royal Highnesses, and loud cheers were given for the Queen. It had been arranged that at 10 P.M. a telegraphic signal should be sent from the Museum to the telegraph offices then open throughout the country, and the invitation to the officers of the Department who could not be present at the celebration in London to join in simultaneous cheering for the Queen met with an enthusiastic response. It will be seen from the extracts given from reports received from the provincial offices to how great an extent the occasion was marked by social gatherings or other celebrations in harmony with the proceedings in London.

Many of the postmasters were, of course, in London at the time, and it was therefore arranged to have a Postmasters' Jubilee Breakfast at Exeter Hall on July 3rd, the morning after the conversazione. The Postmaster-General and the Secretary of the Post-Office accepted invitations, and the gathering proved very interesting.

Throughout the year the Post-Office has been in an especial degree in the minds of the public, and many local events have shown the interest taken in the officers of this great Department. As an example it may be mentioned that on the 24th of August a sermon on the Postal System in its Beneficent and Religious

Aspect, was preached in Llandaff Cathedral by the Very Rev. C. J. Vaughan, D.D., Dean of Llandaff and Master of the Temple, at a gathering of officers of the Cardiff Post-Office, and copies were privately printed as a gift to the Postmaster and his officers.

An interesting indication of the constant growth of the Post-Office was afforded on the 20th of November, when the Postmaster-General laid the memorial stone of the new General Post-Office (North) in Aldersgate Street. After the stone had been laid Mr. Raikes made a speech in which the changes of the past fifty years were admirably described.

The POSTMASTER-GENERAL said that in the inscription on the stone reference was fitly made to the fact that the great work of erecting the new Post-Office was thus auspiciously commenced in the year of the jubilee of the penny postage—the jubilee of that great discovery which had revolutionised the communications of the United Kingdom and the British Empire and of the whole civilised world, and which, during the fifty years it had gone upon its peaceful course of development, had wrought, perhaps, greater blessings for the human race than any other institution, at least of modern times. He was happy to have beside him a gentleman whose own career had been long and distinguished in the service of that Department, and who was even more interesting as a personage present as the son of the great Sir Rowland Hill. They had no doubt seen and read much of the postal literature of the year, to which Mr. Pearson Hill had been a foremost and a most interesting contributor, and they had become more or less familiar with those authentic records, which read almost like fairy tales, of the enormous progress that had been made in the inter-communications of mankind since the penny postage was first established. He (Mr. Raikes) was not going to ask them again to look back over those fifty years, and he would only further refer to the jubilee in expressing his own great satisfaction, and he believed that of the Department generally, that Her Majesty the Queen had been graciously pleased to signalize the fiftieth anniversary of the penny post by conferring distinguished honours upon eminent officers of the department. [Mr. Joyce was made a Companion of the Bath, and Mr. Rea and Mr. Lamb Companions of St. Michael and St. George.] He would only say in connection with those honours that it was also a matter on which they might, he thought, justly congratulate themselves, that the jubilee year of the penny postage in the United Kingdom had also been the first year of the establishment of what he trusted would very soon be a universal postage rate between the United Kingdom and our great Colonies and Dependencies across the sea.

He would ask them that day to look back over the twenty years which had elapsed since the late Mr. Ayrton laid the memorial stone of the General Post-Office West, a work which at that time it was supposed might for a very long time to come suffice to meet the increasing exigencies of that great service. How shortsighted were even the best-informed politicians and officials! Twenty years only had elapsed, and the building, which it was supposed would suffice to house their growing services for, perhaps, a century, had become almost obsolete in its entire insufficiency to cope with the business which they had to transact. He would point out to them that in 1869 the number of postal packets, including letters and all other articles transmitted through the post, was 940,000,000—thirty per head of the population. In 1889 those numbers had grown to 2,511,000,000, nearly treble in twenty years, and representing sixty-six per head of the population. That was considerably more than double the number proportionally delivered per head twenty years ago, after making allowances for the great increase of the population in the meanwhile. In 1871 the number of telegrams was nearly 10,000,000, and in 1889 it was 62,500,000. The telegrams in the United Kingdom in those eighteen years had increased by 500 to 600 per cent. In 1869 the amount of money sent by means of money-orders was £19,500,000, and in 1889 £42,000,000, or more than double. In 1869 the savings bank deposits amounted to £13,500,000, and in 1889 they amounted to nearly £63,000,000, or about five times what they were twenty years ago. In 1869 the gross receipts of the department from all sources fell short of £5,000,000, and in 1889 they exceeded £12,000,000. He did not suppose that there was any other institution that had ever existed which could point to such a record of universal progress in every branch.

He would remind them that when the General Post-Office West was designed it was intended to accommodate the Postmaster-General's office, the Secretary's office, the Solicitor's office, Receiver and Accountant-General's office, and the Central Savings Bank. There was also intended to be a central hall for the transaction of all kinds of public business. The number of persons originally intended to be accommodated was about 700. Now, what was the staff to-day? The transfer of the telegraphs to the Government in 1870 altered the arrangement altogether. The upper part of the building, which had been intended for the Savings Bank, was appropriated to the Central Telegraph Office, and an entirely new building for the Savings Bank had to be erected in Queen Victoria Street, and that accommodated a staff of no fewer than 1,250 persons. An additional story had had to be added to the General Post-Office West in 1884, and further accommodation had been found at the Mount Pleasant depôt. After all these removals and transfers of staff from the principal building they had still no fewer than 1,070 connected with the branches still housed there who could not find accommodation within the walls of the General Post-Office West.

The new building, which came to meet their patent and obvious necessities, was to be called the General Post-Office North, and the site, exclusive of the Money Order Office, cost no less than £326,000. The structure had been designed by Mr. Tanner, and he was glad to be able to compliment that gentleman upon a design which would group very harmoniously with the fine buildings which already accommodated the Post-Office. He thought we were beginning more to appreciate the merit of plainness and classical outline and of simplicity in public buildings, and he was quite satisfied that when the new building raised its head in the City of London it would be considered worthy of its position even in a city which, perhaps, contained within its limits a greater number of really beautiful buildings than any other city in Europe. The total number of persons to be accommodated would be no less than 1,550.

He knew he was not only addressing a body of gentlemen highly qualified to appreciate their importance, but everything at the present day which concerned the Post-Office was read with interest, not only in London or the United Kingdom, but even in our most remote Colonies and Dependencies; and, as they knew, it was generally the custom with every person who had a letter detained in transit, or whose parcel had gone wrong, to enlist in the discussion of his wrongs half the Press of the United Kingdom. It was as well when fitting opportunity served that the public should be reminded, as he hoped he had reminded them with becoming modesty, of the enormous work which that great department did for their good, and of the continually increasing responsibilities and cares which beset those who were in charge of it. It would be impossible to carry on the service, but for the department being officered by the most devoted public servants which any State had ever had to rely on, and he hoped when people saw in the papers a tirade against the shortcomings of which they were suspected or with which they were charged, there would be borne in mind the great work which they were daily and hourly rendering to the public, the enormous labour, the infinite anxiety which they bore in patient silence, trusting that their countrymen would judge them by their work.

After expressing regret that many of those who witnessed the laying of the foundation stone of the General Post-Office West twenty years ago were not present, he said their absence might be accounted for by the fact that official service was comparatively short. He believed an omnibus horse was supposed to have a life of three years, and he was happy to say that the life of a superior officer of the Post-Office considerably exceeded that span, but still it was, he thought, a melancholy circumstance that there should be present so few of those who were there twenty years ago. He was happy to think that the Postmaster-General of that day still lived and flourished, and was indeed only just about entering what was considered the middle life of a statesman—he referred to the Marquis of Hartington. There was present that day Mr. Walliker, the Postmaster of Birmingham, who attended the ceremony of twenty years ago, and he hoped that gentleman would be spared to see the day when his (Mr. Raikes') successor came to lay the memorial stone of the General Post-Office South, and which he had not the smallest doubt would be called for by the increasing exigencies of the service in the very early period of the twentieth century.

The list of interesting events of the year was brought to a close with the Annual Meeting of the Rowland Hill Memorial and Benevolent Fund, which was held at the Mansion House on the 11th of November. The Lord Mayor (Mr. Alderman Savory) was in the chair, and among those present were Sir James Whitehead, Bart., one of the founders of the Fund, Sir Henry Peek, Bart., and Mr. Causton, M.P. Mr. Baines, C.B., Chairman of the Executive Committee of the Jubilee Celebration, was able to hand over to the Lord Mayor, for transfer to the Trustees of the Benevolent Fund, a cheque on account for £16,000, the result of the several special efforts made during the year; and subsequent subscriptions have raised the total sum thus obtained to £22,000. In other words, the Rowland Hill Fund has been more than doubled, a result which could not have been attained but for the cordial co-operation of officers throughout the service.

A BRIEF ACCOUNT OF THE POST-OFFICE,

WITH ESPECIAL REFERENCE TO THE PROGRESS OF THE FIFTY YEARS ENDED 1890.

THE system of uniform Penny Postage for letters throughout the United Kingdom, originated by the late Sir Rowland Hill, was introduced on the 10th of January, 1840, and during the fifty years which have elapsed since that date the business of the Post-Office has developed to an extent far exceeding his utmost anticipations.

Before 1840 the rates of postage on letters sent from one part of the United Kingdom to another were almost prohibitive. It is true that in regard to letters posted in London and other large cities for delivery within their local posts, there existed, as shown hereafter, a "penny post" and a "twopenny post," but beyond these limits the rates for a "single letter," unless "franked" by a member of Parliament, were as follows :—

From any Post-Office to any place not exceeding 15 miles from such Post-Office		4d.
Above 15 miles and under 20		5d.
,, 20 ,, ,, 30		6d.
,, 30 ,, ,, 50		7d.
,, 50 ,, ,, 80		8d.
,, 80 ,, ,, 120		9d.
,, 120 ,, ,, 170		10d.
,, 170 ,, ,, 230		11d.
,, 230 ,, ,, 300		12d.

And one penny for every additional 100 miles; while as regards Scotland an additional charge of one halfpenny was made on every letter sent across the Border.

Only "single letters," *i.e.* letters written on a single sheet of paper, could be sent at these rates. Hence the use, which some of the present letter writers can remember, of the large square sheets of letter paper, folded in four and secured with a seal.

The use of an envelope or cover, or of two sheets of paper, or the transmission of any inclosure, rendered the letter liable to double postage, and two inclosures involved treble postage.

Also, if the letter weighed an ounce the postage was quadrupled, and every additional quarter of an ounce in weight led to an additional rate of postage.

Thus the postage on a "single letter" from London to Brighton was 8*d.*; to Manchester, 11*d.*; to Edinburgh, 13½*d.*; and to Cork, 17*d.*, instead of one penny, as at present. But if the letter weighed just over 1¾ oz., the postage was, to Brighton, 4*s.* 8*d.*; to Manchester, 6*s.* 5*d.*; to Edinburgh, 7*s.* 7½*d.*; and to Cork, 9*s.* 11*d.*

The inconvenience which these high rates inflicted on the public is stated to have been forcibly brought home to Sir Rowland Hill by the fact that when engaged to his future wife he and she found it necessary, from motives of economy, to sacrifice sentiment and to restrict their correspondence to a letter once a fortnight.

An article in the *Blackfriars Magazine*—a journal the plan of which has since been taken by the *St. Martin's-le-Grand Magazine*—traces the inception of the idea of penny postage:—

"It was the practice of Mr. and Mrs. Thomas Wright Hill to encourage their children to select and discuss, in the long, dark evenings of the winter months, topics of general interest; political questions, social, physical, and other problems. Each was at liberty to contribute his views, the parents guiding the discussion, and throwing in now and again a shrewd remark or two, born of their well-ordered minds and ripe experience. It was, no doubt, a home debating society, at which, however, the 'previous question' was never put, and 'calls to order' were superseded by the sense and moderation of the disputants.

"On a previous occasion they had debated the printing-press and the feasibility of its improvement; on this particular evening

SIR ROWLAND HILL'S BIRTHPLACE, KIDDERMINSTER.
(By permission of the Proprietors of the *Illustrated London News*.)

the family circle discussed the heavy postage which the lightest letter cost between any two distant points—between, for instance, London and Liverpool, for which the postage was elevenpence; or even between places so near each other as Birmingham and Wolverhampton, the postage being in such cases at least fourpence.

"Out of that family council arose great things, with most of which the readers of *Blackfriars*, by reason of their occupation, are well acquainted.

"Of the five boys, Matthew, the eldest, intended for the Bar, took, one may be sure, an active part in the discussion; the budding advocate detecting at once the strong and weak points of a possible adversary's case; Edwin, the next, with a turn for mechanical contrivances, reflecting what sort of machinery a postal service might require, would address himself to locomotion and its cost; Arthur, with an inborn gentleness which never forsook him, would cast about, perchance, for excuses for those who permitted the levying of extravagant rates; Frederic, the fifth son, then but a child (the sixth and youngest being probably in the nursery), waiting with deference for the settled opinions of his elders, would in due season express himself, young as he was, with sagacity and prudence; while Rowland, the third son, debating the whole proposition with such energy and grasp as to make it clear that further inquiry on this important track was his particular *forte*, carried with him the whole of the Councillors in his youthful demand for postal reform. Then the Council resolved that the question of the printing-machine should be for Edwin further to take up, and that the field of the Post-Office should be left free to Rowland. So from that or a subsequent family council the brothers went on their way through life—Matthew to become a Barrister, King's Counsel, and Recorder of Birmingham; Edwin, Chief of the Stamp Office at Somerset House, and Improver of its Printing and Stamping Machinery; Arthur, Head of the famous Bruce Castle School at Tottenham; Frederic, Inspector of Prisons in Scotland, and afterwards Assistant Secretary in the Post-Office; and Rowland—the great Postal Reformer—Secretary of the Post-Office and Knight Commander of the most Honourable Order of the Bath.

"It has been said that great things arose out of that family council. Among others it has led to the expansion of a total of 76½ millions of letters, delivered annually, into the wondrous aggregate of nearly 1,800 millions. If we throw in some other odds and ends, such as a trifle of 400 millions of book packets, forty millions of parcels, and two or three millions of samples, it may not be wide of the mark to say, for sake of roundness of numbers, that two billions of postal articles under the vivifying schemes of Sir Rowland Hill are passing through the post."

Now Penny Postage brings within the reach of every class the means of correspondence, and that as frequently as the exigencies of the busy life of to-day may require.

The growth of the Post-Office business during the last fifty years has not, moreover, been confined to articles sent through the post.

The establishment in the autumn of 1861 of the Post-Office Savings Bank, the deposits in which amounted in that year to £735,000, but have now reached £60,000,000; the transfer to the State in 1870 of the telegraphs, the number of messages sent by which was then 8,900,000, but amounted last year to 62,368,000; the introduction in 1881 of postal orders, of which upwards of 178,000,000 were issued last year; the introduction in 1883 of the parcel post, by which 2,000,000 of parcels were sent that year, and upwards of 39,000,000 last year, together with the transaction of life insurance and annuity business and facilities for investment of small sums in Government stocks, have all contributed to render the Post-Office one of the largest and most important of the Departments of the State.

The advantages of cheap postage have however been enormously increased by the simultaneous development of railway communication, which has afforded the means of rapidly transporting the immense quantity of matter sent through the post at the present day.

Messrs

The depressed state of the General commerce will appear to some to be a formidable obstacle to the plan. I do not see it in such a light, for several reasons. First, I consider it but temporary, & in the next place there can be no reasonable doubt that a reduction of postage would give a stimulus to ~~maintained~~ commerce which would greatly benefit almost all the other ~~sources~~ sources of revenue. Conceding, however, for the sake of argument, that a more thorough change is desirable, there would be no necessity attendant on reducing the plan to practice, even if it were at once adopted by the legislature in its full extent, there are various modes by which the approach may be made as gradual as the prudence or fears of the controlling authorities may ~~to be requisite~~ dictate. ~~In ~~ It must be

Mail Coaches.

One of the greatest reforms ever made in the Post-Office was effected by the introduction in 1784 of Mr. John Palmer's plan for sending mails by coach. Mr. Palmer, who was the manager of the theatre at Bath, had observed that when the tradesmen of that city were particularly anxious to have a letter conveyed with speed and safety, they were in the habit of enclosing it in a brown paper cover and sending it by the coach, notwithstanding that the charge was much higher than the postage of a letter. He therefore suggested that mail bags should be sent by passenger coaches in charge of well-armed and trustworthy guards, and that the coaches should be so timed that they should all arrive in London, as far as possible, at the same time, in order that the letters might be all delivered together. Up to this time the mail bags had been carried by post-boys on horseback, at an average rate, including stoppages, of from three to four miles an hour; and Mr. Palmer, in submitting his plan to Mr. Pitt, in 1783, pointed out that "the post, instead of being the swiftest, is about the slowest conveyance in the country," and that "the mails were generally entrusted to some idle boy, without character, mounted on a worn-out hack, and who, so far from being able to defend himself or escape from a robber, is much more likely to be in league with him."

The officers of the Post-Office vehemently opposed Mr. Palmer's plan, but its merits were recognized by Mr. Pitt, and under his auspices an Act was passed authorizing its adoption.

Mr. Palmer was appointed Controller of the General Post-Office to carry out his plan, with a salary of £1,500 a year and 2½ per cent. on any excess of revenue over £240,000 a year, and he appears to have performed his duties with great ability. The speed of the mails was at once increased from three and a half to six miles an hour, and subsequently still greater acceleration was attained, accompanied by a large immediate increase of correspondence and of revenue.

In 1792, Mr. Palmer was suspended from his functions, an

allowance of £3,000 a year being made to him in lieu thereof. This sum was much below what he was entitled to under his agreement, and after unsuccessfully memorializing the Treasury against the arrangement he laid his case before Parliament, and in 1813, after a struggle lasting many years, a Parliamentary grant of £50,000 was made to him.

About the year 1814, Mr. Macadam's improved system of road-making enabled a great acceleration to be effected in the speed of the mail coaches. The speed gradually increased to ten miles an hour, and even more, until in the case of the Devonport mail the journey from London of 216 miles was punctually performed, including stoppages, in twenty-one hours and fourteen minutes.

Mails First Sent by Railway.

In 1830, on the opening of the line between Liverpool and Manchester, the mails were for the first time conveyed by railway, and the payment to railway companies for conveyance of mails amounted last year to £900,000.

The first Travelling Post-Office, for the purpose of sorting correspondence in transit, was established on the Grand Junction Railway between Liverpool and Birmingham on the 1st July, 1837, and on the completion of the railway to the metropolis in July, 1838, that Travelling Post-Office began to run throughout between London and Liverpool. The speed was then a gentle twenty miles an hour, as even at a somewhat later period, when the railway northward had been completed as far as Lancaster, the mail train took eleven hours and a half to perform the journey from London to Lancaster, a distance of 241 miles. Now, when the mail train to the north has travelled eleven hours and a half it is pulling up at Forfar, so distant as 471 miles from London. Travelling Post-Offices are attached to numerous mail trains on all the principal lines, those under the control of the London Postal Service running in the aggregate about 3,000,000 miles annually over the principal railway systems of Great Britain. About

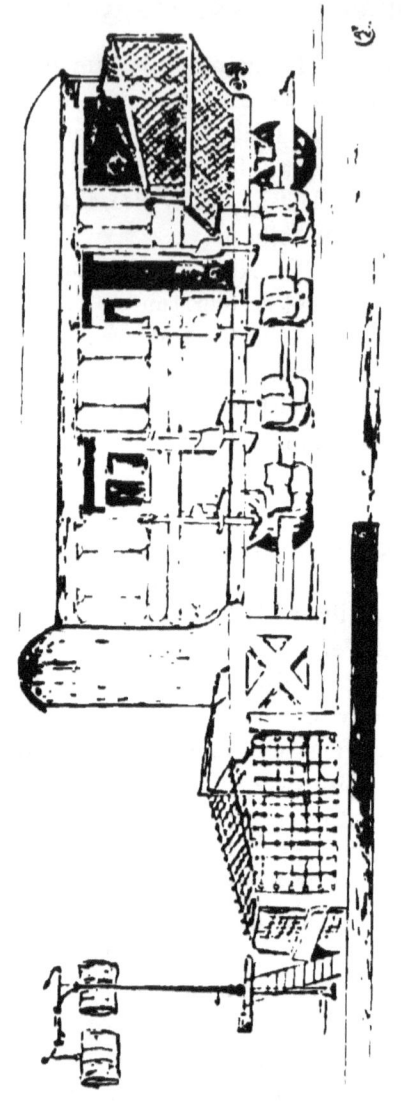

A TRAVELLING POST-OFFICE.
(By permission of the Proprietors of the *City Press*.)

1,800,000 miles, or three-fifths of the total distance traversed by the mail carriages, are run on the London and North-Western and Caledonian Railways; about 270,000 miles are run on the Midland and North Eastern Lines, and nearly 300,000 on the Great Western Railway. The total number of letters, &c., dealt with in the Travelling Post-Offices annually is about 210,000,000, besides about 4,000,000 parcels.

Extensive use is made of the apparatus for receiving mails into, and leaving mails from, mail trains travelling at full speed. Mr. Ramsay, formerly an officer of the General Post-Office, is said to have suggested the machinery for the purpose. To Mr. Dicker, also an officer of the Department, must be ascribed many important improvements of the apparatus, which made it fit for general use, Mr. Dicker receiving his reward in the shape of a grant of £500 from the Board of Treasury, and the appointment of Supervisor of Mail-bag Apparatus. Mr. Pearson Hill, only son of Sir Rowland Hill, is credited with further advantageous changes, and still further improvements have been made of late years by the present supervisor, Mr. Garrett.

The total number of apparatus stations in England, Scotland, and Wales, is 220, and there are 355 standards and 372 nets erected at these stations for the despatch and receipt of mails. There are forty-four Travelling Post-Office carriages to which the apparatus nets, &c., are fixed.

The number of exchanges of mails daily from the station standards into the carriage nets is 516, and from the carriage to the stationary nets 530. The total number of mail bags included in these exchanges is about 2,000. It rarely happens that a bag is missed or dropped. On an average about 110,000 letters, &c., a day are exchanged by the apparatus at a normal period, of which about 85,000, or nearly four-fifths, are sorted in the Travelling Post-Offices, the remainder being sent direct in bags from one town to another through the Travelling Post-Offices unopened.

Foreign and Colonial Mail Packet Service.

The Foreign and Colonial Mail Service benefited almost as much by the introduction of steam packets as the inland service did by the introduction of railways. The state of the mail service to Ireland in old times is illustrated by the fact that in 1693 a piteous petition was received from James Vickers, the Captain of the *Grace Dogger*, who, while his vessel lay in Dublin Bay waiting for the tide to take him over the bar, was captured by a Privateer, the Captain of which, he complains, stripped the *Grace Dogger* of all her rigging and the furniture "wherewith she had been provided for the accommodation of passengers, leaving not so much as a spoone or a nail-hook to hang anything on." The vessel herself had to be ransomed for the sum of fifty guineas, which the Postmaster-General had to pay. The result of this and similar misfortunes was that the Postmaster-General resolved to build swift packet-boats that should escape the enemy, but built them so low in the water that a report states, "We doe find that in blowy weather they take in soe much water that the men are constantly wet all through, and can noe ways goe below to change themselves, being obliged to keep the hatches shut to save the vessels from sinking, which is such a discouragement to the sailors that it will be of the greatest difficulty to get any to endure such hardshipps in the winter weather." It is difficult to realize this state of things now, when the mail packet service is performed by splendid steam vessels of extraordinary power and speed—the voyage from Dover to Calais being performed in little over an hour, and that from Holyhead to Kingstown in three hours and a half; while the mails for the United States, India, and the colonies, are conveyed with the utmost rapidity and regularity by magnificent fleets of the finest steam vessels in the world. When the Pilgrim Fathers settled in America they could never have imagined that the mails would traverse the Atlantic in less than six days in floating palaces like the *Teutonic*, nor could the East India Company have anticipated that the mails which occupied six months in voyaging round the Cape in a sailing vessel, would complete the journey to Bombay in seventeen days by means of the splendid steam vessels of the Peninsular and Oriental Company; while it would have been equally incredible to the first settlers in Australia that the vast distance intervening between them and the mother country would be accomplished in thirty-two days.

The great facilities which thus exist for communication with India and the colonies have, of course, been still further enhanced by the recent reduction of the postage to $2\frac{1}{2}d.$ for a letter under half-an-ounce in weight.

The feat of delivering letters in London within a week of their despatch from New York was accomplished for the first time in October last.

The Inman steamer *City of New York*, and the White Star liner *Teutonic*, passed Sandy Hook at 7.35 A.M. and 7.51 A.M. respectively on Wednesday, the 15th October. Mails were carried by both vessels, those on board the *City of New York* numbering 392 sacks, and those on the *Teutonic* 31 sacks. The bulk of the mails was sent by the Inman steamer, while only correspondence specially addressed was forwarded by the *Teutonic*. The White Star liner, however, made the quicker passage, and arrived off Roches Point at 12.45 P.M. on the 21st, or 1 hour, 47 minutes in advance of her rival.

The mails were sent on from Queenstown by the 1.40 P.M. mail train, and reached London with the Irish mail at 6.50 A.M. on Wednesday, the 22nd, in time for the correspondence to be distributed by the second delivery in the City and other town districts of London, and for the closed mails for the Continent to be forwarded by the first day mails.

The mails conveyed by the *City of New York* were landed at Queenstown at 2.30 P.M., and every effort was made to overtake the *Teutonic's* mail by the employment of a special train to Dublin, a special boat to Holyhead, and a special train thence to Euston.

By these means the mail reached London only 2 hours, 18 minutes after that conveyed by the *Teutonic*, and the letters, &c.,

fell into the next or third delivery throughout London, and the Continental mails were forwarded by the second day mails at about 10.30 A.M.

If this mail had been forwarded from Queenstown by the ordinary arrangements it would not have reached London until late in the day on Wednesday, and, consequently, letters, &c., would not have been in the hands of business men before four or five o'clock.

Post Office Savings Bank.

The establishment in 1861 of the Post-Office Savings Banks afforded great facilities for thrift to the industrial classes. In that year 3,532 Post-Offices throughout the kingdom were opened for Savings Bank business, but the number is now upwards of 9,000. The public appreciation of these facilities is shown by the fact that the number of depositors has increased from 91,965 to 4,220,927, and the amount annually deposited has increased from £735,253 to £19,052,226, while the average amount of each deposit has diminished from £3 12s. 8d. to £2 10s. 6d.

Since 1880 depositors have been enabled to invest their savings in Government stocks with little or no trouble. In this way £3,785,600 of stock is now held by 43,000 persons, the dividends being credited to their Savings Bank accounts. The smallest sum which a depositor can invest in the purchase of Government stock is one shilling.

The Post-Office Savings Bank is much used by friendly societies, provident institutions, and penny banks as a safe place of deposit for their funds.

The idea of establishing this branch of the department is largely and with justice attributed to the late Sir C. W. Sikes, a merchant of Huddersfield. The machinery which rendered the idea practicable was in the main reduced to a workable form within the department, the late Mr. F. I. Scudamore, C.B., and Mr. G. Chetwynd, C.B., being those chiefly concerned.

TELEGRAPHS.

The year 1870 was rendered notable in the history of the Post-Office by the acquisition by the State of the telegraphs, which had previously been in the hands of various companies. On the 29th of January in that year the transfer of the business to the Postmaster-General took place, but for another week the telegraph companies continued to perform, as agents of the Post-Office, most of their practical functions, until at midnight (or more strictly speaking at seven o'clock on the morning) of the 5th of February the Postmaster-General—then the Marquis of Hartington, M.P.—took up the management of inland telegraphy.

The history of telegraphy in this country yet remains to be written. The postal share of it may perhaps be briefly indicated by Parliamentary papers, which show that in 1854 Mr. Thomas Allan, a well-known electrician, published a paper entitled *Reasons for the Government annexing an Electric Telegraph System to the General Post-Office.* Mr. Allan proposed a uniform charge for telegrams of one shilling for twenty words.

In 1858 Mr. F. E. Baines, C.B., an officer of the department, submitted to the Lords of the Treasury, by permission of the Duke of Argyll, then Postmaster-General, and with the concurrence of the late Sir Rowland Hill, a plan *For the establishment in connection with the Post-Office of a comprehensive system of Electric Telegraphs throughout the Kingdom.* Mr. Baines advocated a sixpenny rate of charge, free delivery within prescribed limits, a legal monopoly, an extension of postal telegraph wires, first to post-towns and ultimately to 8,000 or 9,000 sub-post-offices, separation of the railway from the public telegraph service, consolidation of the public telegraph system under one management, and an extension of underground wires. All these suggestions have now been realized. When Mr. Baines framed his proposal 470 post-towns had no telegraphic communication whatever; at 210 post-towns the telegraph office was to be found only at the railway station, while the smaller towns and villages were without any telegraphs whatever, or at best had to depend on a railway service wire at the nearest railway station.

In 1865 the late Lord Stanley of Alderley, Postmaster-General, took up the question, and he directed the late Mr. Frank Ives Scudamore to examine it. Mr. Scudamore's report was laid before Parliament in April, 1868. At that time the Duke of Montrose was Postmaster-General. He advised the Government to bring in a Bill for the acquisition of the telegraphs. This Bill became law, and was followed by a Money Bill in 1869, which confirmed and extended the Bill of 1868.

The burden of organizing the acquisition of the telegraph companies' property, and of establishing the system of post-office telegraphs, fell on Mr. Scudamore. It was a work of excessive labour, and was performed in an incredibly short space of time.

Under Post-Office management the facilities afforded to the public have been greatly increased, and the business developed in all directions. In 1870 a uniform minimum charge of one shilling for each inland message was introduced and the total number of messages sent in the first year was nearly 9,472,000, excluding about 700,000 press messages; the number of telegraph offices throughout the kingdom being 3,700. In October, 1885, the minimum charge for a message was reduced to sixpence, and the total number of messages last year was 62,368,000.

The cost of the telegraph service last year was £2,042,394, while the total receipts amounted to £2,129,699.

Vast strides have been made in telegraphy since Cooke and Wheatstone, in July, 1837, transmitted their first signals between Euston Square and Camden Town. The Post-Office has now duplex, quadruplex, and multiplex apparatus, transmitting many messages on one and the same wire at the same time, while the capabilities of the more recently invented Wheatstone Automatic Apparatus have been developed to an extent unthought of by the inventor. This apparatus can now transmit as many as 600 words in a minute. The first attempt to connect England and the Continent was made in 1850 by a wire laid from Dover to Calais, and in the following year permanent communication was established by a cable, of which a portion is in use at the present time. There are now no less than nineteen cables between Great Britain and the Continent. Those which were established by the Submarine Telegraph Company between England and the Continent were acquired last year by the British and foreign Governments, the concessions to the company having expired.

On the 5th of August, 1858, the first line to the United States was completed, and telegraphic communication established between the two hemispheres; but the cable soon broke, and, although another cable was laid in 1865, it also failed, and it was only in 1866 that the third cable was successfully laid. The second cable was subsequently restored, and at the present time there are no less than twelve cables crossing the Atlantic.

The telephone and the microphone are recent productions of telegraph science, but although the Post-Office has established several telephone exchanges the application of these inventions, so far as this country is concerned, is chiefly in the hands of companies.

Parcel Post.

The latest great addition to the Post-Office business is the Parcel Post, which came into operation on the 1st of August, 1883. This beneficent measure was introduced into Parliament and carried into law by the energy and skill of the late Professor Fawcett, the blind Postmaster-General. Mr. Fawcett took the deepest interest in every detail of the new post, personally examining all the regulations and satisfying himself of the justice and propriety of every condition attaching to it. During the first year the number of inland parcels (for the Foreign and Colonial Parcel Post was not inaugurated till the 1st of July, 1885) was upwards of 22,900,000, but the number last year, including foreign and colonial parcels, was upwards of 39,500,000, the gross postage upon which amounted to £878,547. Close upon 1,500,000 parcels were dealt with in

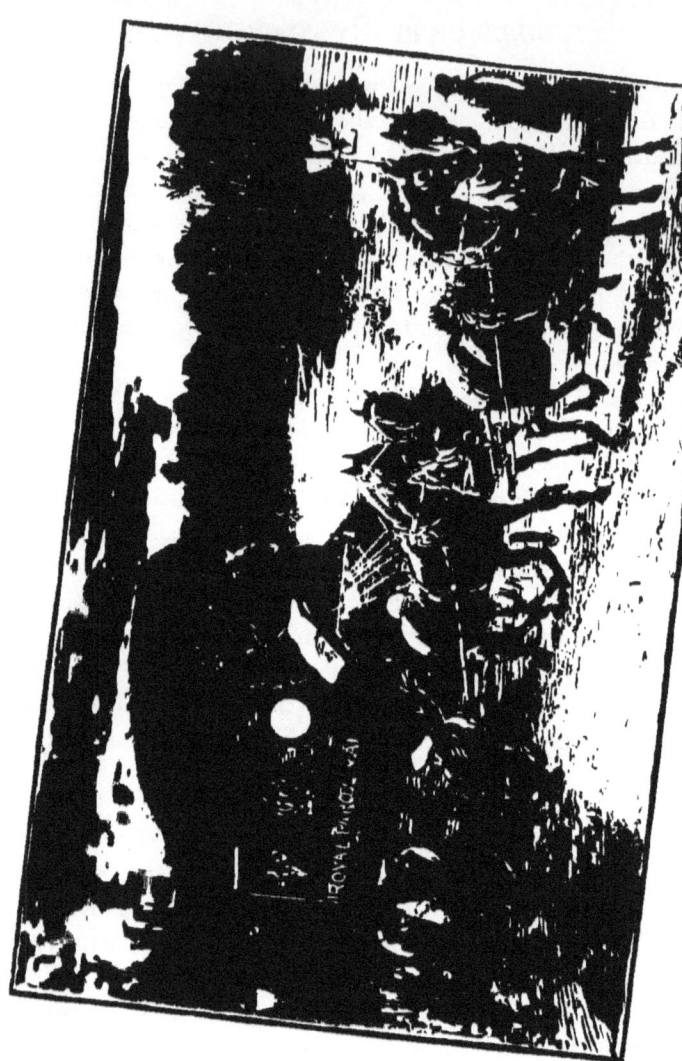

THE BRIGHTON PARCEL COACH.
(By permission of the Proprietors of the Graphic.)

London during the Christmas week of 1890, 185,000 being posted on the 23rd of December alone.

The Parcel Post has been extended to all the colonies, except Queensland, and to almost every foreign state, and the number of parcels sent last year between Great Britain and colonial and foreign states, in both directions, was about 867,000. The total postage amounts to not far short of £100,000 a year. The number of outgoing parcels is to the number of incoming ones in the proportion of almost two to one. Many parcels are of great value, and sometimes contain between £2,000 and £3,000 in gold.

In connection with the Parcel Post the department has, in a few instances, reverted to coach service, and parcel coaches or vans run nightly between London and Brighton, London and Oxford, London and Chatham, London and Tunbridge Wells, London and Ipswich, London and Watford, London and Hertford, and Liverpool and Manchester, a less expensive mode of conveyance being thus obtained than the railways afford.

Post-Office in the Crimea.

During the Crimean war it was found necessary to make special arrangements for the postal service of the army, and in 1854 an experienced officer of the department was, with the approval of the Secretary for War, sent to the East as Postmaster to Her Majesty's Forces, with three assistant postmasters and seven letter sorters. To assist in the postal work soldiers were detached from different regiments who naturally possessed no knowledge of postal work, and this disadvantage added greatly to the difficulties of the undertaking. The late Mr. E. J. Smith, who subsequently became Postmaster of Leeds, was Army Postmaster, and Mr. Mellersh of the Circulation office, Captain T. Angell, now Postmaster of South Western London, Mr. Leonard Bidwell, chief clerk of the Secretary's Office, Mr. Sisson of the Travelling Post-Office, and the late Mr. Bertram also held responsible posts.

Army Post-Office Corps.

When in 1882 it was decided to send an army to Egypt, Mr. Fawcett, the then Postmaster-General, established an "Army Post-Office Corps" upon the basis of a scheme prepared, with the sanction of the War Office, by Colonel Du Plat Taylor, C.B. This corps consists of selected sorters and postmen, who are trained members of the Post-Office Rifle Volunteer Regiment, with officers of that regiment as Army Postmaster and Assistant Postmasters, all being enrolled in the First Class Army Reserve. This newly-created organization was scarcely completed when its services were required with the army in Egypt, and another detachment was again sent out with the expedition to Suakin in 1884. On both occasions the work was most successfully performed to the satisfaction of the army and of the Postmaster-General. The detachments went out under the command of Major Sturgeon, now Postmaster of Norwich, and the late Major Viall.

Reserve of Trained Telegraphists.

In 1884 a somewhat similar body was organized from among the skilled telegraphists in the Post-Office Volunteer Regiment. This body, numbering 100 of the best-trained telegraphists in the kingdom, furnished a detachment to assist the Royal Engineers in 1884 on the despatch of the expedition for the relief of Khartoum, and rendered good service in maintaining telegraph communication along the Nile from Alexandria to Abu-Gus.

These two bodies are now permanently incorporated in the Army Reserve.

Revenue.

The Post-Office Revenue has increased enormously in the last two centuries. When it was settled by Act of Parliament in 1663 upon the Duke of York and his heirs in perpetuity the net amount was £5,000, and in 1685, when, owing to the

Duke having become King, it became necessary to re-settle the revenue upon His Majesty and his heirs, it had reached £65,000; but last year the gross revenue, including the telegraphs, was £11,770,000, and the estimated expenditure about £8,400,000, leaving a net revenue of about £3,370,000; or upwards of six hundred times the amount settled on the Duke of York.

Post-Office Buildings.

The increase in the work of the Post-Office led in 1814 to the adoption of measures to provide a new General Post-Office, but the building in St. Martin's-le-Grand was not occupied till 1829. This building was deemed extravagantly large at first, but it has long ago become insufficient for the needs of the Post-Office, and a much larger building was erected opposite to it in 1873. These combined offices have now proved too small to accommodate the staff, and another large building is in course of erection on a neighbouring site, while portions of the staff are housed in the old prison at Coldbath Fields, now the Central Parcel-Post-Office, and known as "Mount Pleasant," in Moorgate Street, Newgate Street, St. Paul's Churchyard, and other places, besides the large buildings of the Savings Bank Department in Queen Victoria Street, and Knightrider Street.

The work of the Post-Office is carried on by a staff numbering about 108,000 persons. Of this number more than half are on the permanent establishment, the remainder being employed by local postmasters, &c., throughout the country. These numbers include about 20,000 women.

The Service in London.

In order to show what an advance has taken place since 1840, it may be remarked that the staff employed in the Circulation Department and Metropolitan area at that time was about 1,540. In 1890 it had risen to 17,456, or over eleven times as many as in 1840.

The total number of letters, &c., now delivered in London per year is 690,000,000 (or about 30 per cent. of the total for the

United Kingdom), averaging about 138,000 per postman in the year, or about 430 per man per day.

The letters, &c., collected throughout London in one year now number 850,000,000 (or more than one-third of the total number posted in the United Kingdom) as against 564,000,000 in the year 1881.

The number of letters despatched from London on January 10th, 1840, was 112,104. The number of letters and newspapers now sent out from London daily is about 2,000,000. The mails despatched from London to the provinces by railway weigh 28,000 tons a year, and those received in London 18,000 tons.

The number of telegrams delivered in London annually is 18,500,000, and of parcels nearly 8,000,000, the rate of delivery per head of the population being about 138 letters, &c., 3¾ telegrams, 1¾ parcels.

The postmen employed in delivering and collecting letters, &c., were in 1881, 3,751, and now 5,321, or an increase of 41·8 per cent.

The complaints made by the public of late delivery of letters, &c., in the London postal area during the year ended the 31st December, 1889, numbered 220 only.

The Female Staff employed on counter and telegraph duties in the London postal service numbers 560 persons. On the average twenty retirements take place annually. About twelve leave to be married, four on account of ill-health, and three to better their position. The death-rate of the female staff is less than 0·5 per cent.

In 1890 there were in the Metropolitan area eight principal distributing offices for letters and parcels, and six separate depôts for parcels, together with 93 secondary sorting and posting offices for the collection into and delivery from of letters and parcels.

The public business, such as the sale of stamps, &c., is conducted at 98 Crown offices, and 770 letter receiving houses. In 1839 there were about 70 letter receivers in the London district.

Stamps can be purchased by the public from about 3,000

shopkeepers licensed for the purpose by the Inland Revenue authorities.

There are 11 head, 96 branch, and 304 receiving offices in the Metropolis where telegraph business is transacted.

The area included in the London postal system, which extends from Mill Hill and Whetstone in one direction to South Norwood and Sydenham in another; from Chiswick to North Woolwich; from Wimbledon to Greenwich; and from Hanwell to Woodford, is about 250 square miles; and the population is estimated at 5,000,000; this gives about $2\frac{1}{3}$ square miles to each of the 107 centres of letter and parcel distribution. As about 35 miles of new streets, and 15,000 new houses are built in every year new centres have been arranged for letter delivery. The annual increase adds houses and streets to the Postal zone equal annually to Oxford and Cambridge.

The conveyance of the letter and parcel mails between the various districts of London, and to and from the respective railway termini, is performed by means of vehicles of different descriptions amounting to about 550 in number. The total distance traversed daily by these conveyances is about 5,750 miles, or nearly a fourth of the circumference of the globe. The distance travelled by these vehicles in one year amounts to about 1,800,000 miles. About 380 regular and 95 casual drivers are employed, and 1,100 horses are used.

The Valentine has nearly had its day. Missives of this description in London have dropped from 3,000,000 in 1883 to 342,000 in 1890, and of the latter about 12,000 circulated by the comparatively new Parcel Post system. Easter Cards are gaining in public favour. The number circulating within London bounds in 1890 was about 640,000 as against 520,000 in 1889. Christmas Cards dealt with in London have reached the prodigious number of 50,000,000.

And now the commemoration of another festival has to be watched in its effect on postal duties;—that of Primrose day. Last year the delivery of Primrose Parcels by Letter and Parcel Post was 55,000, or about double the number in 1886. Of these over 3,000 were brought into London by the Brighton parcel coaches.

Rowland Hill Benevolent Fund.

In the year 1882 a fitting memorial to the late Sir Rowland Hill, the originator of Uniform Penny Postage, was created by the establishment, under the auspices of the Lord Mayor of London and many influential citizens, of the "Rowland Hill Memorial and Benevolent Fund."

This Fund has for its object the relief of Post-Office servants throughout the United Kingdom, the only condition of relief being that the recipient is, through no fault of his own, in necessitous circumstances. It also affords assistance to their widows and orphans.

The Fund is managed by a body of Trustees, who are assisted by a Committee of Recommendation, composed of officers of the Post-Office. The Trustees are well-known gentlemen, of high standing and repute in the City of London, to whose benevolent efforts on behalf of the Department the Fund owes its origin.

The relief is given only after careful inquiry by the Committee of Recommendation, who possess the means of obtaining authentic particulars of the merits of every case submitted to them. Sometimes the grant is renewed in a succeeding year; but the Funds at the disposal of the Trustees do not admit of annual payments being maintained, even in cases where the circumstances would—funds permitting—abundantly justify such a course.

The Fund is available for the relief of every class of officers employed by the Post-Office, whether in receipt of a pension or not; the only condition being that there shall be actual distress on the part of the person relieved. Aged people, past work and with very small means, or none at all, and widows with young children and few or no resources, are the chief recipients of assistance from the Fund.

The Superannuation Act affords pensions to those who have been in the Post-Office not less than ten years. A pension, even if it should prove to be sufficient for actual support, ceases on death, and the widow and orphans are often left destitute. Sometimes a deserving and distressed Post-Office servant has not served long enough to qualify for a pension, and sometimes persons who have acted for years as auxiliaries in the postal service are not entitled to any pension at all. In such cases the distress is occasionally severe.

There are certainly fifty thousand, and, counting those not on the establishment of the Department, probably one hundred thousand servants in the Post-Office (chiefly in receipt of weekly wages) whose cases might come within the scope of the Rowland Hill Benevolent Fund, but the income at the disposal of the Trustees of that Fund is very limited. In 1889 the total income arising either from investments or from donations and annual subscriptions amounted to £1,673 5s. 2d.; of which amount the Trustees felt themselves warranted, having regard to possible claims in the future, in spending no more than £1,027; to that extent administering relief in 175 urgent cases, in sums ranging from £5 to £10.

At present the Fund is mainly supported by contributions from within the Post-Office itself. Of the Donations and Annual Subscriptions, amounting for the year 1888-9 to £1,024 14s. 9d. the sum of £838 4s. 11d. was so contributed. It was an object to ensure the stability of the Fund by enabling the Trustees to increase their investments, as well as to widen the scope of their beneficent action by adding to the income of the Fund the interest of increased investments. It will be seen elsewhere how, by concerted action, this result has been largely attained.

SOME REMINISCENCES.

(From an article in the *Blackfriars Magazine*.)

When penny postage came into force, the Earl of Lichfield was Postmaster-General. When the Jubilee of that reform of the 10th of January, 1840, was celebrated, the Right Honourable Henry Cecil Raikes, M.P.—Chairman of the feast of the 15th January, 1890—reigned in his stead. When the old rates of postage were abolished, Lieut.-Colonel Maberly occupied the secretarial chair, but the guiding spirit was Sir Rowland Hill. Soon he became sole Secretary. After him, in 1864, came Sir John Tilley, K.C.B., who, at the Jubilee banquet (January 1890), recalled his experiences, gained before most of the guests in the Venetian chamber, in which he spoke, were born; before, indeed, the actual Secretary of the Post-Office himself—the vice-chairman of the evening—Sir Arthur Blackwood, K.C.B., had seen the light.

Between Lord Lichfield and the Right Honourable Henry Cecil Raikes there came as Postmasters-General the Earl of Lonsdale, the Earl of St. Germains, the Marquis of Clanricarde, the Earl of Hardwicke, Viscount Canning, the Duke of Argyll, Lord Colchester, the Earl of Elgin and Kincardine, Lord Stanley of Alderley, the Duke of Montrose, the Marquis of Hartington, Mr. Monsell (Lord Emly), Sir Lyon Playfair, Lord John Manners (Duke of Rutland), Professor Fawcett, Mr. Shaw-Lefevre, and Lord Wolverton. Now, in the administrations of these thirteen ministers of the Crown, assisted by the four secretaries named, what has been accomplished? Who have been active figures in the minor parts? Why is a period of fifty years of official work cause of jubilation?

The army of one hundred thousand Post-Office servants—established and auxiliary—scattered over the face of the land must be as exact and well ordered in their movements as would be an actual army in the field, in the finest condition and under the severest discipline. But, unlike an army whose component parts move in masses, each man in the Post-Office has his distinct sphere of action, and yet must move in such exact harmony with his distant comrades that loitering of the rural postman at John o'Groats may not trouble the dwellers at the Land's End; and in lieu of martial law, the working bees are held together by no more potent bond than the value of their situations, a short set of rules, and a British sense of duty.

What servant of the Post-Office has been ever known to shrink from his post of duty, even when danger threatens? Marine mail-guard Mostleman, on board the *Vivid*, in a storm in mid-channel, knowing that the vessel into whose hold the water was swiftly pouring must soon be lost, goes down darkling into the flooded mail-room to rescue, if it may be, the bags in his charge, and so, dying in the act, leaves his life a memory. The Scotch rural messenger, blinded and frozen by the snowstorm, hangs the mail-bag on a tree, so that it may at least be saved, and then lies down to die beneath it. The mail-guard, Bennett, sorely hurt in a railway collision, thinks less of his mangled body than of collecting the fragments and contents of the scattered mail-bags. The Northumberland mail-cart contractor, not daunted by a raging storm, heroically drives across the moor because he sees his duty plain before him, and lays down his life in doing it. So in all grades of the Service, in all the varying conditions which official duty presents, and regardless of time and circumstance, the grand old signal of what England expects her sons to do is ever to the fore.

Who would not find cause for jubilation in belonging to a service whose honourable watch-word is "duty," and whose labours rarely cease; a service in which there is daily something to be attempted, and, if Heaven wills, to do? Who would not see in the completion of fifty years of the operations of a great and world-wide fiscal reform, which has brought unnumbered blessings to the human race, a fit occasion for giving utterance to some not unreasonable rejoicings?

In these fifty years the plan of penny postage has been worked out, a book-post established, half-penny post-cards introduced, a sample-post set at work, a parcel-post which benefits the million cheap and widely extended telegraphy, telephones, and the vast Savings Bank established. Perhaps, after all, these are trifles and more remains for mightier men to do.

Lord Canning sanctioned the book-post, and Sir Lyon Playfair the post-cards and postal orders. Mr. Raikes introduced the sample-post, Professor Fawcett, parcels. The Duke of Montrose began upon, and Lord Hartington finally brought out, the telegraph system. The name of Lord Stanley of Alderley is linked with the Savings Bank, and Mr. Shaw-Lefevre, although out of office, virtually carried in Parliament the sixpenny rate for telegrams.

Few can remember the first posting of penny post letters on the 10th of January, 1840. Some can. Mr. William James Godby is certainly able to do so. He was a surveyor for fifty years—so that he can recall 1840 with ease, and, as a young clerk, have a good margin to spare.

A few months ago, there died a very ancient Post-Office servant—Mr. Job Smith, of Islington, N. He had been a postman in the old days, nearly seventy years ago, and was in 1889 still a pensioner, aged 93. He died on the very day on which, trudging to St. Martin's-le-Grand, as usual, he received his monthly stipend.

Mr. Moses Henry Nobbs, the last surviving mail-guard, began work June 27th, 1836, and still does duty as mail-officer at Paddington. He could remember a good deal in his fifty-four years of service. Old memories must have revived as he went down from London to Brighton, two or three years ago, as guard-in-charge of the special trip of the new Brighton parcel coach. He was fully equipped, as of yore, for that perilous journey, a timepiece from Jamaica serving to complete the outfit. A blunderbuss from Exeter was handed in at the last moment to make the armament fourfold; and had to be tied on to the hind seat with official string. Several valued colleagues still in active service date from pre-historic, that is, ante-penny-postage times. If we knew their names for certain, we would chronicle in these pages all the good men and true who have for so many years borne, like our famous flag, "the battle and the breeze" of official life.

Once some time in November, 1867, when Mr. Disraeli was Chancellor, there came a little note from the late Mr. George Ward Hunt at the Treasury, to the late Mr. Scudamore. It contained only a few words: "You may give the notices for the Telegraph Bill."

That brief intimation, like the magician's wand, has largely changed the face of the Post-Office, given the postal side perhaps eighteen or twenty thousand colleagues, erected 183,000 miles of telegraph wire; produced an annual transmission of fifty millions of telegrams, and an annual receipt of two millions of money.

Many years ago some miscreants blew down a prison wall in Clerkenwell with gunpowder. As a result, fifteen hundred special constables were sworn in at the Post-Office. The astute Colonel John Lowther du Plat Taylor, C.B., an old servant of the Post-Office, and a soldier born, swiftly saw his opportunity, and formed therefrom, and has ever since maintained, his splendid Post-Office regiment of a thousand volunteers, fit to go anywhere and do anything, as was shown by their services in Egypt. More power to his elbow—and theirs.

Once, half a dozen clerks in the Post-Office bought a chest of tea, kept it in a cupboard, and dealt it out among themselves at cost price, a few pounds at a time. Look out of the windows of the Savings Bank, craning your head a trifle, and there you will see the modern *replica* of the postal cupboard, a building and a business with an annual turnover of a million and three-quarters sterling. So do great things grow from small beginnings.

One day, about thirty years ago, a bank director of Huddersfield, Sir Charles William Sikes, wrote a little paper on a possible Postal Savings Bank. How many hundreds of millions

LOADING THE BUCHLON PARCEL COACH.
(By permission of the Proprietors of the *Graphic*.)

sterling, the savings of the people, have passed—mainly, as a result of Sir Charles's suggestions, through the coffers of the Post-Office on their way to the National Debt Office for care and investment?

In the past there have been (as there are in the present) many active figures on whom, uniting, as they did, a sound discernment with an absorbing power for official work, must rest in large degree the merit of what has been accomplished. Of the brilliant statesmen who have adorned the office of Postmaster-General, a volume could be written. But good as were their services to the State at the Post-Office, it is mainly in other spheres of public duty that their substantial reputation has been acquired.

Sir Rowland Hill rests in Westminster Abbey, and he "though dead yet speaketh" in the administration of the Post-Office. A foreign grave has closed over the remains of one of the ablest and most devoted of officials, the late Mr. Frank Ives Scudamore, C.B. He might often be seen dictating official minutes from nightfall until daybreak with untiring vigour when time was known to be of consequence, and when personal convenience had to be wholly thrust aside. His power of work was prodigious, his faculty of attracting men to work with him unsurpassed. Organization had a charm for him; the Telegraphs pre-eminently, the Savings Bank, the system of accounts, the packet service, and the registered letter system, all felt the power of his grasp.

His pupil, as it were, and, perhaps, his favourite disciple, the late Mr. C. H. B. Patey, C.B., justified all Mr. Scudamore's confidence, and realized all—perhaps more than all—that he had foreseen of aptitude and capacity. The absorbing nature of the duties in connection with the telegraphs withdrew Mr. Patey in great degree from an active participation in the management of the purely postal side of the department. But not altogether. For he could find time, even amongst his most pressing engagements, to identify himself with the inner life of the office, to share in its social or benevolent gatherings, and to stamp his mind on whatever official questions came before him. In fact, in the later years of his life, important branches of postal work were added to the main duty of conducting telegraph business which was confided to his care, and in all of these he showed the insight and good judgment which made him eminent in the Post-Office.

The late Mr. Benthall was a valued and most trustworthy servant of the State. He had taken a good degree at Cambridge, and soon rose in official life. He supervised the relations of the department with the railways with an astuteness and cordiality which left nothing to be desired. He was greatly respected in the railway world. Numerous Crown Post-Office buildings throughout the country are witnesses of the careful hand and experienced judgment of John Strange Baker. He was much beloved. Mark Beauchamp Peacock, W. H. Ashurst, and Henry Watson bore the brunt of the legal work of the department in London, as did the genial and accomplished Robert Thompson in Dublin. They were all men of capacity and honour.

William Bokenham, Thomas Boucher, and Thomas Jeffery will long be remembered as Controllers in succession of the Circulation-Office, and men of great experience and shrewd judgment.

Controllers of the Savings Bank who have passed away are no fewer than four in number—the energetic and many-sided Chetwynd, better known, however, as Receiver and Accountant-General; A. Milliken, A. C. Thomson, and G. Ramsay. They built up that great edifice in which so many of our officers look after the finance of the toiling million.

The " eyes of the department," once said a great authority, " are the Surveyors." Since penny postage times how many of these valued officers have fallen away from the side of their old and honoured colleague and *doyen*, Mr. W. J. Godby. South Wales still remembers Mr. Gay; Cambridgeshire the versatile Anthony Trollope; and Manchester has reared a monument to the beloved St. Lawrence Beaufort. There are other names to be recalled — Creswell, Smith, Johnson, Rideout, Stow, and Neal of old; those of Edward Page, Hodgson, and Churchill; of Wedderburn and West; of John Allen, Henry James, T. B. Harkness, and J. P. Good; and of John Kains in the far away West Indies. The telegraphs are still young in the history of the Post-Office. Mr. R. S. Culley is with us yet, but for Mr. T. H. Sanger, and Messrs. Shaw, Tansley and Walsh, the tale of years is told.

What would the Post-Office be without accounts? Where could abler men be found than in the latest three—George Richardson (the last to pass away), G. Chetwynd, C.B., and F. I. Scudamore, C.B., who filled in turn the heavy post of Receiver and Accountant-General? What wonders the three accomplished in making accounts clear and simple, in dealing with the vast mass of financial work which presents so many aspects as that arising out of the postal revenue, and how the last-named two especially, diverging from the beaten track, were always ready successfully to grapple with new problems and untie the tightest knots. As to the medical department, Dr. Gavin, of the cholera year, sleeps in the far-off Crimea, and Dr. Waller Lewis in his native land.

Happily, all that have written *Finis* on their postal work have not yet gone to the great majority. Sir John Tilley, K.C.B., is as vigorous as ever. Fifty or sixty years of hard and responsible work have made little difference in him. He built, or, at his instance was built up, the new Post-Office now about to be devoted to the purpose of a central telegraph station. He reduced rates of postage, and prepared the way for a parcel post. Mr. Frederic Hill still lives at Hampstead, at an age frosty yet kindly; advanced indeed, but still, at eighty-six, full of vigour. At the Post-Office he was the main agent in reducing the cost of the packet service, in cheapening postage to the Continent, and in, at least, preparing the way for the postal order scheme, which the late Mr. Chetwynd brought to maturity. In a hundred other ways he did good service to the State.

Mr. Francis Abbott, at about the same green old age, flourishes in Edinburgh, where he was so long the secretary. His name will be found as a subscriber of £5 to the special effort of 1890 on behalf of the Rowland Hill Benevolent Fund. Mr. C. B. Banning, Mr. Warren, Mr. Milliken, Mr. Barnard, Mr. Stow, Mr. Guinness, Mr. Newman, Mr. South, Colonel Taylor, Mr. Mellersh, and Mr. Teesdale, and a hundred others, whose names escape me at the moment, deserve to be cherished in the memory of their colleagues. Are these recollections out of place amidst our jubilation?

Shall we not rejoice that the Post-Office is so rich in the record of good and faithful servants—men whose lives have been spent within, as it were, the official walls; of whose labours, diligence, devotion, and consummate skill the general public have heard but little, but who have done—some, perhaps, unseen, unthanked, unknown—with all their might, the duty which lay to their hand. Long may this spirit still prevail with us, and keep our office foremost in efficiency, usefulness and zeal for the public good amongst the several branches of Her Majesty's Civil Service.

For fifty years the Post-Office, in its modern garb, has been before the public, working under its eye, and even though it be its servant, hand in hand with it. So a strong bond of mutual good will and confidence has grown up. The servant has been not ungenerously treated—and the master is, with no ungrudging hand, heartily well-served. Shall we not rejoice that it is so; that, looking back on these fifty years of labour, whether of ourselves or our predecessors, we are conscious of ever striving for the public good? We might, perhaps, claim that, as officials, we are not always mindful of what is pleasant and convenient, and in giving of our best, whether of brain or muscle, we have at least earned the right to hug the flattering thought that Diogenes, looking around for the State's bad bargains, need not trouble himself to bring his lanthorn to the POST-OFFICE.

FREDERIC HILL, ESQ.
Sole surviving brother of the late Sir Rowland Hill
(From a photograph taken in his 87th year.)

THE JUBILEE OF THE PENNY POST.

(From *Punch*, January 18, 1890.)

"On Jan. 10, 1840, the Penny Post became an accomplished fact."—*Times.*

ATTEND, all ye who like to hear a noble Briton's praise !
I tell of valiant deeds one wrought in the Century's early days ;
When all the legions of Red Tape against him bore in vain,
Man of stout will, brave ROWLAND HILL, of true heroic strain.

It was about the gloomy close of Eighteen Thirty Nine,
MELBOURNE and PEEL began to melt, the P.O. "sticks" to pine,
For vainly the Official ranks and the Obstructive host
Had formed and squared 'gainst ROWLAND HILL'S plan of the Penny Post.
Still poor men paid their Ninepences for sending one thin sheet
From Bethnal Green to Birmingham by service far from fleet ;
Still she who'd post a *billet doux* to Dublin from Thames shore,
For loving word and trope absurd must stump up One-and-four ;
Still frequent "friendly lines" were barred to all save Wealth and Rank,
Or Parliamentary "pots" who held the privilege of "Frank ;"
Still people stooped to dubious dodge and curious device
To send their letters yet evade the most preposterous price ;
Still to despatch to London Town a business "line or two"
Would cost a Connemara peasant half his weekly "screw ;"
Still mothers, longing much for news, must let their letter lie
Unread at country post-offices, the postage being too high
For their lean purses, unprepared. And Trade was hampered then,
And Love was checked, and barriers raised—by cost—'twixt men and men.

Then up and spake brave ROWLAND HILL in accents clear and
    warm,
"This misery can be mended! Read my *Post-Office Reform!*"
St. Stephen's heard, and "Red Tape" read, and both cried out
    "Pooh! Pooh!
The fellow is a lunatic; his plan will never do!"
All this was fifty years ago. And now,—well, are there any
Who do not bless brave ROWLAND HILL and his ubiquitous
    Penny?
One head, if 'tis a *thinking* one, is very often better
Than two, or twenty millions! That's just why *we* get our letter
From Aberdeen, or Melbourne, from Alaska or Japan,
So cheaply, quickly, certainly—thanks to one stout-soul'd Man.

Fifty years since! In Eighteen Forty, he, the lunatic,
Carried his point. Wiseacres winced; Obstruction "cut its
    stick."
He won the day, stout ROWLAND HILL, and then they made
    him Knight.
If universal benefit unmarred by bane gives right
To titles, which are often won by baseness or a fluke,
The founder of the Penny Post deserved to be a Duke.
But then he's something better—a fixed memory, a firm fame;
For long as the World "drops a line," it cannot drop his name.
'Tis something like a Jubilee, this tenth of Janua-*ree!*
Punch brims a bumper to its hero, cheers him three times three,
For if there was a pioneer in Civilisation's host,
It was the cheery-hearted chap who schemed the Penny Post.
And when the croaking cravens, who are down on all Reform,
And shout their ancient shibboleth, and raise their tea-pot
    storm,
Whene'er there's talk of Betterment in any branch of State,
And vent their venom on the Wise, their greed upon the Great,
Punch says to his true countrymen, "Peace, peace, good friends
    —be still!
Reform does *not* spell Ruin, lads. Remember ROWLAND
    HILL!!!"

TO THE HONOURED MEMORY OF SIR ROWLAND HILL.

His is no victor's wreath of blood-stained bay,
   No humbled foemen cowered before his name,
   No martial multitudes with loud acclaim
Placed on his brow the laurel green to-day
Though half a hundred years have rolled away.
   Far happier he, whose clear, keen-sighted aim
   By patient service won a peaceful fame
Nor Time can touch, nor envious tongues gainsay.

We reap what he hath sown: his fostering hand
   Sheltered the sapling: from the spreading tree
   'Tis ours to pluck the fruit, and celebrate
The strength that laboured and the skill that planned
   To closer draw the bonds of unity,
     And make our England's greatness yet more great.

HENRY F. SMART.

January, 1891.

THE DINNER

IN THE

VENETIAN CHAMBER, HOLBORN RESTAURANT,

JANUARY 15, 1890.

THE RIGHT HON. HENRY CECIL RAIKES, M.P.
(Postmaster-General.)
(*From a negative kindly lent by Messrs. Barraud.*)

PENNY POSTAGE JUBILEE DINNER.

(From the *Times*, Jan. 16, 1890.)

LAST evening a large party of officers and ex-officers of the General Post-Office dined together at the Holborn Restaurant, to celebrate the jubilee of the penny postage. The chair was taken by the Right Hon. H. C. Raikes, M.P., the Postmaster-General, who was supported by two of his predecessors, the Right Hon. Sir Lyon Playfair, K.C.B., F.R.S., M.P., and the Right Hon. G. J. Shaw-Lefevre, M.P. The vice-chair was occupied by Sir Arthur Blackwood, K.C.B., secretary of the Post-Office, and those present included Sir J. Tilley, K.C.B., secretary of the Post-Office from 1864 to 1880, Mr. Pearson Hill, son of the late Sir Rowland Hill, K.C.B., and late of the secretary's office in the General Post-Office; Mr. Algernon Turnor, C.B., financial secretary of the Post-Office; Mr. H. Joyce, third secretary; Mr. F. E. Baines, C.B., assistant secretary and inspector-general of mails; Messrs. E. H. Rea and J. C. Lamb, assistant secretaries; Mr. A. M. Cunynghame, surveyor-general for Scotland; Mr. H. L. Creswell, secretary for Ireland; Mr. W. H. Preece, electrician to the Post-Office; Mr. Philbrick, Q.C., Mr. R. Hunter, solicitor to the Post-Office, and upwards of 250 more members and ex-members of the staff, including among the retired members Mr. Edmund Yates. The speaking was interspersed with quartets and songs, given by Messrs. E. Richardson, Sealey, Barnes, and Sydney Beckley. Mr. W. G. Gates, of the secretary's office, had acted as secretary of a large general Jubilee Committee.

The Marquis of Hartington had intended to be present, but

was prevented by illness. On the 12th inst., his secretary, Mr. H. A. Lascelles, wrote from Devonshire House to Mr. F. E. Baines :—

"Lord Hartington has been suffering for some time past from a very severe cold, but he hoped to recover from it in time to allow him to come to London to attend the Post-Office Jubilee dinner. I regret to say that the cold has turned into congestion of the lungs, which will of course make it impossible for him to come to the dinner. The last account of Lord Hartington is a very good one, and I trust the attack may not prove a very severe one."

Lord Emly wrote from Limerick expressing regret that it was impossible for him to be in London.

The following letters had been received from the Dukes of Argyll and Rutland :—

"INVERARY, ARGYLLSHIRE, *Dec.* 19, 1889.

"SIR,—I am much flattered by the very kind invitation conveyed to me in your letter received to-day, and I very much regret that I am unable to take advantage of it. In recent years I have been compelled by my health to give up attending public dinners, and I shall be in Scotland at the time you refer to. I have a very pleasant recollection of my time, or rather times, at the General Post-Office, and of my connection with its officers. No public department is better served—perhaps few so well, and certainly none with such almost unfailing success.

"Your obedient servant,
"ARGYLL."

"3 CAMBRIDGE GATE, REGENT'S PARK, *Dec.* 20, 1889.

"DEAR MR. BAINES,—It is with very great regret that I find myself obliged to forego the pleasure of joining the departmental dinner by which it is proposed to celebrate the jubilee of the penny post. An engagement in the country, which I cannot evade or postpone, will not allow my attendance on January 15. I must therefore content myself with asking you to be good enough to convey to my kind friend the Postmaster-General, and to the officers of the department present, my cordial good wishes for their health and happiness throughout the new year, and the expression of my confidence, founded on pleasant experience, that in their hands the great organization, to which Sir Rowland Hill's invention has given so enormous a development, will in an increasing ratio continue to merit and receive the confidence and gratitude of the community.

"I remain, dear Mr. Baines, yours faithfully,
"RUTLAND."

The CHAIRMAN, in proposing "The Health of the Queen," said,—Although the inception of the penny postage does not exactly synchronize with the beginning of her Majesty's reign, yet that half-century of progress which we are met to celebrate to-day coincides so nearly with the more than fifty years during which Queen Victoria has reigned over us as to establish something like a special connection between this toast and the occasion which has brought us together. I cannot but believe that her Majesty the Queen has been no unmoved spectator of the progress of this great department, which indicates, perhaps, more than any other the wonderful march of civilization under her reign; and we who are here to-night, being nearly all persons in her Majesty's service, should be, and are, the first to recognize the virtues, the wisdom, and the steadfastness which have endeared our Sovereign to her people.

The toast was cordially drunk.

The CHAIRMAN, in proposing the toast of "The Prince and Princess of Wales," said that some anxiety had been felt because of the announcement in that morning's papers as to the state of her Royal Highness's health. He was happy to be able to say, however, that the statements in the newspapers seemed to have been exaggerated. There was no reason to suppose that the Princess of Wales had gone out of her way to show sympathy with the Post-Office by succumbing to the epidemic of influenza.

The toast was warmly responded to.

The CHAIRMAN, in proposing the toast of "The Post-Office," said,—Before I venture to address myself to the toast which I have risen to propose I should like to read to you a short telegram received at the General Post-Office this morning, which appears to me to be exceedingly interesting in connection with the subject of our meeting here this evening. This is the telegram:—"On the occasion of the penny postage jubilee the Egyptian Administration, which is just adopting Rowland Hill's great reform, sends to the Department which initiated it half a century ago, best congratulations and cordial greetings.—SABA PASHA, Postmaster-General, Egypt." I may mention also that, among other congratulatory telegrams and messages which have been received, a most kind and cordial message was received on Friday last, the actual jubilee day, from our esteemed and respected friend Dr. von Stephan, the Postmaster-General of Germany.

I think we are all sensible that what has brought us here to-night is not an ordinary occasion. Congratulatory banquets, congratulatory celebrations, have become so common in these days of advanced civilization that they seem to some to have almost lost their point and meaning. But in meeting here to-night we are celebrating what perhaps, although the subject of it seems in the first instance inconsiderable, has really been one of the greatest peaceful revolutions of the century, and we who sit within the walls and under the roof of the establishment which has benefited so greatly by the foresight and the practical genius of the great man who initiated this reform would, indeed, be the most ungrateful of mankind if we did not assemble here to-night to congratulate each other upon the progress of his great idea, and to do honour to his venerated name.

I have seen in one of the many notices with which the Press has teemed a touching anecdote—I am not prepared to vouch for its absolute accuracy, but it is one of those anecdotes which one wishes to believe to be accurate—that an old schoolmaster of Sir Rowland Hill's lingered outside the post-office of Birmingham on the night of the 9th of January, 1840, with a letter in his hand in order to be the first person, when the clock had finished striking twelve, to place it in the box and to send a letter under the system inaugurated by his pupil. I am glad to be corroborated by the highest living authority on that subject, and I only wish to point out the interesting succession of ideas in the fact that it was an old master of Sir Rowland Hill's who was the first to do honour to his inventive genius on that occasion; so we, fifty years later, who sit here are proud to consider ourselves the pupils of that distinguished man.

You are all so familiar with the circumstances in which Sir Rowland Hill began his crusade for Post-Office reform that it would be idle, and indeed almost impertinent, to dilate upon them to-night. Most of us who are present here to-night have probably

His Grace the Duke of Argyll, K.G., K.T.
(From a photograph by the London Stereoscopic Company.)

seen that most interesting work published by Sir Rowland Hill's son, giving a most vivid sketch of the difficulties and the embarrassments which attended postal communication fifty years ago. We most of us know that in those days the charge for a letter within the British Islands was multiplied by the distance which it had to travel, and I confess that I do not greatly blame those Ministers and administrators who thought there was a sort of rude fairness in a system of that sort. It would look at first sight to those who are not versed in the minutiæ of postal matters as if there ought to be an increasing charge for the distance travelled within the British Islands; but it was the courage, the sturdiness, and tenacity, as well as the inventive faculty, of Sir Rowland Hill that demonstrated that, in point of fact, the distance travelled was almost an infinitesimal element in the cost of the transmission of a letter. That was the great point that had to be established.

Sir Rowland Hill, who was an amateur, who was what I suppose people would have called an outsider, had grasped the fact, which had not at this time become patent to the officials at St. Martin's-le-Grand. He had not only the ingenuity and the fertility of resource to discover and develop this idea, but he had also that rare faculty of moderate and reasoned eloquence which brought the country at once to his side. No doubt he was a little sanguine; where is the inventor who is not a little sanguine? He believed that the revenue would recoup itself within a shorter time than it actually did recoup itself; but the revenue has more than recouped itself, and that the net profit upon the Post-Office at the present time, enormously as its business has increased, is double what it was at that time is one of those facts which are familiar to every schoolboy in the fourth form.

Sir Rowland Hill was aided to a certain degree by circumstances. He brought forward his scheme at a time when public opinion was varying rather rapidly between the two great parties in the State, and no administration that could be formed could be certain very long of continuous life; and it was, perhaps, owing to this, I must call it, happy accident on that occasion that Sir Rowland Hill was able to press successfully on the Government of that day the adoption of his great scheme, although it involved, as he was prepared to admit, at all events for the first year, a very considerable loss of revenue. I think it is gratifying to those who have sat for many years in the House of Commons that it was through one of its oldest and most respected members, the Right Hon. Charles Pelham Villiers, that Sir Rowland Hill's scheme was first brought to the knowledge and pressed on the attention of the Government of the day. The scheme was adopted: the volume of postage instantly increased by leaps and bounds. The revenue, as was expected in the first instance, declined, but the country was quite prepared to meet the declining revenue in order to secure the great boon which this simple schoolmaster with no administrative experience, with no special advantages of fortune or position, had thought out for himself and had verified by a labour and an attention to detail which may even be commended to the reformers of any other day.

From that time, as we know, the progress has been continually increasing, until at the present time the letters that are carried represent, I understand, forty-two letters per annum for each head of the population, whereas at the time before the penny post was instituted it was only three. The actual volume of letters carried is twenty times what it was fifty years ago. I am speaking only of letters, because there are subsidiary services—the post-cards, the circulars, book-post, and parcel-post—which would swell up the total from 1,500 millions to 2,365 millions of missives. I may mention to you what is, I think, a very striking fact, that in the course of the last two years the increase in the number of letters annually despatched and received in the kingdom has been no less than 172,000,000—that is to say, that in those two years the increase has been more than twice the whole number of letters which were posted in the year 1840.

I have not come here to-night to weary you with statistics, and to give to you the marvellous details of the development of this great Department, but you may be interested if I remind

The Right Hon. the Marquis of Hartington, M.P.
(From a photograph by Mr. A. Bassano.)

you that at the present moment there are 18,000 post-offices in the United Kingdom, as well as 20,000 other receptacles for letters, and that the force which now carries on the postal service of the country consists of 58,000 established officers as well as 50,000 other persons employed in the service of the Post-Office. I think this will justify me in saying that it is probably to that happy thought, that patient research, that heroic persistency of Rowland Hill that this Department has become the most important administrative Department of the State.

Talk of armies! Why, the numbers of officers I have just mentioned to you, and of whom I may say I am for the time being the commander-in-chief, are more numerous than any regular forces which the Secretary of State for War can show within the compass of her Majesty's dominions. The fleets over which the Postmaster-General exercises control are faster, better found, and more efficient than any which obey the bidding of the First Lord of the Admiralty. Talk of the Foreign Office!—or the Colonial Office! Why, half of the work of those Departments is what we make for them, and in which we have to assist them. I believe in fact that the growth from this grain of mustard seed, this little penny post which was invented by the Worcestershire schoolmaster, has been such that we are approaching a period, if we have not reached it, when the Post-Office will be regarded with eyes of envy and suspicion by every other Department in the State.

Let me just recall the other steps of this great Department. After the penny post there comes, about twenty years later, the institution of the Post-Office Savings Bank. The result of that institution, by which the Post-Office became the banker of the poor, is that, at the present moment, the deposits amount to £62,000,000, and we have been able, in consequence of recent legislation, to act not only as the bankers, but also as the brokers for the labouring classes, and to invest no less than £4,000,000 of their money in the public funds of the country. Ten years later came the telegraphs, and that enormous new Department was added to the control of the Post-Office. Do you suppose that the country would have been prepared to confide those new and vast fields of business to the Post-Office of the day if they had not been thoroughly well satisfied that the spirit which had been initiated by Rowland Hill was still permeating, as it does to the present day, every branch of the Department?

When you see a few carping critics who find fault, in the columns of the daily papers, with the administration of this great Department, because they have had to pay a halfpenny surcharge, or because their fish sent by parcel post arrived too late for dinner—atoms of criticism which float in the sunshine of public opinion—be satisfied that they are the very rare exceptions, and it is because that confidence which Rowland Hill obtained for the Department has continued to subsist that the Post-Office has continually had fresh fields of labour thrust upon it.

Let me give you one fact as regards the telegraphs, and I think it will please my right hon. friend on my left (Mr. Shaw-Lefevre), who took a great interest when he was Postmaster-General in the extension of our telegraphic system at the time the sixpenny telegram was introduced. I think you will be glad to know that the number of telegrams sent in the last financial year amounted to 57,000,000, and I think my right hon. friend may also be congratulated, because I know he was rather sanguine on the subject of the revenue—that the revenue which, when I came into office in 1886 showed a deficit of £145,000, mainly in consequence of the adoption of the sixpenny telegrams, has shown in the last year a surplus of £85,000. Those have been two great additional labours, the savings bank and the telegraphs, but the Post-Office has not been idle in other spheres.

You have a great development of the money-order system brought about by the institution of the postal orders. I have a figure here about postal orders which will show the enormous amount of use made of this mode of transmitting money by the poor. I think that last year no less a sum than £39,000,000 was transmitted by means of money orders of one class or another. Then you have the parcel post, of the enormous convenience of which we are all so sensible. We cannot all perhaps achieve the greatest triumphs, but I may point to things that have been done during my own tenure of office in the reduction of the price of postal cards, and the establishment, as I believe, of a method of calculation with regard to them which would have satisfied the mathematical aptitude of Sir Rowland Hill himself. We used to pay 8d. per packet of twelve cards until a year ago. It occurred to me that people did not calculate money in eightpences or things in dozens. There are only two things that I know of in this country that are counted by dozens, and these are wine and silver articles; but by the arrangement then subsisting the duo-denary system of calculation was withheld from the silver while it was applied to the post-cards. It occurred to me that it would be an enormous simplification if you put the money basis on the basis of the shilling calculation, under which we count money, and if you put the basis of the number of the article supplied on the duo-denary scale. If you wish to buy 100 post-cards you send 5s., and if you want £1 worth of post-cards you get 400, and I have always felt that if in anything I should have deserved the approval of the great founder of postal reform this matter would have met with his approving regard.

There is another matter which is perhaps picturesque, but it is also practical, and that is the establishment of parcel coaches. I observed the other day some strictures from some antiquated and Rip Van Winkle Radical, who was shocked at the idea of reversing the magnificent railway system by going back to the old coach and four. I read that letter with some amusement, because it showed me how a man who believed himself to be possessed of the newest ideas may be the representative of the most antiquated prejudices. I am happy to believe that we have saved a considerable sum of money to the State by the institution of the parcel coach to Brighton. We mean to save by our parcel coach between Manchester and Liverpool. I was particularly anxious to run this coach, because I thought it was the most picturesque and telling manner of bringing home to the attention of the nation the fact that in existing circumstances the contract between the railways and the Department is one which is not beneficial to the public service.

We are always told that we ought to be making a new departure. We are always making new departures. If the public only knew the secrets of the Post-Office they would find that there is no Department on the face of the earth which is so prone to ventilate and push new ideas. We are being held up occasionally by ill-informed persons to public obloquy as if we did not go with the times, when the fact is that our endeavour is, not merely to go with the times, but to keep ahead of the times. But we have a partner—Mr. Jorkins. The Post-Office is never in the position to give effect to its own promptings without consulting that very formidable person in the background. There is another Department of the Government which may literally be said to be paved with good intentions, and it is because our good intentions only go to pave that Department that we have not been able to show to the public what we realize among ourselves—the strenuous progressive spirit which still animates every rank in the service.

But it is not only that we have this difficulty at which I have hinted; we have also difficulties created by those who sometimes wish to pose as postal reformers. There are people, you know, who make the best of causes ridiculous, and there are those whose advocacy is so unfortunate as to provoke hostility and antagonism. I would illustrate that for a moment by reference to a question of which we hear a great deal in the newspapers, and something occasionally in the House of Commons—the question of what is called international penny postage. I am not going to say that there may not be reasons of high State policy calling for a great reduction of our external postage rates. I do not propose to discuss that question here this evening, but I wish to point out the hollowness of the agitation which has been maintained upon this question by simply putting it to the test of the example of Sir Rowland Hill. Now Sir Rowland Hill, when he devised the penny postage for the United Kingdom, had satisfied himself of what I will call the enormous area of productivity which he might look to in order to recoup the revenue.

There are 36,000,000 people in the country; there were about 25,000,000 at the time when the penny post was established;

THE RIGHT HON. SIR LYON PLAYFAIR, K.C.B., M.P.
(*From a photograph by the London Stereoscopic Company.*)

but if those 36,000,000 of people were each to write one letter a day—and I think it is not impossible—if we may arrive at that happy state of inter-communication, we should have a circulation of letters nine or ten times greater than that which subsists at present. In fact the area of productivity is almost immeasurable, and to that Sir Rowland Hill looked for the recovery of revenue. Take the cost of the Indian post. There are 200,000 British-born persons in India, including the Army. Suppose that each of them writes a letter by each post. There are only fifty-two posts to and from India in the year, not 365. Supposing four times as many of the native community write their letters, say, one a year, you would have 1,000,000 people writing fifty-two letters in the year as against 36,000,000 people writing a letter 365 times a year. If you take the case of Australia, although the figures are more favourable to the reformer, they still land him in the hopeless position of inability to prove that he has that area of productivity, or anything approaching to it, which Sir Rowland Hill saw before him when he proposed his scheme. Sir Rowland Hill had satisfied himself that in the British Islands the cost of transmission was so small that it might be absolutely disregarded. But in the case of the transmission of a letter between this country and India, China, or Australia, we know that the cost of such transmission must be three times, if not more, the total sum which the reformer proposes to levy by way of postage. I would sum it up in this way—Sir Rowland Hill proposed a great change because he believed it was for the good of all, especially of the poor, at the same time that it was shown to increase the revenue. We are asked, on the other side, to adopt a change, which must necessarily largely diminish the revenue, and must do it for the sake of the few at the expense of the many.

What I have said to you has no reference to those larger questions of general State policy to which I adverted earlier, but I venture to believe by conjuring from the shades the venerable shade of that great name, and by putting to the test of merciless logic this bubble which is blown before your eyes. It has been burst. I feel that this occasion is one which appeals to us on every side except one; happily it does not appeal to us on the side of party politics. You may dwell upon it as the man of business, as the family man, as the administrator and statesman, as the humble emigrant, but every member of the community takes the same interest in this great question. We should remember that in the days when it was first produced it stirred the fire even of the cold intelligence of Harriet Martineau, who spoke in the language of romantic sympathy of the wealth of ideas that would occupy the weary mind and of pleasures which would refresh the sleepless affections. Not only did this discovery stir to unwonted expression of feeling one of the clearest and keenest intellects of our century, but it actually made my Lords of the Treasury themselves turn poets. In a Treasury minute penned on the occasion of Sir Rowland Hill's retirement from the office he had so long adorned, a Treasury minute salutes him, not merely as a faithful servant of the country, but as a benefactor of the human race.

It is with that great example before us that every man in this service does his daily work. As long as that example is cherished and honoured as it is to-day there need be no fear for this great Department, which goes step by step and stride by stride in advancing the welfare of mankind. I ask you to-night to drink the toast of the Post-Office as one of the first civilizing agencies of our century, and as embodying year by year, one after another, those peaceful revolutions which make up the happy history of man.

Sir A. Blackwood, being called upon first to respond, desired that he should be allowed to yield precedence to Mr. Pearson Hill, as the only son of Sir Rowland Hill.

Mr. Pearson Hill said,—As the representative of Sir Rowland Hill's family, I rise to offer our most hearty thanks to the Postmaster-General for his kindly reference to my father's services and to all old friends who have assembled here to-night to do honour to his memory, and to Sir Arthur Blackwood I am especially indebted for his thoughtful generosity in wishing that I should take precedence in replying to the toast with which our names have been associated.

The Postmaster-General has made a generous reference to the benefits which the world has reaped from the uniform penny postage system which it was Sir Rowland Hill's lot to devise and carry to completion; but there are one or two points connected with that reform upon which, from my intimate acquaintance with my father's views, I am perhaps more qualified than any one else to bear testimony, and to which it may not be out of place for me to refer to to-night. In all his earnest endeavours to carry his plan to completion, there was one great point of which he never lost sight, and that was to do so with the least possible injury to the officers of the Post-Office, and of this strong desire on his part I can perhaps give a sufficient illustration by stating what took place when, thirty-four years ago, the work of dividing London into its ten postal districts was commenced.

The investigation then made into the working of the London district postal system soon brought to light endless abuses which had gradually accumulated in that department. In those days the letter-carriers were expected to perform ten hours' work daily, but if employed beyond that time they received extra pay; but numerous instances were discovered where letter-carriers received such extra remuneration, not only when they did no extra work, but when their ordinary hours of employment fell far short of the official standard. One glaring case I remember, where a letter-carrier was found to be working only four hours a day instead of ten hours, and yet in addition to full pay he was receiving, I think, 28s. a week in addition for extra work, not a single stroke of which did he perform. Such an abuse had, of course, to be stopped at once; but in this case, and in all others, Sir Rowland Hill laid down the rule that the letter-carrier's pay should not be reduced if he were willing to perform the amount of duty which that pay represented. Again, many cases occurred where by simplifications which Rowland Hill introduced into the duties of some branch department it was found possible to work with a much smaller staff of officers; but I can remember no instance of any officer being turned adrift because his work had been abolished. Places were found for redundant officers in other departments of the Post-Office, or the desired reduction of force was accomplished by the simple process of not filling up vacancies as they occurred.

I need scarcely say that it is impossible for any one to reorganize a great institution like the Post-Office without making many enemies amongst those who prefer that things should be left as they were; and at one time it was the fashion of some newspapers to represent Sir Rowland Hill as a hard taskmaster who constantly overworked his men and ruthlessly cut down salaries. Perhaps the two facts I am about to mention will best show the injustice of any such accusation. At the present moment a demand is being put forward on behalf of the working-classes that their daily task of labour shall not exceed eight hours; but more than thirty-four years ago Rowland Hill, as regards the Post-Office *employés*, anticipated this demand, and reduced the regular working day of the letter-carriers from ten hours to eight, and I believe there is still a rule in force at St. Martin's-le-Grand that any letter-carrier who, taking one day with another, finds his work exceeds eight hours is entitled to apply for relief. As regards Rowland Hill's supposed eagerness to cut down the remuneration of those employed in the postal service, I may mention one fact to which he once called my attention—viz., that while he was Secretary of the Post-Office the salaries of every class of *employés* had been raised, with scarcely more than two exceptions, those exceptions being the salaries of the Postmaster-General and of the Secretary himself.

And now I would like to say a word or two with reference to uncomplimentary observations that are sometimes made with respect to the officers of the Post-Office who long ago, when Rowland Hill's scheme of postal reform first came before the public, met that scheme with the most uncompromising hostility, and who, to quote an amusing expression which I read in one of the recent notices of the jubilee of the penny postage, were thereby "damned to everlasting fame." I must admit that when some forty years ago I entered the postal service I used to regard such opposition as something little short of sacrilege, but I am bound now to say that so long as Colonel Maberly, and the other gentlemen who were responsible for the

His Grace the Duke of Rutland, K.G.
(*From a photograph by the London Stereoscopic Company.*)

well-working of the Post-Office, conscientiously believed that the uniform penny postage system would be detrimental to the public welfare, such opposition on their part was not only justifiable but was the only course they could take with honour; and that Sir Rowland Hill himself held that view will, I think, be clear when I tell a little bit of postal history which will, no doubt, be new to most of those here present.

One of the most earnest opponents of Sir Rowland Hill in early days was a gentleman who has long since passed away, but whose memory is held in the warmest esteem in the Post-Office for his sterling worth, not only in official matters, but in his private life. I need only mention the name of Mr. William Bokenham to awaken the pleasantest memories amongst all old postal servants here present. Before Rowland Hill became Secretary of the Post-Office, an old gentleman who took the greatest interest in his scheme of postal reform said to him, " When you become Secretary of the Post-Office the first thing you must do is to get rid of Master Bokenham." I am glad to say that, having by that time learned thoroughly to respect Mr. Bokenham for his many sterling qualities, one of the first things Sir Rowland Hill did after he became Secretary to the Post-Office was to raise his salary.

I must apologize to you, Mr. Raikes, and to all old friends round St. Martin's-le-Grand, for having already taken up so much of your time, and will only say, in conclusion, that in the brightness of this celebration of the jubilee of the uniform penny postage system one cannot help looking back with amusement to the darker days when Rowland Hill's name was not altogether that of a welcome guest at the Post-Office—though I am sure you will believe me that in referring to that time I do so in no hostile spirit, but merely for the purpose of heightening the contrast between the past and the present. In those days the name of St. Martin's-le-Grand was associated in the mind of Rowland Hill with a sense of trouble, vexation, heartburn, and sometimes of grievous injustice; but even had the trials of that period been tenfold what they were, I am certain that he would have regarded them as a light price to pay for the cordial respect—I may almost say veneration—with which his memory is now regarded by all who knew him, and for the strong friendship which the officers of the Post-Office have for years past been good enough to extend to myself and every member of Sir Rowland Hill's family.

SIR A. BLACKWOOD, who was most cordially received, said,— In now rising to acknowledge the toast which you have been good enough to propose I am conscious of two very distinct feelings—one, that of an unaffected sense of very great personal inferiority to my distinguished predecessor, whose famous reform we are met to celebrate to-night; the other that of pardonable pride that I have the honour of sitting in his chair, who may be said almost to have created the vast service to which we belong, and consequently of being the spokesman of such a body as the Post-Office of the present day. In the name of that service, Sir—of the 100,000 officers of whom you are the head—I desire to return most sincere and hearty thanks for the exceedingly kind terms in which you have spoken of us. The expressions which have fallen from your lips have, I can assure you, gratified us extremely, and they will give a sincere thrill of pleasure to the many thousands who cannot be with us to-night, but who will read your words to-morrow. In the discharge of our arduous duties it is no small encouragement to receive the approbation of our political chief; and I am sure that not only the high officers who are gathered here, but also the great army of Post-Office servants elsewhere, male and female, veteran and juvenile, down to the most diminutive telegraph boy, are grateful to you.

And now, Sir, I confess to a feeling of embarrassment and difficulty in attempting to follow my friend Mr. Hill, upon whom it devolved to speak of the achievements of his distinguished father, since no such deeds of world-wide renown can be pointed to in the history of the fifty years which have passed since that memorable 10th of January, 1840. It has been the duty of the Post-Office in succeeding years to follow faithfully the lines which Rowland Hill traced, to carry out in their ever-extending ramifications the principles he proclaimed, and to apply them to the changing circumstances of each day and to the requirements of the highly organized life of modern society; and I think, Sir, that not only have you yourself to-night, but the Press of this country has also borne witness to the fact that that duty has been discharged with some measure of success. But if such startling reforms as uniform penny postage cannot be repeated, and if Rowland Hills cannot reappear, the past fifty years have not been without important events in the history of the Post-Office or without great and able men in the service. Telegraphs, savings banks, parcel post, as well as great extensions of cheap postage rates have marked those years, and the names of such men as Scudamore, Chetwynd, and Tilley are in themselves evidence of the ability and zeal for the public advantage which have been developed within our ranks.

Although a well-abused Department, as I know to my cost by the indignant letters I receive when a post-card is misdelivered, a telegram mis-spelled, a newspaper belated, or a parcel damaged, yet, on the whole, working as we do in "the fierce light that beats" upon us from every home and from every place of business in the kingdom, our labours, carried on under difficulties of which the public at large know very little, are not unappreciated, and we are glad to think that they are favourably recognized. For we do claim to be public benefactors. Talk of a free breakfast table! What is a free breakfast table compared to one loaded with letters, post-cards, newspapers, and halfpenny circulars? The ladies fly to the letters we bring them with swifter flight than to their cups of tea, and the man of business turns with disgust from his toast and coffee if we do not hand him his daily paper. Now, to pass from these universal benefits to smaller matters, have we not conferred imperishable fame on politicians otherwise unknown by furnishing them with materials for at least half a hundred conundrums wherewith to scare Postmasters-General out of their five senses? Where would such individuals be but for the Post-Office?

But, turning from the pleasant memories that such achievements as these awaken, I desire to say, in all seriousness, that the Post-Office has a very deep sense of its responsibility. We are aware that upon no other institution or service in the country depend consequences affecting so keenly and so immediately every home—nay, almost every citizen—of this country. I do not undervalue the other great Departments of the State, but the efficiency of either the Army or the Navy might be temporarily affected without the nation feeling it. No dismay would be experienced if, during January, the ubiquitous tax-gatherer did not visit our homes; but if our energies flagged, if our machinery got clogged, if the pulse of the postal and telegraph system ceased to beat but for half a day, and its circulation by rail, road, and wire were impeded, the very life of the community would stand still. I can imagine no greater disaster than the breakdown of the Post-Office system except the contemporaneous cessation of all railway communication.

We work, therefore, under a sense of great responsibility and with a proud consciousness of the trust which our fellow-citizens so generously repose in us. We hope to prove ourselves more and more worthy of it. We have many critics, many candid friends. We touch every imaginable interest, and are in contact at all points with humanity on its most sensitive side; for I know that nothing raises such passions in the human breast or elicits such violence of language as the non-receipt of a letter, newspaper, or post-card. We are necessarily much criticized and closely watched. I do not complain of this. It is right and good for us. I would only ask that those who are so ready with blame for our failures—for we are not perfect—and for our alleged inability to move with the times, would remember that, with a complicated and highly-organized machinery like ours, and working under constant high pressure, reforms and changes must be carefully and slowly made. That which seems very easy to the outsider who wants a change of a particular kind affecting his own interests may disturb the balance of working and affect the convenience of millions of persons and a revenue and expenditure of millions of pounds.

But I do not say this either to deprecate criticism or to advocate standing still. As the servants of the State—that is to say, the State in its character of the general public—our one and foremost object should be, and, indeed, I may say it is, to supply the wants and to administer to the convenience of that public. Though styled a revenue department, and most valuable as a machinery for indirect and unfelt taxation, I should deeply regret if we came to be regarded, or to regard ourselves, as a mere tax-collecting department. Nothing, in my opinion, would be worse for the Department, and consequently for the public, than for the former to consider as the be-all and end-all of the Post-Office service the extraction of a large revenue from the country; and, indeed, such a limitation of its functions would defeat the very object for which it exists—namely, the greatest possible convenience to the public by the multiplication and acceleration of every form of communication which properly falls within its limits. Nothing would be so calculated to chill the ardour, to stunt the energies, and to repress the inventive zeal of the officers of the Post-Office as for them to feel that there are barriers in the path of postal progress which they are forbidden to surmount.

There may be many ways in which the service can render itself more useful to the community at large, and thus minister to the general progress and prosperity of the country; and I cannot but regard it as the bounden, if not the paramount, duty of a great commercial department like the Post-Office to do its utmost, without undue interference with private enterprise, to invent and bring into operation such methods of general utility as will best promote the common weal. I believe that there is a variety of directions in which the Post-Office could render very great service to the community which have as yet been unattempted, and that, with its unexampled facility for reaching the public in every corner of the kingdom, it might do much to help forward the social and commercial interests of the country.

It is not for me as a servant of the State to attempt to criticize the doings of my superiors, but I confess that I should like to see the Post-Office, which is the greatest commercial department in the country, administered on something like true commercial principles, and a portion at least of its large annual profit (which in reality is larger than it seems, owing to the system which charges capital expenditure against income),

F

utilized for developing and extending its work for the general benefit of the public.

It may be true that in some respects other countries which at first followed us in the great postal reforms introduced by Rowland Hill have, here and there, outstripped us; and I cannot but confess a feeling of some humiliation when attending as representative of this country at our great international postal congresses, where all the civilized countries of the world are represented, at being asked by my foreign colleagues whether England, which had so long been in the van of postal reform, was now going to take a second place. I hope, for the honour of our country, as well as for its advantage, that that will never be permanently the case, and I beg to assure you, Sir, that I speak the mind of the whole Department when I say that nothing shall be lacking in the way of a high sense of public duty, of energy, and, if need be, of inventive skill to keep Great Britain in the proud position in which the determination and ability of Rowland Hill placed her—that of the first country in the world for the perfection, as it is for the magnitude, of its postal service.

Mr. A. TURNOR proposed "The Past Postmasters-General," of whom he said two not the least distinguished were present. They regretted very much the absence of four others, and had received letters expressing sorrow that they could not attend. He was sure he was expressing the feelings of all present when he said they sympathized with the reason which prevented Lord Hartington from being present; and they wished him a speedy and a complete recovery. Looking at the eminent roll of statesmen who had filled the office of Postmaster-General, he could not help dwelling on the name of one who had been taken away—a man whom they would always regard with affection and respect, one who initiated and carried through great reforms in the Post-Office—he alluded to the late Professor Fawcett.

The duties of a Postmaster-General did not terminate with his departure from the office, and the Department and the public often received valuable aid from those who had held the office. A notable example of this was furnished by the assistance which Mr. Shaw-Lefevre gave to the passing of the Sixpenny Telegrams Bill when there was only an hour and twenty minutes available for passing it through the House of Commons. If it had not been for his skill and intimate knowledge of the subject it was probable that the Bill would not have been passed in that Session.

The duties of a Postmaster-General differed very considerably from what they were when Henry VIII. appointed Sir Brien Tuke at a salary of £66 a year, and designated him "Master of the Posts." Probably the greatest anxiety which troubled the breast of that worthy knight was how he should enjoy his salary. In the Victorian era the duties of a Postmaster-General were far different. The British public desired him to do everything and yet wished to pay for nothing. During the last hundred years there had been thirty-eight Postmasters-General, and that number gave an average reign of two years, seven months, and thirteen days. In the face of so many changes it seemed extraordinary that so many improvements were made.

Mr. SHAW-LEFEVRE, M.P., in responding, said,—As one of the ex-Postmasters-General, I have the honour to return thanks for the very cordial manner in which you have received the toast. I very much regret that two of the most distinguished among our number—the Duke of Argyll and Lord Hartington—are unable to be present, and still more that serious illness is the cause of the latter being absent. I am sure that I express the hopes of all that he may speedily be restored to public life, of which he is so distinguished an ornament. My own career as Postmaster-General was not a long one. It did not extend over more than a few months, but my connection with the Department was not confined to this, for twice I served as Deputy-Postmaster —on the first occasion for many months—during illnesses of my lamented friend and colleague Mr. Fawcett, whose name is imperishably connected with Post-Office improvements, and than whom no one since Sir Rowland Hill has more adequately grasped the needs of the people, or done more to popularize the service and to increase its functions. It so happened that in my capacity as deputy, or as the successor to Mr. Fawcett, I was largely responsible for the regulations to carry into effect the parcel post and also sixpenny telegrams; and I think I may say that I had unusual opportunities of forming an opinion as to the willingness and capacity of the permanent officials of the Department in carrying out such great extensions.

I have a very vivid personal recollection of Sir Rowland Hill. I frequently saw him at my father's house, when I was a young man, between the years 1848 and 1855. I have often heard him discuss and explain the difficulties which he encountered in carrying the great scheme in the four years before 1840. I recollect well his saying on many occasions that what most surprised him was, the opposition and obstruction which he met with from the Post-Office officials of that day. He was anything but complimentary to those officials; fortunately the genus is now extinct, and if there is one he would be worthy of a place in the museum of eccentricities which turn up in the Dead Letter Department. Sir Rowland used to say that he could quite well understand the opposition of the Financial Department of the Government, who looked to receiving a large revenue from the Post-Office, and who feared any measure which might even temporarily endanger that revenue.

It must be admitted that Sir Rowland was somewhat oversanguine as to the immediate financial results of the change, and, in fact, it was many years before the loss to the revenue was recouped. When we blame such great statesmen as Sir Robert Peel for opposing the change in the interest of the revenue, we may perhaps recollect that statesmen in the present day have been heard to pronounce in the most emphatic manner that they will brook no interference with the revenue derived from the Post-Office; and if they had lived fifty years ago, they would probably have taken the same view as Sir Robert Peel and Lord Melbourne. What Sir Rowland could not understand was, how the Post-Office officials could have ranged themselves in opposition to the scheme, why they should have sided with the financial authorities, and have done their utmost to defeat the scheme. They must have known the absurdities, the inequalities, the complexities, the injustice of the old system, how hardly it pressed on the poor, how it was the engine of privilege under which one-half of the letters forwarded were forwarded free of charge under the system of "franking."

It is difficult to conceive how they could fail to understand the simplicity and equality of the new scheme. I know nothing more amusing than to read the evidence given before the Committee of 1838 by the Post-Office officials. The secretary to the Post-Office, Colonel Maberly, said that the scheme was utterly fallacious, a most preposterous one, utterly unsupported by facts, and resting wholly on assumption. Every experiment in the way of reductions which had been made in the Post-Office had shown its fallacy. If the rates were reduced to a penny the revenue would not recover itself for forty or fifty years. The assistant-secretary boldly stated his opinion that there would be no increase of correspondence. Every possible objection was raised to every part of the scheme. They maintained that uniformity would be unjust and impracticable; that payment in advance was impossible; and that the charge by weight could not be entertained.

Sir Rowland Hill not only carried his great scheme, but gave a great blow to the obtuse and ignorant and prejudiced officialism from which it has, I rejoice to think, never recovered. It survived in fact for a time; but Sir Rowland inspired the Department with a new spirit, and founded a new school of officials. Up to that time he has stated no improvement had ever been devised in the Department. Post-Office reformers had always forced their schemes upon the Department after a long struggle. They were taken into the office to carry them out, but were later turned adrift. It is demonstrable that of late years there has been a great change in this respect. All the great changes and improvements and extensions have been devised and carried out within the Post-Office by such men as Mr. Chetwynd, Mr. Scudamore, and Mr. Patey, and I have often heard Mr. Fawcett say that he owed all his schemes to men within the Office, and found them the most ready agents for carrying them out; and I can bear the same testimony from my short experience. I desire to emphasize this, as there is a disposition in the Press to complain of the tardiness of the Post-Office to adopt improvements.

The difficulty does not rest there. It rests rather with the Financial Departments of the Government. Every change and improvement costs money; most of them risk for a time some more revenue. If it is insisted upon that there shall be an ever-increasing net revenue, it stands to reason that many reforms and extensions which the public desires must be postponed. He would be a bold man who would beard the Chancellor of the Exchequer and ask him to give up the whole of this net revenue for Post-Office improvements, though it is to be remarked that no other country in the world draws a revenue from its Post-Office. It is not, however, necessary to contemplate this. What I have at various times suggested is that we should estimate at a liberal amount what net revenue we should draw on the average of years from the Post-Office, and that what there is beyond this of growing net revenue should be applied year by year to the improvements and extensions the public desires.

The present would be a very good opportunity for applying this principle, for the net revenue is growing by giant bounds. In 1888 the net revenue increased by £300,000, in 1889 by another £400,000, and in the current year I doubt not it will be £500,000, or an increase of £1,200,000 in three years, and the net revenue is now double what it was before the introduction of the penny post. I can conceive no better way of celebrating the jubilee or in commemorating its great founder than by applying at all events the increase in the growing net revenue to improvements. The essence of his scheme was simplicity, uniformity, universality, cheapness, and there are many directions in which these great principles may be carried further to the benefit of the people and the improvement of trade.

Sir Lyon Playfair, in responding, said,—Our chairman has made such an exhaustive speech as to the occasion of the jubilee, and the progress of the Post-Office during the last fifty years, that he has left to the following speakers little to say, except to refer to their own memories during that period, if, like myself, they have lived all through it. In my historical readings

THE LATE RIGHT HON. HENRY FAWCETT, M.P.
(From a photograph by Mr. J. B......)

I remember a curious instance of the cost of letters long ago. Six hundred years since, on August 17, 1290, a letter-carrier called on Edward I. with an important letter announcing the arrival of the Maiden of Norway on the coasts of the kingdom. The king, after some grumbling, paid him 13s. 4d., a large sum in those days, for the delivery of the letter. The letter-carrier was a Scotchman, called William Playfair, who held the office of letter messenger to the Earl of Orkney. As the name is not common, and as he hailed from Scotland, this letter-carrier of 600 years ago may have been my ancestor, and if so, it is natural, in the Darwinian process of evolution, that I should have become a Postmaster-General.

Unfortunately for myself, a change of Government prevented me from holding this office for more than a few months, so that it is good of you even to recollect the fact that at one time I was Postmaster-General. My only useful work in regard to the Post-Office was prior to this appointment. In 1870 I entered into a conspiracy with the late Lord Advocate of Scotland, Mr. Macdonald, to press upon the Post-Office a system of open letters, which we called post-cards. At that time Mr. Macdonald was not in Parliament, so the Parliamentary advocacy of post-cards fell upon me, but my ally in Edinburgh was most efficient in getting up influential memorials in its favour. Our work was short, because Lord Hartington—then Postmaster-General—saw the value of the suggestion and adopted the system of halfpenny post-cards, which now number 201,000,000 annually, or nearly twice as many as the letters were the year before our jubilee. Excuse my egotism in recalling my connection with the introduction of the post-card, for I value this humble service as a pleasant memory.

I now turn to my recollections of Rowland Hill, whose memory we are now to a great extent celebrating. When I first came to London, like other Scotch youths looking for occupation, the penny post had been established for one year. It was my good fortune to become acquainted with some men of light and leading, among whom were Rowland Hill, John Stuart Mill, Edwin Chadwick, Neil Arnot, and others. We formed a club to dine at each other's houses, calling ourselves "friends in council," in order to discuss various economical subjects. Among these postal reform was one of the most prominent. Even at that early date the penny post, which had been so vehemently opposed, had got to the stage when people denied its novelty, and decried the merits of Rowland Hill as an inventor. All successful inventions go through this stage of denial and ingratitude; why, even a court of law has left a solemn decision that Watt did nothing to improve the steam engine!

It is a matter of perfect indifference to me whether Rowland Hill alone, or a dozen men before him, proposed a penny post. As a fact, we know that there were private companies which carried letters for a penny in various cities. The mere idea of making a local rate a uniform rate throughout a country was sure to suggest itself to some people. When the tree ripens much of the fruit gets ready about the same time, but it was Rowland Hill who grasped the idea and made it his own, who grappled with prejudice and monopoly, who awakened public conviction, who showed that a great agitator could be a great administrator, and who ultimately conferred the inestimable blessing of the penny post on the toiling millions of the people.

I recollect that, at our friendly dinners, Rowland Hill delighted to discuss the effect of cheap postage on the affections and education of the people. I illustrated my own case, which was by no means rare, of a family living in India, with whom it was difficult to keep up constant correspondence on account of the cost. At that time a letter consisted of a single sheet, crossed and often recrossed, and this cramped and stunted family affections. A quarter of an ounce of love even from Scotland cost 1s. 4d.; from India much more; whereas now we can get a whole ounce of love for 1d. As an educational agency the penny post has been most powerful. The three R's given in our public schools form such a thin veneer of knowledge that it is rubbed off in three years' wear and tear of life. Reading, writing, and arithmetic, as taught in elementary schools, are plants of weak growth, but they are watered and made to thrive by the penny post.

I recollect giving Rowland Hill an illustration which pleased him much. I had been travelling in Norway and Sweden, and found that they were abandoning their Sunday secular schools. On asking the reason I was told that since the introduction of the penny post they were no longer found to be necessary, as cheap letters kept up education better than Sunday schools.

On a day of rejoicing and remembrances like this, let me say a word of appreciation of one of the greatest and best officials in the history of the Post Office—I allude to the late Mr. Scudamore. When I entered upon my duties as Postmaster-General he was in official difficulties with the Treasury and Parliament, because in his zeal he had used the revenue of the Department for the rapid extension of the system of telegraphs. Of course this was a grave official error, for the money ought to have been voted by the House of Commons. I entered the office believing that I would have much trouble with this impetuous secretary, but I left it feeling the highest admiration of his administrative capacity, and unselfish zeal. The country owe him a debt of gratitude for the rapid and efficient extension of the telegraphic system. One night of anxiety remains vividly in my memory. The new Post-Office buildings, with their fine telegraphic halls, were ready, but it was an anxious thing to disconnect the whole telegraphic communication of the country and re-establish it in the new building. Mr. Scudamore was equal to the occasion, and the change was made without the loss of a single message or more than one hour's delay. Like so many of our friends Mr. Scudamore has gone to the great majority, but his memory should not be forgotten on this occasion.

There is one feature of the Post-Office which has contributed greatly to its success—I allude to its perfect freedom from political action. I believe that the only survival of politics in it is in the appointment of rural messengers by members of Parliament for the district. This miserable remnant of patronage ought to be swept away. I do not think that I ever knew, and certainly never asked, what were the political convictions of any candidate for office when I had to deal with the patronage, and this must be the practice and experience of my successors.

How different is the administration of the Post-Office in the United States! At every change of a political party in the Presidency there is a sweeping change of officers, on the principle that "spoils belong to the victors." The present President has been in office only a few months, but when I left America in November, 17,000 postmasters had been dismissed because they were Democrats, and the party newspapers were urging increased activity in the process of disorganization. It is because our Post-Office has been an efficient servant of the public, having only one thought as to how to do its duty without fear or favour, that it stands so high in public estimation. Its work has been great in the past fifty years, and it is a joy for us who are present to-night, to aid in the celebration of the benefits which half a century of pure and active administration has conferred on the public.

Mr. F. E. BAINES proposed "The Retired Officers of the Post-Office," and mentioned several to the merits of whom he paid tributes which were endorsed by the company. The deceased included the following : Secretaries :—Colonel Maberly, Sir Rowland Hill, F. I. Scudamore, C.B., Arthur Benthall, and C. H. B. Patey, C.B. Controllers of London Postal Service :—W. Bokenham, T. Boucher, and T. Jeffery. Inspectors-General of Mails :—G. Stow (mail coaches), West, and Edward Page. Receivers and Accountants General :—Hyde, Chetwynd, Richardson. Surveyors :—Gay, Creswell, Johnson, Anthony Trollope, James, and Beaufort. Savings Bank :—A. Milliken, C. Thompson, and Ramsay. Telegraphs :—Shaw and Sanger. Doctors :—William Gavin and Walter Lewis. The living included Sir John Tilley, K.C.B., Frederic Hill, Francis Abbott, W. J. Page, F. R. Jackson, Pearson Hill, H. Mellersh, C. B. Banning, C. Teesdale, R. S. Culley, J. H. Newman, Ernest Milliken, and finally E. Yates, of whom the speaker remarked that, finding the yoke of the Post-Office too easy, he took on himself the cares of the *World*.

SIR J. TILLEY, in responding, said that, if he were a useful servant at the Post-Office, he owed such usefulness in great measure to the assistance he obtained from those about him.

The Right Hon. G. J. Shaw Lefevre, M.P.
(From a photograph by the London Stereoscopic Company.)

He heard with intense pleasure the generous remarks of Sir L. Playfair about Mr. Scudamore. Probably his own knowledge of Sir Rowland Hill was larger than that of any one present except the members of his family. With all Sir Rowland Hill's foresight, it was probable he never contemplated that the civilized world would take up his scheme in so short a time. When he was first appointed the General Post-Office occupied the site of the present branch office in Lombard Street, and his room was the kitchen of the old rectory house of St. Mary Woolnoth. The *personnel* was somewhat different from what it is now. At that early date if gentlemen wanted to increase their incomes they did not write novels or their autobiographies or edit editions of Shelley. The Secretary had occasion to send for one gentleman, to whom he said, "I have the greatest admiration for trade and commerce; but you must decide between the Post-Office and a cabbage stall in the New Cut." The increased business was now carried on as easily as the small amount of work that had to be done in Lombard Street. It had grown largely since he left the Office ten years ago, and he believed it was conducted with greater ability than he could have brought to bear upon it.

Mr. Edmund Yates also responded, and said it was very kind of the company to drink to the health of a body of bygone and feeble old men, for whom he tremblingly returned thanks. He could scarcely bring himself to believe that it was nearly eighteen years since he gracefully retired from the public service. In that retirement he had acted on the principle of the proverbial well-bred dog, who went before he was kicked; and as soon as he saw his friend Sir John Tilley's boots shuffling on the floor he made his salaam. Times had changed in the Post-Office, and he understood that more work was done there than previously. So far as he was personally concerned he admitted the possibility of such a change. His first chief, Colonel Maberly, used to impress upon him the necessity of not overworking himself: he had given the Colonel the pledge that he would not, and had solemnly adhered to that sacred obligation.

Sir A. Blackwood rose to propose the health of "The Postmaster-General," and said,—If my unfortunate and intolerant principles forbid my asking you to pledge Mr. Raikes in flowing bumpers and no heeltaps, I can none the less invite you to join me in wishing him most heartily all happiness and prosperity. It has been extremely kind of Mr. Raikes to identify himself so thoroughly with the Department by presiding on the present occasion, and the postponement of our gathering for a few days has been well worth the advantage of his presence which we have thereby secured. The tenure of the office of Postmaster-General by Mr. Raikes has been remarkable for this fact—that it has comprised no less that three jubilees. First, his own—for he completed his fiftieth year of life since he came to St. Martin's-le-Grand; secondly, that of her Most Gracious Majesty's reign; and, lastly, the jubilee of the great event we celebrate this evening; and I am sure that this occasion will ever be remembered by him as an interesting episode in his Post-magisterial career. If Mr. Raikes may fairly be congratulated on his good fortune in that respect, we also may consider ourselves fortunate in having so distinguished and able a statesman as our present Parliamentary chief.

It is a happy coincidence that the Post-Office, which is nothing if not a literary Department, should have at its head the representative of one of the most famous seats of learning and letters in the world; and not less fortunate are we in having as the Minister responsible to the country for our service one who, by his tact and courtesy no less than his ability, is so successful in his Parliamentary conduct of the business of the Post-Office. It has been my lot to communicate instruction—or, perhaps, I ought to say, lest I unduly magnify my office, to supply information—to several successive Postmasters-General, and, without any reflection on his predecessors, two of whom we are proud to have with us this evening, I may say that I never met with any one who more rapidly or more completely mastered the complicated details of our very intricate system. There is not one of those details with which the present Postmaster-General is not conversant, and I may add—what is perhaps of greater importance—there is not one of the 100,000 people over whom he presides whose interests he is not anxious to promote whenever he can legitimately do so, and for whose welfare he is not solicitous.

I am sure that no more laborious Postmaster-General has ever occupied Mr. Raikes's chair in St. Martin's-le-Grand. Not only has he succeeded to more arduous labours than any of his predecessors by the mere growth of Post-Office business, but he has materially added thereto by the self-imposition of branches of work which he felt it right personally to undertake; and the mass of papers which the secretaries have to send him every day must make him one of the hardest-worked men in the Department. For the Postmaster-General can never have a day's leave; others may have their month or fortnight, but the Postmaster-General never rests. He is the official Flying Dutchman of modern times, for the wheel of the Post-Office never stops. Once or twice, indeed, overburdened, he has endeavoured to flee, not leaving his address behind: but the Post-Office, which is never at fault, tracked him to his hiding place wherever he was, on the shores of the Riviera or in the fastnesses of Wales, and delivered to him with unfailing regularity his daily official papers. Still, I know that it is for him a work of love no less than of duty, and that, so long as he continues to preside at St. Martin's-le-Grand, the important service of which he is the head will be most ably administered.

Our respected chief is not only a statesman of eminence and ability, but one who is susceptible to the claims of sentiment in even so prosaic a Department as the Post-Office. This statement will, I am sure, be appreciated when I say (and I hope Mr. Raikes will forgive me for alluding to it) that when, on a very recent occasion, a candidate for postal employment, not perhaps in all respects quite unexceptionable, came forward, bearing fortuitously the name of Rowland Hill, Mr. Raikes could not bring himself to reject a candidate nominally so distinguished at the present time.

We wish you, Mr. Raikes, all health and happiness, and

we hope that the recollection of this evening's gathering, where you are surrounded by so many loyal and devoted servants of the State, will nerve you for every conflict. We thank you most heartily for honouring us with your presence to-night.

Mr. RAIKES, in responding, said,—I wish to thank you most sincerely for the extremely kind manner in which Sir Arthur has proposed my health and in which you have received it. I cannot deny that perhaps I have multiplied my duties at the Post-Office, and so far deprived myself of any claim to sympathy. It is quite true the Postmaster-General has no repose; pouches follow him with unerring accuracy. Entertaining the postmen at home at Christmas, I learned that the local postmaster believed the Postmaster-General had a sinecure until I took the office, and then he realized his mistake from simply counting the pouches which came from London. Some of my predecessors have done more distinguished service to the State, and if their terms of office had been as prolonged as mine they might have earned imperishable names.

It is an easy and pleasant task to encounter criticism when you feel that you have the whole service with you, and as long as you are endeavouring to do your duty by every member of the service, so long you have a right to count upon their cordial and loyal assistance. I have enjoyed that privilege in a conspicuous degree, and I am quite satisfied that as long as the Department is united we shall always be able to meet an enemy in the gate and render increasingly valuable service to the country. Interesting as this occasion has been, it is only a Departmental festival, and it is not to be regarded as a full and entire consummation of our wish to do honour to the jubilee of the penny post.

I trust that in the course of the next few months there will be a public celebration in which we may be permitted to participate, and which will, I trust, assume a really national aspect; and if it is carried out I hope it may not only redound to the honour of the illustrious name of Rowland Hill, but that it may also be made a means of improving the position of many of the poorer and unfortunate servants of the Department whose difficulties are now but imperfectly met by the fund which bears Rowland Hill's name. We have had a jubilee Sir Arthur did not refer to—that of the telegraphs, and I refer to it for the purpose of expressing my affectionate regard for that brilliant, capable, kind, considerate, and disinterested man, my late friend, Mr. Patey, whose valuable assistance on many occasions I feel bound to recognize. Nothing will afford me greater pleasure than that in the course of the year a real national movement shall be set on foot, and that it shall be the means of improving the circumstances of the most necessitous and distressed members of the service. Once more thanking you, I can only wish that there may be present some who will attain even to the official term of service of Sir John Tilley and live to be present at the next jubilee.

The company then separated.

THE CONVERSAZIONE

AT THE

GUILDHALL,

MAY 16, 1890.

Sir James Whitehead, Bart.
(Chairman of Corporation Committee.)
(From a photograph by Mr. Walery.)

THE CONVERSAZIONE AT THE GUILDHALL.

[*Extracts from the Catalogue of Articles arranged by Mr. G. A. Aitken for exhibition at the Guildhall.*]

A COLLECTION ILLUSTRATING THE HISTORY OF THE POST-OFFICE.

Postal Sorting Office, 1890; showing stamping, sorting, and despatch of letters posted in the City of London.

Exterior of a Post-Office of 1790, with notices of the period exhibited.

Model of Street Lamp, Fire Alarm, and Pillar Letter Box, combined. *Mr. Theodore Lumley.*

Guildhall Branch Post-Office; at which all kinds of postal and telegraph business will be transacted.

Army Postal Corps Tent, fittings, and appliances, with staff.

The first Rifle Volunteers under fire. The Post-Office Corps at Kassassin (September, 1882). *Captain Dickson.*

Collapsible Sorting Tables, used in sorting offices at times of special pressure.

Model of Royal Mail Steamer *Hare*. Built 1887. Runs between Ardrossan and Belfast. *Mr. J. Burns, Glasgow.*

Model of S.S. *Umbria*. *Cunard Steam Ship Company.*

Paintings of Cunard R.M. Steamers :—
P.S. *Britannic* (1840), P.S. *Persia* (1856) S.S. *China* (1862), S.S. *Russia* (1867), S.S. *Gallia* (1879), S.S. *Servia* (1881), S.S. *Umbria* (1884). *Cunard Steam Ship Company.*

Model of P.S. *William Fawcett*. Dimensions 74 ft. 3 in. by 15 ft. 1 in. by 8 ft. 4 in. Tonnage 206; horse-power 60.

Built of wood, 1829. The first Vessel employed in the Contract Mail Service to the Peninsular Ports, 1837.
Peninsular and Oriental S.N. Company.

Model of S.S. *Oceana*. Dimensions 465 ft. 5 in. by 52 ft. 1 in. by 34 ft. 6 in. Tonnage 6,362; horse-power 7,000. Built of steel, and fitted with gun platforms as a War Cruiser. A type of the Company's Jubilee ships *Victoria*, *Britannia*, *Oceana*, and *Arcadia*, now carrying the Mails.
Peninsular and Oriental S.N. Company.

Painting of the *Victoria*—the first of the Company's Jubilee ships—surrounded by pictures, showing points of departure in the history of the Company and of the Mail Service from 1837. *Peninsular and Oriental S.N. Company.*

Model of Paddle Mail Steamer *Connaught*, 1860.
Messrs. Laird Brothers.

Model of Paddle Mail Steamer *Ireland*, 1885.
Messrs. Laird Brothers.

Model of H.M.S. *Dover*, 1840. Employed for years in the Mail Service between Dover and Calais.
Messrs. Laird Brothers.

Model of the *St. Columba*, 1847. Built for the Holyhead and Dublin Mail Service. *Messrs. Laird Brothers.*

Model of the Liverpool and London Mail Coach.

Model of Locomotive, Great Northern Railway.
Mr Curtin, Doncaster.

Model of Locomotive. *Great Eastern Railway Company.*

Model of Broad-Gauge Mail Locomotive, "North Star."
Dowager Lady Gooch.

Sign of a Post-Office of 1790.

Mail Guard's Post Horn in use during the earlier years of this century. *Mr. Billson.*

Models of a Travelling Post-Office, with apparatus for receiving and despatching mail bags.

Travelling Post-Office Standard, with two full pouches suspended, to illustrate the actual working of the system.

Apparatus Net for receiving bags from Travelling Post-Office.

Staff issued to letter carriers in London at time of Chartist Riots, 1848.   *Mr. Watson.*

Books of Curious Addresses.

Albums of Foreign Post-Office Christmas Cards.

Special Postal Train between London and Aberdeen. Established in 1885.

Notice of Postal Changes on the 1st July, 1885.
> On this date the Mail Service to Scotland was greatly improved, and a Special Mail Train, devoted to Post-Office purposes, was established between London and Aberdeen. Other postal facilities in London and the provinces, and in the colonial and foreign services, also came into operation in July, 1885.

Brass Memorial Plate (rubbing of) at St. George's Chapel, Windsor, to the memory of Edward Phillips—"The said Edward Phillips also served King Charles the II. and King James the II. in the General Post-Office." Afterwards he was one of the 100 Yeomen of the Guard to William and Mary, Anne, and George I.   *Mr. Bambridge.*

Photographs of Railway Travelling Post-Office.

Medal or Badge, having on the obverse side the Royal Arms, and on the reverse side "Letter-Bearer, General Post-Office."   *Mr. Billson.*

Flint pistols, and watch, carried by Guard of Mail Coach running between Clapham and Lancaster in 1835.
   Mr. Fletcher

Pistol in holster, carried by Mail-man in Sussex, in 1839.
   Mr. Knight, Hawkhurst.

Cutlass used by Mail Coach Guard in 1800.
   Mr. T. C. Bokenham.

Original Bell, used by Bellmen who collected letters by ringing a bell in the City in 1840.   *Mr. Finch.*

Blunderbusses and Flint Pistols used when conveying the Mails across the Isthmus of Panama.   *Mr. Bennett, Exeter.*

Revolver and Sword Bayonet, as used by Guards to Parcel Coaches now on the Road.

Engravings of the Interior of General Post-Office, East. About 1840.   *Mr. Billson.*

Departure of Mail Coaches from General Post-Office and Piccadilly.

Introduction of an Inland Parcel Post, August, 1883. Notice to the Public.

Parcel Post Vehicles. Four framed drawings.

Photograph of Chief Officials despatching the first Parcel Mail to Australia.

Despatch of first Parcel Mail to India.

Photographs of the Brighton and Watford Parcel Coaches.

Chart showing the progress of the Inland Parcel Post, from 1st August, 1883.

Chart showing the progress of the Foreign and Colonial Parcel Post, from 1st July, 1885.

View of the Yard of the General Post-Office, showing Mail Coaches preparing to start (Coloured Print by J. Pollard).
Mr. Pamphilon.

Mail Coach and Stage Waggon. *Mr. T. C. Bokenham.*

A Post-Office on St. Valentine's Day. *Mr. T. C. Bokenham.*

Act of 1657, by which the General Post-Office and the office of Postmaster-General were established.
Mr. J. E. Hodgkin, F.S.A.

Early Postal Guide (before 1681). *Mr. J. E. Hodgkin, F.S.A.*

The Penny Post (London). Broadside notice. 1680. Dockwra was the "chief undertaker." *Mr. J. E. Hodgkin, F.S.A.*

Portrait of the last of the Mail Guards, James Nobbs, still in the service of the Post-Office.

Portrait of the only Letter Carrier in Wolverhampton in 1854.
Mr. Kewley.

Arrival of the Mail after a great victory. (Engraving after painting by Mr. Goodall). *Mr. Smith.*

Royal Mails starting from Post-Office, in Lombard Street, in 1827. *Mr. Dixon.*

Plan of Aldersgate Ward, as it existed in 1754, showing the streets, courts, &c., which were afterwards to be demolished in 1824 to 1829, to make room for the present General Post-Office. *Mr. Billson.*

POSTMEN'S UNIFORMS DURING THE LAST FIFTY YEARS.

Rowland Hill's Chapel. View of the G.P.O., issued in 1849, in opposition to the then suggested Sunday Deliveries.
Mr. Billson.

Painting of Postmen's "Accelerator," formerly used for conveying Postmen to the starting-point of their Deliveries.

The Interior of Sorting Office, General Post-Office, by candle-light, at the time of the Gas Stokers' strike in 1872.
Mr. Finch.

Letters sent by Balloon Post from Paris in 1871.
Messrs. Salmon and Clayton.

Collections of English Postage Stamps. V. (crown) R. design; &c.

Specimens of Foreign Postage Stamps.

Long-lost Letter. Cover of Envelope delayed in the post twelve years.

Seal and Stamp of the Baschurch Penny Post.
Mr. Phillipson, Shrewsbury.

General Post-Office, Lombard Street, formerly the residence of Sir Robert Vyner, Lord Mayor of London, 1675. View showing the interior of the old courtyard.
Mr. J. E. Gardner, F.S.A.

General Post-Office, Lombard Street, exterior. Original drawing by S. Ireland, 1799. *Mr. J. E. Gardner, F.S.A.*

St. Martin's-le-Grand. Site of the New Post-Office, 1815 (Girtin). *Mr. J. E. Gardner, F.S.A.*

Crypt of the ancient College of St. Martin's-le-Grand, discovered on clearing for the New Post-Office. (Five views.) 1819.
Mr. J. E. Gardner, F.S.A.

Bull and Mouth Inn. (Original Drawings by Nash, and by Shepperd.) 1806. *Mr. J. E. Gardner, F.S.A.*

The Bull and Mouth, St. Martin's-le-Grand. Despatch of the Glasgow Mails (Henderson). *Mr. J. E. Gardner, F.S.A.*

General Post-Office. Interior of Inland Office. (Two views.)
Mr. J. E. Gardner, F.S.A.

The Letter Woman (with a bell). 1768.
Mr. J. E. Gardner, F.S.A.

Postman Delivering Letters. 1813. *Mr. J. E. Gardner, F.S.A.*

Costume of the London Postman, 1820 (T. Busby).
Mr. J. E. Gardner, F.S.A.
Departure of the Mails from the General Post-Office. About 1830. *Mr. J. E. Gardner, F.S.A.*
Mulready Envelopes and Caricatures. (Thirteen.)
Mr. J. E. Gardner, F.S.A.
Edinburgh Mail leaving St. Martin's-le-Grand on a foggy night, 1829. (Pollard.) *Mr. J. E. Gardner, F.S.A.*
Bull and Mouth Inn. Interior. Mails preparing for departure ("All the World's a Stage").
Mr. J. E. Gardner, F.S.A.
General Post-Office in Lombard Street (Robert Cruikshank), 1825. *Mr. J. E. Gardner, F.S.A.*
St. Martin's-le-Grand. Post-Office, Bull and Mouth Inn.
Mr. J. E. Gardner, F.S.A.
The General Post-Office. (Pollard.) 1829.
Mr. J. E. Gardner, F.S.A.
Royal Mails starting from the Post-Office, Lombard Street (E. Jones). *Mr. J. E. Gardner, F.S.A.*
North-East view of the New General Post-Office. Mails preparing to start. *Mr. J. E. Gardner, F.S.A.*
The Great Snowstorm of 1836. Four views of Mail Coaches stopped by the Snow. The Mail Bags were sometimes carried on by horse. *Mr. J. E. Gardner, F.S.A.*
Map showing the boundaries of the General and Two-Penny Post Deliveries, the districts of the Two-Penny Post-Office, and the number and situations of the General and Two-Penny Post-Office Receiving Houses. 1830. Printed by order of the House of Commons.
Mr. J. E. Gardner, F.S.A.
Map showing the boundaries of the General Post-Office Delivery, of the Foreign Delivery, of the Town Delivery, of the Two-Penny Post Department, and of the country Deliveries. 1830. *Mr. J. E. Gardner, F.S.A.*
Franks of Members of the House of Commons, 1784-1832. 4 vols. *Mr. E. Walford, M.A.*
Showing the franks of Burke, C. J. Fox, David Ricardo, and Mr. Lawson.

The last-named is written on blank paper, and the abuse of franking by Members who sold their signatures led to the Act of 1784, by which Members were compelled to date their franks.

Franks of the Members of the Houses of Lords and Commons, 1837-1840 (the Queen's first Parliament).
Mr. E. Walford, M.A.

Letter and last Frank of Lord Nelson, 1805.
Mr. E. Walford, M.A.

This is the last complete letter Nelson wrote. It is addressed to Lady Hamilton, and was sent on shore by a boat after Nelson had set sail from England for the last time. Another letter, commenced by Nelson after he was fatally wounded at Trafalgar, five weeks later, was never finished; it is in the British Museum. The present letter has the Portsmouth post-mark.

The Mail Coach (Fittler, 1803). *Mr. A. M. Ogilvie.*
Dedicated to John Palmer, Esq., Surveyor and Controller-General of the Post-Office.

Views of the General Post-Office, Lombard Street: Exterior, 1793; Interior (pencil sketches), 1815. *Mr. A. M. Ogilvie.*

The Quicksilver Royal Mail, 1835. *Mr. A. M. Ogilvie.*

Mail Coach in a Thunderstorm on Newmarket Heath (Pollard), 1827. *Mr. A. M. Ogilvie.*

Mail Coach in a Storm of Snow (Pollard), 1826.
Mr. A. M. Ogilvie.

Mail Coach in a Drift of Snow (Pollard), 1825.
Mr. A. M. Ogilvie.

Mail Coach in a Flood (Pollard), 1827. *Mr. A. M. Ogilvie.*

Mail Coach Days. Five prints (Pollard). *Mr. A. M. Ogilvie.*

The Royal Mails leaving the General Post-Office (Pollard), about 1830. *Mr. A. M. Ogilvie.*

A Dead-lock. The turnpike-keeper asleep. *Mr. John Mitford.*

Exchange of Mail Bags, early morning. (Bath and London Royal Mail.) *Mr. John Mitford.*

Collections of Postage Stamps. *Mr. Matthews.*

Dormouse forwarded through the Post. Print. *Mr. R. F. Pitt.*

Robbery at the Wetherby Post-Office of the Portmantua, with Bags from London for Knaresborough, Harrogate, &c., 1819. Offer of £30 reward.

Attack upon an armed Horse-Post Rider, near Spofforth, 1826. Offer of 20 guineas reward.

Robbery of Bags from the Dover Mail, 1826. Offer of 100 guineas reward.

Robbery of the Leeds Mail Coach between Kettering and Higham Ferrers, October 26th, 1812. Two notices, giving list of Bags stolen, with a reward of £200 for the arrest and conviction of the thieves.

Robbery of the Mail from London to Ipswich, September 11th (1813?). Large Notice, with particulars of Country Notes lost. £1,000 reward.

Robbery of the Mail between Leatherhead and Dorking, July 12, 1827. Driver fired at by two men and severely wounded. Notice offering 100 guineas reward.

Robbery from a Rider with the Foreign Mail from Dover, 1804. Offer of £50 reward.

Robbery of Twopenny Post Bags in Abchurch Lane, 1814. Offer of £50 reward.

Mail Bag stolen from the Selby and York Post-boy in 1798, and found in the roof of an old public-house pulled down in 1876.

Saxon and Roman Pottery found in excavating for the foundations for the General Post-Office (West).

Mr. Lawrence.

The Universal Magazine, July, 1753. Containing an account of the Execution of Two Highwaymen for the Murder of a Postman at Winchmore Hill. On the application of the Postmaster-General it was ordered that the bodies of these two men should be hung in chains near the spot where the murder was committed. *Mr. Knight.*

Pictures illustrating Travelling on the Liverpool and Manchester Railway in 1831 and 1833.

London and North Western Railway Company.

H.M. Cable Ship *Monarch* (photograph).

Delegates to the International Postal Commission, Paris, 1863.

Mr. H. Buxton Forman.

Delegates to various Postal Union and Telegraph Congresses.

Way Bill of a Mail sent by Express, 1807.
Mr. C. B. G. Banning, Liverpool.

Document appointing Mr. Worth Deputy-Postmaster of the Stage of Chatteris, in the County of Cambridge, 1784.
Mr. C. B. G. Banning, Liverpool.
Signed by the Earl of Tankerville and the Right Hon. H. F. Carteret (Postmaster-General), and Anthony Todd (Secretary).

Time Bill of the London and Edinburgh Mail Coach, 1836.
Mr. Mawson, Sheffield.
The journey occupied forty-two hours.

Order of the Procession of Her Majesty's Mail Coaches, 1838.
Mr. R. Gray, London.
This is believed to have been the last year in which the mail coaches went through London in procession on the birthday of the Sovereign.

Invitation Card to a Cold Collation, and to see the Procession of Coaches (about 1830). *Mr. R. Gray, London.*

Two Notices forbidding mail guards on the Treasury scale of wages to receive fees from the passengers, 1841.
Mr. R. Gray, London.

Contract for the Conveyance of Mails between Dover and Calais and Dover and Ostend, 1721.
The contract, made in April, 1721, was for seven years, dating from December 25, 1720. Charles Lovel, of Dover, gentleman, agreed with the Postmaster-General to defray all the expense of extraordinary boat hire whether for transporting of the mails or of his Majesty's messengers, to pay the charge for supporting his Majesty's poor subjects in their passage between Dover and Calais or Ostend, and to establish a correspondence with several persons in France and England, in order (if possible) to suppress the Bye Passage boats on those stations. In consideration for these services Lovel was to receive all the passage money paid by passengers in the Pacquet boats between Dover and Calais or Ostend.

Peninsular Steam Navigation Company. Notice issued by the Company, 7th August, 1837, that as they now conveyed mails they could not carry letters not forwarded through the Post-Office.

Consolidation of General and Twopenny Post Receiving

THE CONVERSAZIONE AT THE GUILDHALL. 93

Houses within the Three Mile Circle. Notice, December, 1838.

Sir Rowland Hill, K.C.B. Painting by Mr. J. A. Vinter.
Mr. Vinter.

Photograph of Heber Dale (height 4 feet, age 51), postman between Brailsford and Shirley, 1889. *Mr. S. Court, Derby.*

The Post-Office. A comic song sung at the Lyceum Theatre, &c., by J. Sanderson (about 1840). *Mr. Salt.*

Photographs of Locomotives, "North Star," and "Lord of the Isles." *Great Western Railway Company.*

Sheepskin Bag for Town Collections, formerly used in Edinburgh.

Rates of Post-Letters, both Inland and Outland (1685 ?).
Mr. W. J. Godby.

The only Postman in Newcastle-on-Tyne, 1824.
Mr. Hunter, Newcastle.

Regulations for the Uniform Penny Post, 7th January, 1840.
Mr. T. Coltherd, Edinburgh.

Quarterly Account of Postmaster of Ruthven, 1758.
Mr. T. C. Laws, Edinburgh.

Photograph of Letter fired in hollow Cannon Ball, at the Siege of Neuss, Germany, 1475. *Mr. J. W. Hyde.*

Portrait of the late Mr. Robert Paton, Morpeth and Rothbury Mail Driver. *Mr. J. W. Hyde.*

Mr. Paton met with his death in a snow-storm during the winter of 1889–90, while endeavouring to proceed with the mails.

York Four Days' Stage Coach (Notice), 1706.
Mr. J. W. Hyde.

Nest of a Tom-Tit built in a Letter-Box; with Tom-Tit in a glass case. *Mr. J. W. Hyde.*

Description of New Penny Post Delivery, London, 1794.
Mr. J. W. Hyde.

Portrait of a Manchester Postman in Livery worn prior to the Uniform Penny Postage. *Mr. J. W. Hyde.*

Scotch Letters. July 22, 1813. Notice that the new tax of one halfpenny on Scotch letters did not apply to letters to and from Coldstream, Hawick, and certain other towns in the neighbourhood.

News supplied by Postmasters. Notice, July 4, 1816, stating that the instruction—which had not been invariably attended to—that all Postmasters should send to the Secretary, for the information of the Postmaster-General, an immediate account of all remarkable occurrences in their district, that the same might be communicated if necessary to the Secretaries of State, must henceforth be carefully carried out.

Irish Letters. Two notices, July 1818, respecting surcharges on letters for Dublin or other Irish towns. The British and Irish revenues were to be kept distinct.

War with France. Three notices:—

(1) April 16, 1814. Communication with France re-opened (after the abdication of Napoleon, April 4). Four mails a week from London; postage (from London) 1s. 2d. a letter.

(2) March 30, 1815. Mails to Calais discontinued (outbreak of war after the escape of Napoleon from Elba).

(3) July, 1815. Mails for France resumed (after the battle of Waterloo and the occupation of Paris).

Valentines. Notice, May 5, 1829, to Postmasters. They were not at liberty to use their own discretion as to the disposal of what are called "Valentines" put into their offices for delivery. *All* undelivered letters must be sent to the Dead Letter Office.

Post-Office Expresses. Notice, December 21, 1825, directing that Post-boys conveying expresses must deliver them at the Post-Offices, and not at the Inns in the different towns.

Mr. Cary, editor of *Cary's Road Book*. Notice, January 14, 1820, directing Postmasters to give any information they may be able to Mr. Cary, in his inquiries about country seats or roads.

Newspapers, and Votes or Proceedings in Parliament. Regulations for forwarding free of postage. March, 1828.

Mr. Price, Ware.

Newspapers. Further regulations respecting the examination of newspapers sent by post; with cautions against delaying or tampering with them. November, 1830.
Mr. Price, Ware.

Votes of Post-Office Officials. Notice, 23rd November, 1832, giving extracts from Acts forbidding Post-Office *employés* and others to vote in Parliamentary elections, or to endeavour to influence the votes of any electors.
Mr. Price, Ware.

Notice prohibiting the sending to Postmasters of parcels containing prospectuses, bills, &c., with a request that the contents may be distributed. 12th January, 1830.
Mr. Price, Ware.

Notice forbidding Postmasters to receive packets containing several letters sent to them for distribution in the neighbourhood.
Mr. Price, Ware.

Receipt for Newspapers, 1816. *Mr. Kewley, Wolverhampton.*
The Clerks of the Roads had a monopoly until 1834.

Newspapers. Notice, 26th March, 1834, informing Postmasters that the Clerks of the Roads would now be prohibited from being concerned in dealing in newspapers.
Mr. Price, Ware.

Their Newspaper Privilege was abolished on April 5th.

"The New State of England"; about 1694.
Mr. A. M. Cunyngham.
Contains various particulars of the Post-Office. The head office of the Penny Post was at Crosby ("Grosby") Hall.

General Account of the Post-Office Revenues for a year, to 5th April, 1775.
The account of William Tanquier the younger, Esq., Accountant-General; on a very long parchment roll.

Surcharged Newspapers (three).
These papers were surcharged in amount varying from 8s. 6d. to 15s. 4d., because they were marked for reference, or bore words of the nature of a letter on the wrapper.

Report of the Postmaster-General (Lord Lichfield) on the Recommendations of the Committee on Postage, and their effect on the Revenue. 6th May, 1839. (About eighty pages.)
The Treasury.

Treasury Minute inviting competitors to suggest the best plan for covers under the Uniform Postage Act. 23rd August, 1839.
The Treasury.

Sir Rowland Hill's Report on the proposed Franking Stamp. 6th December, 1839. With specimens of stamps and paper suggested. *The Treasury.*

Treasury Minute upon the communications (more than 2,600 in number) received from the public with reference to the Postage Stamps, and upon the regulations for the Uniform Penny Post. Signed by Sir Francis Baring, 26th December, 1839. *The Treasury.*

> By this minute it was decided that as far as possible the postage of letters should be prepaid by stamps of various kinds ; that there should, on and after January 10th, 1840, be a uniform minimum rate of one penny ; and that the privilege of franking should cease.

Treasury Warrant for regulating the Rates of Postage, 22nd November, 1839. Signed by Lord Melbourne, Sir F. Baring, and Mr. Tuffnell. *The Treasury.*

> This warrant directed that on and after December 5th all letters should be charged by weight, and not according to the sheets of paper or enclosures. The minimum rate for letters not exceeding half an ounce in weight was 4d. in the case of inland letters, 1s. in the case of packet letters, and 8d. or 1s. in the case of ship letters (*i.e.* letters conveyed by private vessels) according to whether they were posted at the port from which the ship sailed or not. In cases where under existing arrangements the postage would be less than 4d., only the existing lower rate was to be charged. This arrangement lasted for one month, when Uniform Penny Postage was introduced.

Treasury Warrant authorizing a uniform minimum rate of Postage of One Penny for Inland letters, 27th December, 1839. Signed by Lord Melbourne, Sir F. Baring, and Mr. Wyse. *The Treasury.*

> After repealing the warrant of November 22nd this warrant fixed the minimum rate for Inland letters at 1d. The minimum rate for ship letters, wherever posted, was to be 8d. These alterations came into effect on January 10th, 1840.

Report, signed by Sir Rowland Hill, upon the Obliteration of Postage Stamps ; September 17th, 1840. *The Treasury.*

> Contains proofs of stamps, printed with various inks, and in different colours.

Original manuscript of Sir Rowland Hill's pamphlet on Post-Office Reform; with other papers. *Mr. Pearson Hill.*

The Post-Office of Fifty Years Ago, containing a facsimile reprint of Sir Rowland Hill's pamphlet *Post-Office Reform*, 1837. *Mr. Pearson Hill.*

Letter from the Treasury, January 4th, 1837, acknowledging the receipt of Sir Rowland Hill's first proposals for Post-Office Reform. *Mr. Pearson Hill.*

The Ninth Report of the Post-Office Inquiry Commission, containing Sir Rowland Hill's first evidence, and the proposal of adhesive postage stamps. *Mr. Pearson Hill.*

Specimens of Postal charges in 1839; showing the absurdity of the system of charging according to the number of sheets in a letter. *Mr. Pearson Hill.*

Letter from Mr. Henry Warburton to Sir Rowland Hill, May 22nd, 1839, stating that he had just heard that Penny Postage was to be granted. *Mr. Pearson Hill.*

Draft memorandum of Sir Rowland Hill to the Chancellor of the Exchequer upon the arrangements connected with the first introduction of the Penny Post; November 1st, 1839. *Mr. Pearson Hill.*

Letters from Richard Cobden and Charles Knight upon points connected with the new Penny Post. 1840, &c. *Mr. Pearson Hill.*

Sir Rowland Hill's Journal while at the Treasury, 1839 to 1842; containing particulars of the first day's sale of stamps, &c. *Mr. Pearson Hill.*

Freedom of the City of London and of the Fishmongers' Company, presented to Sir Rowland Hill. *Mr. Pearson Hill.*

Introduction of (temporary) minimum rate of fourpence for general post letters. Two Notices, November, 1839.

Instructions issued to the Post-Office Letter Receivers relative to the introduction of the Penny Post, December, 1839.

Notice to the Public, and to all Postmasters in the United Kingdom, relative to the introduction of the Penny Post, December, 1839.

> This is the draft copy submitted to the Postmaster-General for approval, and it bears Lord Lichfield's signature.

Penny Postage Handbill, with regulations, January 7th, 1840.

Notice respecting printed letter covers prepared for the use of Members of both Houses of Parliament only. January 16th, 1840.

Letter from Mr. Joseph Hume, M.P., requesting that—in order to give effect to the Uniform Penny Post—all Inland letters for him which were not prepaid might be opened and returned to the writers. 10th January, 1840.

Notice to Postmasters, enclosing specimens of stamps, including the stamp with the letters V.R. at the upper corners, which was intended for official correspondence, but which appears never to have been brought into use.

Notice to Postmasters, enclosing specimens of adhesive stamps, and stamped covers and envelopes, April, 1840.

Introduction of Postage Stamps, May 6th, 1840. Notice to the Public, April, 1840.

"It must be distinctly understood that it is optional with the public either to use stamps, or to forward their letters, &c., prepaid or unpaid as at present."

Introduction of Postage Stamps, May 6th, 1840. Directions as to their obliteration, April 25th, 1840.

Obliteration of Stamps, May, 1840. Notice to Postmasters, &c., that care must be taken to cancel all label stamps with the obliterating stamp, and the proper ink.

Notice pointing out how adhesive stamps should be affixed to letters, May 7th, 1840.

Postage Label Stamps and Stamped Covers, June, 1840. Notice to postmasters. Stamps were to be sold in future by all postmasters, sub-postmasters, and letter receivers.

Registration of Letters, introduced on January 6th, 1841. Notice to the Public.

Twopenny Post-Office, May 1st, 1815. Letter-Carriers' general instructions. *Mr. C. J. Stevens, London.*

The Bradford Post-Office in 1840 and 1890. (Two views.)
Mr. Sayers, Bradford.

The Bideford Post-Office in 1840 and 1890.
Mr. Cadd, Bideford.

Keswick Post-Office, past and present.
Mr. Crosthwaite, Keswick.

Edinburgh Post-Office Directory, 1829. *Mr. G. A. Aitken.*
> Printed for the letter-carriers of the General Post-Office. Under the patronage of Sir David Wedderburn, Bart., Postmaster-General for Scotland.

"The Muses Mercury; or, The Monthly Miscellany," 1707-8.
Mr. G. A. Aitken.

> In the number for January, 1708, is an account of a Post-Office Feast on Her Majesty's birthday, 1708, with a song by Mr. Motteux, set by Mr. Leveridge. The songs were made up as letters from Parnassus, and were brought by a post-boy who blew his horn as he rode into the hall.

"The Penny Post Act." *Mr. G. A. Aitken.*
> A comic song sung at Vauxhall Gardens in 1840. The picture outside represents Sir Rowland Hill as a postman, distributing letters to crossing-sweepers and a crowd of other people who had hitherto rarely made use of the post.

Hatton's "A New View of London." 1708. *Mr. G. A. Aitken.*
> In Vol. II. (pp. 710-12) there is an account of the Post-Office, with a list of offices.

The Post-Office Annual Directory for 1801. By the Inspectors of Inland Letter-Carriers.
> This is the second issue of the Official Post-Office Guide. The editors state that nearly 5,000 copies of the first Directory were sold.

The Post-Office London Directory for 1840.
> On pp. 631 *seq.* are full particulars of the new Penny Postage.

"Cary's New Itinerary;" from an actual admeasurement, made by command of His Majesty's Postmaster-General, for official purposes. By John Cary, Surveyor of the Roads to the General Post-Office. 1798. *Mr. Carter, Hastings.*

Open Letters for Paris. Transmission by Carrier Pigeons. Notice dated 16th November, 1870.
> During the siege of Paris letters were sent by carrier pigeons from Tours. No letter was to exceed twenty words in length, and no envelopes were allowed. The charge was fivepence a word.

"Bulletin Official de la Délégation du Government de la Défense Nationale," Tours, 27th November, 1870.
> Giving further facilities for brief communications on cards.

Letters Patent appointing various Postmasters-General. 1735-1880. With Seals of the several Sovereigns.
> Until 1823 there were generally two Postmasters-General.

Instrument empowering the Right Hon. G. J. Shaw-Lefevre, M.P., to act as Deputy Postmaster-General during the illness of Mr. Fawcett. 1882.
>This is the only occasion upon which there has been a Deputy Postmaster-General.

The first warrant issued for repayment of money in the Savings Bank. September 16th, 1861. (Sir Charles Sikes, of Huddersfield, payee.)

Counterfeit Letters. March, 1832.
>Notice respecting counterfeit letters made up in imitation of twopenny post letters, and delivered by men who demanded and received money as the postage payable thereon.

"The Post-Office Letter Weight," in the form of a copper medal.
Mr. A. Bell, Redhill.
>On the reverse, "For Rowland Hill's plan of Penny Postage. H. Hooper, August 12th, 1839."

Mail Coach Token, payable in London. Two copies.
Mr. J. Willkley and Mr. T. Sherwin, London.
>On the reverse, "To J. Palmer, this is inscribed as a token of gratitude for benefits received from the establishment of Mail Coaches."

Window Notice respecting Mails from Oxford (about 1760).
Mr. T. Arnall, Oxford.

Penny adhesive Stamps, black, 1840. Proofs before letters, from first plate engraved.

Original Sketch for adhesive Stamp, by Wyon.

Proofs taken while deciding the question of colours.
Mr. Pearson Hill.

Petitions from Postmasters who lost their places or otherwise suffered during the Civil Wars; or from persons desiring postmasterships in compensation for their losses during that time. *H. M. Public Record Office.*

First declared Account of T. Randolphe, Master of the Posts (afterwards Ambassador to Scotland and France). 1st October, 1566, to 30th September, 1571. Signed by Lord Burghley and Sir Walter Mildmay. *The Audit Office.*

First declared Account of Stephen Lilly, Receiver-General of the Post-Office. 25th March, 1695, to 25th March, 1696.
The Audit Office.

The King to the Governor of Barbados, June 1, 1663: To establish within the Caribbee Islands Public Offices for the receipt of letters and postage, according to the establishment made in England by Parliament.

The Colonial Office.

The Governor of Barbados was strictly to conform to the orders of Daniel O'Neil, Groom of the Bedchamber, who had been appointed Postmaster-General and Master of the King's Post and Carriers.

By the King. A Proclamation for quieting the Postmaster-General in the execution of his office, January 16th, 1660.

The British Museum.

Forbidding the conveyance of letters by unauthorized persons, and exempting the Postmaster-General and his deputies from serving on juries, &c.

By the King. A Proclamation for the better quieting the Postmaster-General in the execution of his office, and for his future encouragement therein, 25th May, 1663.

The British Museum.

Repeating the above, and forbidding Postmasters to open letters except by warrant from a Secretary of State.

By the King. A Proclamation for quieting the Postmaster-General in the execution of his office, 26th July, 1667.

The British Museum.

A similar notice, in favour of Lord Arlington, now Postmaster-General.

By the King. A Proclamation for enforcing the due execution of the Act of Parliament, entituled, An Act for setling (*sic*) the profits of the Post-Office on his Royal Highness the Duke of York and his Heirs males: and for prevention of the inconveniences arising by the infringement of the said Act, 21st June, 1669.   *The British Museum.*

By the King. A Proclamation for enforcing the due execution of the Act of Parliament, entituled, An Act for settling the profits of the Post-Office on his Royal Highness the Duke of York and his Heirs males, and for prevention of treasonable correspondencies, and other inconveniencies arising by the infringement of the said Act, 25th August, 1683.   *The British Museum.*

By the King. A Proclamation for quieting the Postmaster-General, his Deputies and Assigns in the execution of his office, 7th September, 1685.   *The British Museum.*
No soldiers to be quartered at an Inn belonging to a Postmaster.

By the King. A Proclamation for enforcing the due execution of the Acts of Parliament for erecting the Post-Office, and for settling the profits thereof upon us, our Heirs and Successors, 7th September, 1685.   *The British Museum.*

The names of all the Towns where the Posts are between Berwick and the Court.

The names of Post-Towns coming out of Ireland, from the seaside to London, with the number of miles distant one from the other.

Orders appointed by the Queen's most excellent Majesty, to be generally observed by her Highness' Posts throughout her Majesty's Realm. May, 1574.   *The Home Office.*

Orders agreed on between Sir Francis Walsingham, Thomas Wilson, Principal Secretary of State, and Thomas Randolph, Master of her Majesty's Posts, for the conveyance of packets or letters into France or Flanders. Original Draft, with corrections by Lord Burghley; also a fair Copy of the same. May 19th, 1579.
The Home Office.

Ordinances for the order of the Posts and Hackneymen between London and Dover.

The Wages of the Posts northwards, as they have continued from the beginning of the Queen's Majesty's Reign unto this present. [Endorsed by Thos. Randolph.] Total sum, £981 3s. 4d.

Wages of the Posts from the Court to Berwick. Total sum, £997 9s. (About 1566.)   *The Home Office.*

Queen Elizabeth to Thos. Randolph, Master of the Posts. To discharge all the posts unless they will serve for half their wages, except the posts of the Court.

Draft, with corrections by Lord Burghley. February 4th, 1568.   *The Home Office.*

Models of the *Scotia* and *Connaught*. *South Kensington Museum.*

The Indian Post Cart. *South Kensington Museum.*
The last letter by Post from Gordon.
South Kensington Museum.
The Pigeon Post. *South Kensington Museum.*
Copy of Treaty between the Post Offices of England and France, made in 1713. Signed by Mathew Prior, Minister and Plenipotentiary of the Queen, and Lewis Pajot, Count of Ousenbray, &c., Comptroller-General of the Posts of France. With an authority to the Postmaster-General to ratify the Treaty signed by Lord Bolingbroke.
Dies used in the making of the plates from which were produced the first Postage Stamps, printed under the control of the Board of Stamps and Taxes by Messrs. Perkins, Bacon & Petch, 69 Fleet Street.
Inland Revenue Department.
Mulready Envelopes and Covers. One Penny and Twopence.—Mulready design, engraved by Thompson. First proof from original plate before lettering.—Mulready design. First proof from plate after lettering, but before insertion of Post rate. India paper. Signed by Sir Rowland Hill.
Inland Revenue Department.
Recess-Printed Stamps (produced by Messrs. Bacon and Petch) :—
Duty, One Penny.
Plates from the Heath die. Hand-made paper with watermark of a small crown. These stamps were issued unperforated.
Inland Revenue Department.
Recess-Printed Stamps (produced by Messrs. Bacon and Petch and their successors in business, Messrs. Perkins, Bacon, and Co :—
Plates from the Heath die. Hand-made paper with watermark of a small crown. These Stamps prior to 1854 were unperforated. *Inland Revenue Department.*
Recess-Printed Stamps (produced by Messrs. Perkins, Bacon, and Co. :—
Duty, One Penny.
Plates from the Heath die, deepened by Humphrys. Hand-

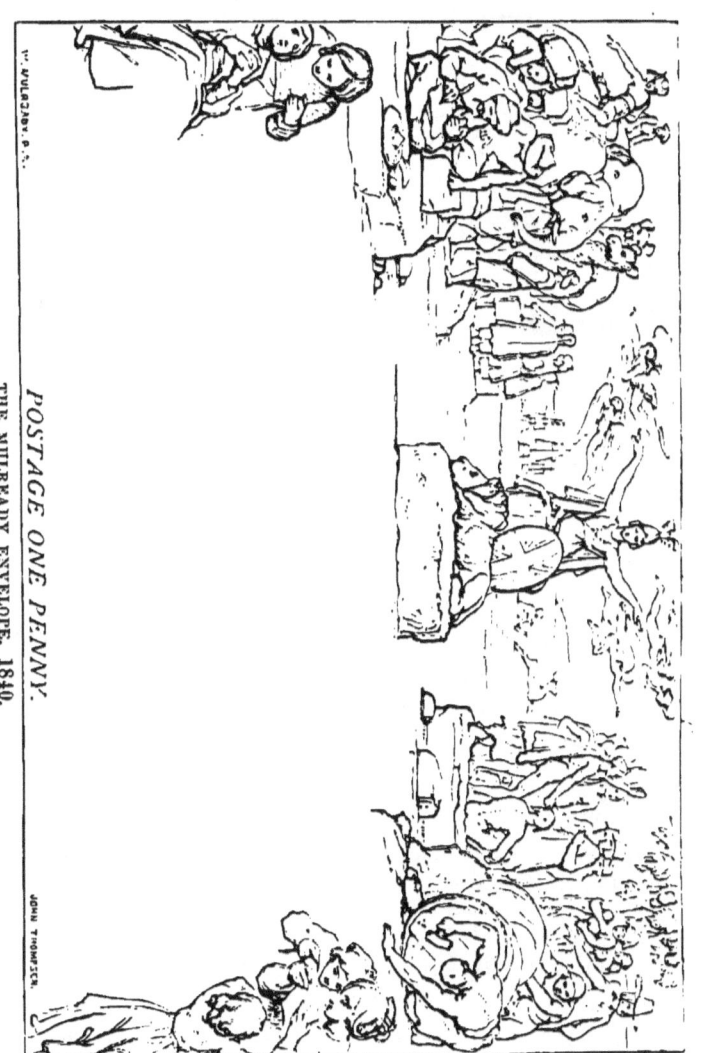

POSTAGE ONE PENNY.
THE MULREADY ENVELOPE, 1840.

made paper with watermark of a small crown to plate 22 inclusive, followed, in plate 23 and subsequently, by a watermark of a large crown.

Inland Revenue Department.

Recess-Printed Stamps (produced by Messrs. Perkins, Bacon, and Co. :—

Duty, One Penny.

Plates from the Heath die, deepened by Humphrys. Hand-made paper with a watermark of a large crown.

Inland Revenue Department.

Recess-Printed Stamps (produced by Messrs. Bacon and Petch and their successors in business, Messrs. Perkins, Bacon, and Co. :—

Duty, Two Pence.

Plates to No. 6 from the Heath die. No. 7 and subsequent plates from the Heath and Humphry's die. Hand-made paper with watermark of a small crown to plate 5 inclusive, followed, in plate No. 6 and subsequently by a large crown. The stamps produced prior to 1854 were unperforated.

Duty, One Halfpenny.

Plates from a die produced by Messrs. Perkins, Bacon, and Co. Hand-made paper with a watermark of the word "Halfpenny."

Duty, Three Halfpence.

Plates from a die by Messrs. Perkins, Bacon, and Co. Hand-made paper with a watermark of a large crown.

Embossed adhesive Stamps at 1s., 10d., and 6d. Die by Wyon. The 1s. and 10d. on Dickinson paper; the 6d. on V.R. paper.

Inland Revenue Department.

Surface-printed adhesive Stamps, produced by Messrs. T. De La Rue and Co., from electrotype plates made from dies prepared by themselves. Machine-made paper; watermark, a crown. Duties, $\frac{1}{2}d.$, 1d., 1$\frac{1}{2}d.$, 2d., 2$\frac{1}{2}d.$, 3d., 4d., 5d., 6d., 8d., 9d., 10d., 1s., 2s., 2s. 6d., 5s., 10s., £1, £5.

Inland Revenue Department.

Adhesive I.R. Official, Government Parcels and Telegraph Stamps.

Inland Revenue adhesive surface-printed and embossed Stamps, which may be used for Postal purposes. Embossed Envelope Stamps. Newspaper Stamps, hand printed, and Newspaper Wrapper Stamps. Post Cards. Registration Envelopes and Telegraph Forms. Postal Orders. Specimens of Irish Dog Stamps (De La Rue & Co.); with original drawing of design. Impressions from plates under Grenville's Stamp Act for America. Almanack Stamps, 4d., 8d. Specimens of Hat Stamps. *Inland Revenue Department.*

Print of old Stamp Office, by Rowlandson and Pugin.
Inland Revenue Department.

The last of the Four-Horse Royal Mail Coaches leaving Newcastle-on-Tyne for Edinburgh upon 5th July, 1847, with Union Jack hoisted half-mast, &c. Painting.
Mrs. Brandon.

Coaching Days. Paintings and Prints. *Mrs. Brandon.*

Telegraphic Apparatus.

Historical.

Cooke and Wheatstone's Four Needle Telegraph, 1838.
 In this instrument some of the letters were indicated by the convergence of two needles, the other letters being indicated by the deflection of one needle only. Four line wires were required. The signals were transmitted by the simultaneous depression of two out of ten finger keys.

Cooke and Wheatstone's Double Needle Telegraph with Crutch Handles, 1844.
 Two line wires were used. The letters were indicated by the movements of one or both needles. Two movements were required for indicating certain letters and three movements for others. An alarm bell was originally used for calling attention, but it was soon found that the "click" of the needles acted sufficiently well and the alarm bell was abandoned.

Double Needle Telegraph with Drop Handles, 1850.

Double Needle Instrument, 1851.

Highton's Single Needle, 1848.

The letters were indicated by the movement of the needle from side to side. Certain letters are formed by one or more movements of the needle to either side, other letters requiring combinations of movements to both sides. The signals were transmitted by two "tapper" keys. Only one line wire was required.

Tapper Key.

Used with Highton's Single Needle and also with Bright's Bell Instrument. The depression of one key transmits a current in one direction and the depression of the other key a current in the other direction.

Dering's Single Needle Telegraph, 1852.

The movement of the needle in this instrument is effected by means of an electro-magnet instead of a coil, as in the Cooke and Wheatstone and Highton instruments.

Bright's Bell Telegraph, 1855.

Worked with a relay. The single needle alphabet is produced by striking two bells of different tones, the hammers being actuated by electro-magnets each worked by a relay and local battery. The relay consists of two electro-magnetic bobbins placed side by side, their ends being furnished with pole pieces turning inwards. Between these pole pieces at each end of the bobbins the ends of permanently magnetized needles pivoted on vertical axes play; these needles are so placed as regards their polarity that a current in one direction moves the needle which closes the local circuit of the right-hand bell, and a current in the opposite direction moves the other needle which closes the local circuit of the left-hand bell. The signalling key used with this instrument is similar to that used with Highton's Single Needle Telegraph. The instrument is still in use.

Henley's Magneto-Electric Single Needle Telegraph, 1848.

The dots and dashes of a modification of the Morse alphabet are represented by the duration of the deflection of the needle on *one* side only of its normal position. It is worked by the magneto-electric current generated by moving the handle.

Cooke and Wheatstone's A B C Telegraph Receiver, 1840.

A step by step instrument. The letters of the alphabet are arranged round a disc fixed on the axle of an escapement wheel. The letters are presented at an opening in the front of the case. There is an escapement wheel, on the axle of which the disc is fixed, which is controlled by electro-magnets. There are as many teeth in the escapement wheel as there are letters on the revolving disc; the latter moves from one letter to the following one for each current sent.

Cooke and Wheatstone's A B C Telegraph Transmitter, 1840.

Battery commutator for transmitting the currents for working the A B C Receiver.

Cooke and Wheatstone's A B C Telegraph Transmitter, 1840.

Magneto transmitter for generating and transmitting the currents for working the A B C Receiver. This transmitter is so arranged that a magneto current is sent when its spoked-wheel is turned through a distance equal to that dividing the letters engraved upon it.

Wheatstone's A B C Telegraph Transmitter, 1858.

In this transmitter the electro-magnet, which by its rotation over a permanent magnet produces electric currents, is kept in continuous rotation by the hand of the operator, and finger stops, corresponding with the letters on the dial of the telegraph, are respectively pressed down and regulate the passage of the currents to the telegraph circuit. The keys are arranged to work by a lever movement, and they are so connected by an endless chain that the depression of one key raises up the one previously depressed.

Siemen's A B C Telegraph, 1862.

A magneto-electric telegraph. The transmitter currents are generated by the rotation of an elongated electro-magnet between the poles of a series of horseshoe magnets. The receiver works by a propelment action.

Bright's Relay, 1855.

Used with the Bright's Bell Instrument. A relay or repeater for relaying the signals of the Bright's Bell instrument. In construction it is similar to the relay fixed on the bell instrument itself, but it consists of duplicate bobbins and magnetic needles.

Earliest Form of Relay with an Inducing Magnet, 1855.

Invented by Varley. The coil is wound on a reel of soft iron, upon each end of which a hollow casing or cap of the same material is fitted, almost completely encasing the coil in soft iron. The armature is crescent-shaped, and is magnetized by induction from a compound bar magnet placed behind. The crescent-shaped portion plays between the inner end of the casings, which for that purpose do not quite meet, but leave the central portion of the coil exposed. An ordinary magnetic needle pivoted below the coil is acted upon by the latter, and serves as an indicator to call attention. The armature is held up against knife-edge bearings by two helical springs, and the adjustment is effected by varying the tension of one of them.

Varley's Relay, 1856.

A horizontal bar of soft iron is pivoted vertically, and is free to move in the interior of two cylindrical bobbins. The ends of the bar which project beyond the bobbins, play between the poles of horseshoe permanent magnets fixed at each end. The relay is adjusted by moving the stops, and consequently the soft iron bar, to one side or the other. The weak currents received from the line pass through the bobbins and actuate the horizontal bar which connects up the local battery and coils of the reading apparatus.

Double Current Key, 1855.

A key for sending a short reversal after each signal, two sets of batteries being required. When the key is up the line wire is connected to the receiving apparatus. Known as the "Slate" key, from its being mounted on a base of slate.

Varley's Wheel Key, 1855.

A double current key. So called from the wheel shape of the commutator. A constant current is maintained to line, and signals are made by depressing the key and thus reversing the current. A switch is used for making the necessary alterations to the connexions for sending and receiving.

Morse Embosser, 1853.

This instrument superseded the Bain instrument, and was in turn superseded by the Ink-writer. The dots and dashes of the Morse alphabet are made by a rounded steel point fixed at one end of a lever, the other end being furnished with an armature, which is attracted by an electro-magnet worked by a relay and local battery.

Early Form of Galvanoscope, about 1850.

Used as a means of indicating a call when the recording apparatus was out of adjustment.

Old Form of Circular Sliding Rheostat.

An instrument used for comparing electrical resistances of wires.

Early Form of Single Needle Telegraph.

Wheatstone's Automatic Telegraph Transmitter, 1858.

In this apparatus the transmission of electric currents is regulated by the action of three vertical rods, which are caused to move up and down by the rotation of a wheel worked by hand.

A slip of paper punched with holes corresponding to the signals to be transmitted passes over the upper end of the rod, and through these holes the ends of the rods can pass. When one or other of two of the rods passes through a hole a current is transmitted in one direction or the other; if when a rod is moving upwards there is no hole for it to pass through, then no current is transmitted. The third rod only acts as a guide to the paper slip. A battery is used to transmit the currents.

Wheatstone's Automatic Telegraph Receiver, 1858.

In this apparatus two pens or styles are depressed by the polarized armatures of an electro-magnet; when the electric current passes in one direction through the magnet one of the styles is depressed, and when it passes in the contrary direction the other style is depressed. The ends of the styles when depressed pass through small holes in the bottom of a shallow reservoir containing ink, and carry with them a sufficient amount of ink to make a legible mark on a strip of paper which moves under them.

Wheatstone's Automatic Telegraphic Puncher, 1858.

An apparatus for perforating the paper strip for use with Automatic Telegraph transmitter. There are three finger keys, the two external ones being used to punch the holes which grouped together represent letters and other characters, and the centre key to punch holes which mark the intervals between the letters.

Nott and Gamble's Step by Step Pointer Telegraph, 1846.

Electro-magnets act on a ratchet-wheel by means of clicks attached to their armatures. On the axle of the ratchet-wheel the pointer is fixed; the latter is moved forward through a space equal to the distance between two letters for each making and breaking of the battery contact. A simple tapper or pedal key is used for sending the currents, and the pointer is allowed to rest for a short interval of time when it is opposite to the letter desired to be indicated. The instrument is furnished with an alarum, the bell being struck by a hammer attached to the armature of an electro-magnet provided for the purpose.

Railway Block-Signalling Telegraph.

Early form of instrument used for signalling trains on the "block" system.

Comb Lightning Protector.

Consists of metal plates whose edges are placed in close proximity to each other, the edges being serrated with sawlike teeth. One of the plates is connected to earth and the other to line.

Early Form of Lightning Protector.

Varley's Globe Vacuum Lightning Protector, 1861.

A number of platinum points connected to the line wire are arranged in close proximity to the end of a platinum wire connected to earth, the whole being enclosed in a small glass globe (through which the wires pass, and into the sides of which the wires are sealed) exhausted of air.

APPARATUS AT WORK.

Double Needle Instruments.

Single Needle Instrument.

This instrument does not require adjustment, and is therefore extensively used both by the Post-Office and the railway companies upon circuits where it is desired to connect several small offices together and communicating with one central office.

The depression of one pedal transmits a current in one direction and the depression of the other pedal a current in the other direction, the movements of the needle, which are read by the receiving operator, corresponding to those of the pedals.

Double Sounder.

This instrument is used principally at the "Central" Office on single needle circuits to facilitate the reception of messages from the various small offices. It can be more rapidly worked than the single needle. The signals are acoustic.

The alphabetic code corresponds to that of the single needle; a signal on the left-hand side representing a deflection of the needle to the left, and a signal on the right-hand side representing a deflection of the needle to the right.

A B C or Alphabetical Telegraph.

This is used for private wires and at small village offices, where the number of messages is small and where the operator is not a skilled telegraphist.

The large horizontal dial surrounded by keys is the transmitting portion, and the smaller sloping dial the receiving portion of the apparatus.

It is worked by magneto currents generated by turning the small handle in front.

Direct Writing Morse Inker.

The advantage of this instrument (which is used in almost every country) over the Morse embosser consists in the greater legibility of the signals, which can be read in any light, and requires much less power to work it. This form (which is fitted with a signalling key and galvanometer) is used on lines of moderate length, where the direct line current is sufficient to actuate the electro-magnet without the assistance of a relay and local battery.

Working to the *City Press* and *Citizen* newspaper offices.

Direct Writing Morse Inker Duplex.

Morse Sounder Set.

The receiving sounder is similar to the electrical portion of the direct writing Morse inker, the clock-work, with its recording slip and inking mechanism, being dispensed with. The signals are acoustic, the sounds being produced by the lever striking the screws which limit its movement. The alphabet is formed of short and long audible signals (dots and dashes) corresponding with those recorded upon the slip of the direct writing Morse inker. The transmitting key is arranged to reverse the battery connections at every movement. This is of great advantage on long lines, as it obviates the necessity for keeping the armature of the receiving instrument under mechanical control. By this system the speed of working on long lines is also considerably increased.

Working to Penzance. The adjoining instrument, which is similar, is working to Aberdeen.

Morse Sounder Duplex.

This apparatus is similar to that working to Penzance and Aberdeen, but it is fitted with the additional apparatus necessary to enable messages to be transmitted in opposite directions simultaneously.

Working to Manchester.

Quadruplex.

By this system four messages are sent at the same time and on the same wire. This is accomplished by combining double current and single current working in such a way that one portion of the apparatus is worked by one system of currents, and the other portion by the other system of currents.

Working to Bristol.

Multiplex.

By this system six messages are transmitted over one wire at the same time.

The line wire is in electrical connection with the revolving arm. A wire brush attached to the arm passes over the small segments forming the circle surrounding the axle. These segments are grouped together at intervals, and connected to the different sets of apparatus, A to F, worked by the operators.

As the arm revolves the brush is successively brought into contact with each group of segments, and each set of apparatus is thus momentarily connected to the line. The "Distributor" at each end of the line is controlled by a vibrating "Reed," driven electrically.

The distributors are caused to run synchronously within a small fraction of a second, and the synchronism is maintained by means of connecting currents sent automatically through the line from certain of the segments of each distributor as the arms revolve.

Working to Birmingham.

Hughes Type-Printing Telegraph.

This apparatus is mainly mechanical, the electrical action being confined to the sending a single short pulsation of current at the instant the type wheel is in the proper position, and only one wave of current is needed to produce a letter. The sending and receiving instruments are combined.

The keyboard consists of as many keys as there are letters and signs to be printed.

Connecting with the keys and corresponding with them and also with the type wheel is a set of pins arranged radially in a circular horizontal plate. An arm revolves over these pins without touching them until a key is depressed, when a current is sent into the line. The instruments are caused to run approximately isochronously by means of suitable adjustments, and they are afterwards maintained in synchronism automatically by the actual working.

The instrument is eminently suitable for continental message traffic, for which purpose it is largely used.

The two working instruments shown are connected with Paris and Berlin.

Wheatstone's Automatic System.

In all Automatic systems the messages must first be prepared on a slip of paper. This work is done by means of a machine called a "Perforator," operated by a clerk. The Morse characters are perforated along the slip which is afterwards passed through the Transmitter.

The Transmitter is an instrument arranged to do mechanically, and at a much greater speed, exactly what is done by the hand-worked keys of the instruments connected with Manchester, Penzance, and Aberdeen.

The strip of perforated paper regulates the movement of the contact levers, determining when currents shall pass to line in the same manner as the perforations in the cards of the Jacquard loom determine the lifting of the threads of the warp.

The signals appear at the Receiving points in the ordinary dots and dashes of the Morse Code.

The apparatus is most useful as a means of transmitting news, speeches, &c., and during a general breakdown of the wires.

The speed of the apparatus has been raised from 100 to 400 words per minute in the hands of the Post-Office, and a speed of over 600 per minute has been attained between London and Bristol.

Transmission of News by the Automatic System.

This apparatus shows a complete news circuit and consists of the Transmitting Instrument and three Receiving Instruments representing offices, say, in London (sending office) and Newcastle, Edinburgh and Glasgow (receiving offices).

The Repeater.

All the systems described can be relayed, or repeated at various points by means of suitable apparatus.

The instrument shown is used for repeating the currents of the automatic system, and such instruments are introduced into the London Glasgow wires at Leeds or Manchester; into the London Dublin wires at points in North and South Wales near the landing places of the cables; into the Belfast wires at Preston; and into the Aberdeen and Dundee wires at Newcastle-on-Tyne.

These repeaters act automatically.

The effect is that the currents reaching the repeater actuate it and another current is sent forward from batteries connected with it.

This mode of cutting up a long line into shorter sections enables a high speed of working to be attained.

Railway Block-Signalling Instruments.

Telephone Switch Station.

Showing the automatic indication of the completion of a conversation.

Pneumatic Tube.

As used for sending messages from a counter to an instrument or other room where the rooms are situated apart from each other.

The system is extensively used throughout the country.

Cable Specimens.

Case containing Early Forms of Cables designed by Cooke and Wheatstone.

Piece of the First Submarine Cable.

    Laid between Dover and Calais in 1850. The gutta-percha was not protected. The cable was sunk by means of lead weights attached at intervals throughout its length.

    It worked for one day only. The specimen shown was picked up in 1875.

Piece of the First Sheathed Submarine Cable.

    This cable had four separate conductors. It was laid between Dover and Calais in 1851, and in portions of it recovered after twenty-seven years submersion, the gutta-percha was found to be both electrically and mechanically as good as when first laid.

Piece of Seven Wire Irish Cable.

    This cable was laid by the Electric and International Telegraph Company between Killantringan (Wigtownshire) and Whitehead (Antrim), June 1866.

    It was not then new, but had been previously laid between Orfordness and The Hague.

Piece of Submarine Cable laid in 1858.

    This cable consisted of four conductors, and was laid between Dunwich and Zaandvoort. Two of the conductors are insulated with gutta-percha and the other two with gutta-percha and Chatterton's compound.

Piece of Telegraph Pole showing Hole made by Woodpeckers.

    This pole was removed from the vicinity of Shipton-on-Stour in the autumn of last year. It had been erected only about three years. The perforations were made by the common green woodpecker. It is supposed that the birds are attracted by the humming of the wires produced by the wind, and imagine that there are insects in the pole. A specimen of the bird is shown upon the pole.

Pole with specimens of Ancient Insulators for Aerial Lines.

Pole with specimens of Insulators for Aerial Lines, as now used by Post-Office.

A Model Locomotive, worked by Electricity. Lent by the North London Railway Company.

The Phonograph in operation.

INSTRUCTIONS FOR POSTAL DUTY

TO BE PERFORMED IN CONNECTION WITH

THE UNIFORM PENNY POSTAGE JUBILEE CONVERSAZIONE AND EXHIBITION

AT GUILDHALL,

ON

FRIDAY, SATURDAY, AND MONDAY, MAY 16TH, 17TH, AND 19TH, 1890.

16TH MAY.—GUILDHALL.

Yard.

The Royal Mail Four-Horse parcel coach to leave the yard at 9 P.M. for Brighton, carrying parcel mails made up in the Guildhall.

A mail coach, to illustrate the royal mail coach of the past, drawn by four grey horses, will take up and discharge mails, passengers, and luggage. The coach will drive off after H.R.H. the Prince of Wales has arrived, about 10.30 P.M.

The coachmen and Post-Office servants who look after the vans which will be stationed in the yard will implicitly act upon the instructions they receive from the police.

Corridor leading from Entrance to Library.

To be lined with two mail guards, sixty postmen, and forty telegraph boys in uniform. Seven telegraph messengers will distribute programmes and leaflets.

The postmen will assemble in the Guildhall yard at 6 P.M.,

and take up their positions in line in the corridors as soon afterwards as possible. They will remain in the corridor until 7.30 P.M., and then break off until 9.30 P.M., when they should reassemble and reline the corridor until 11 P.M., so as to be in attendance when H.R.H. the Prince of Wales arrives.

16TH, 17TH, AND 19TH MAY.

The curious address books of the Inland Branch, the albums of Christmas cards from other offices, and a collection of postage stamps, Mulready envelopes, &c., will be exhibited, in charge of Mr. W. Matthews, Inland Branch, assisted by Mr. Thomas, Controller's office.

The officers in charge of the various sections of the London Postal Service Exhibition will take care not to leave the exhibits without proper custody until the Guildhall is closed each night.

At 8 P.M. on the evenings of the 16th, 17th, and 19th, there will be an exhibition of dissolving views by Mr. A. Hunter, viz:—

1. Ancient Egyptian letter, 1500 B.C.
2. Cursus Publicus, or ancient Roman post.
3. Fac-simile of original sketch of first postage stamp.
4. Fac-simile of original sketch of Mulready envelope.
5. Flag used on Post-Office sailing packets.
6. The stage waggon.
7. The post-boy.
8. Mail coaches starting from General Post-Office.
9. The mail coach snowed up.
10. First train run from Manchester to Liverpool.
11, 12, and 13. The Travelling Post-Office.
14 and 15. The General Post-Office.
16-23. Curious addresses.
24. Sir Rowland Hill.
25. Her Majesty the Queen.

Public Post-Office Business.

16th, 17th, and 19th May, 1890.

A post-office will be established for the occasion. It will be situated in the north-west corner of the Central Hall, and will be designated the "Guildhall Post-Office, 1890."

In order to illustrate the postal system in operation at the present day, public business of all kinds will be transacted at the Jubilee Office.

> Postage stamps of all denominations sold.
> Inland and foreign post-cards sold.
> Letters registered and insured.
> Parcels (Inland and Foreign) posted and insured.
> Postal orders, money orders, issued and paid.
> Savings bank deposits received, and withdrawals cashed, and new accounts opened.
> Licenses issued.
> Life insurance and annuities business transacted.
> Telegrams accepted for transmission, and received for delivery.

Visitors expecting telegrams should look at the notice board near the post-office.

On the night of the 16th May the post-office business will be conducted from 6 P.M. to midnight by Miss Straker, inspecting telegraphist, acting as supervisor; Miss Gunston of the South Kensington B.O.; Miss Parsons of the Regent Street B.O.; Miss Turner of the North-Western District Office; and Miss Brown of the Westminster Palace Hotel B.O.

The telegraph business will be undertaken by Mr. Bolton, inspecting telegraphist of the Controller's office.

On Saturday the 17th, from 10 A.M. to 4 P.M., the postal business will be performed by Miss Gunston and by Miss Turner. From 4 P.M. to 10 P.M. by Miss Brown and Miss Parsons.

The telegraph business will be undertaken by Mr. Gilbert

between 10 A.M. and 4 P.M., and by Mr. Morgan between 4 P.M. and 10 P.M.

The same officers will perform the duties on Monday the 19th instant, but they will reverse their times of attendance.

The necessary stocks of stamps, &c., will be supplied.

A special card in commemoration of this event will be sold in the Guildhall on the 16th, 17th, and 19th instant.

The card will be of a light drab colour. In the left-hand corner will appear a Crown, with the letters "V.R." and a rose, shamrock, and thistle beneath. In the centre the City arms, with the words "Penny Postage Jubilee, 1890, Guildhall, London"; and in the right-hand corner an impression of a penny stamp similar to that used for foreign post-cards. The printing of the whole will be of red colour. The cards will be made up in packets of twelve and one hundred. They can be sold singly or in larger quantities, at 6d. per card, and can be obtained at the branch office and in the Art Gallery.

There will be a speaking-tube from the combined pillar letter-box and lamp-post to the telegraphist at the public counter at the Guildhall Post-Office.

Arrangements for the Performance of Postal Sorting Work.

Fittings for postal work will be supplied as follows :—

    1 Bag opening, facing, and stamping table.
    1 Sorting table (eight divisions).
    3 Roads for district despatches.
    1 Rack for parcel duty.
    1 Collapsible packet sorting table.

"Pearson Hill" stamping machines will be affixed to the stamping table, and hand stamps will also be available for use on packets, newspapers, &c.

A supply of bags, string, sealing-wax, sealing-pot, and gas jets, and other necessaries for the conduct of the postal duty will be at hand.

The correspondence collected from forty-nine pillar letter boxes in the E.C. District will be entirely dealt with at the Guildhall, the town letters, &c., being faced, stamped, sorted, and despatched to the respective district offices, *viâ* the E.C.D.O. for inclusion in the several rides.

The despatching officers at Guildhall will enclose special letter bills in the bags for the districts and for the G.P.O.

The bags to bear red neck labels, "From Guildhall Jubilee Post Office."

The postmasters concerned have been advised.

The country correspondence will be selected, and that entitled to despatch the same night will be forwarded to the Inland Branch by messenger every ten minutes from 7.30 P.M. The late fees must be sent in separate labelled bundles.

Each despatch will be accompanied by a way bill numbered consecutively, and the last out of each collection will be marked "Final."

The letters, &c., collected at 9.30 P.M. not being entitled to despatch to the provinces the same night, will be forwarded at 11 P.M. to the Inland Branch, labelled, "Posted too late for Midnight Mails."

Special way bills for the three collections at 8 P.M. by van, and collecting cards for the postmen, have been provided.

Pillar letter-box dockets will be placed in the boxes for the 9.30 P.M. special collection.

Collections will be made at 8 P.M. by van from thirteen offices, and the bags for Guildhall will be unloaded at the corner of Fountain Court, Aldermanbury.

Instructions have been given for these offices to make up bags as follows :—

1. Town letters, news, &c., for the Guildhall.
2. Bag for E.C.D.O. (to contain registered letter bag) to be labelled "Town Letters for E.C.D.O."
3. Country letter bag for Inland Branch.
4. Country newspaper bag for N.P.B.

The town bags will be taken into the Guildhall by porters *viâ* Fountain Court, and the town correspondence will be faced, stamped, sorted, and despatched.

The country bags and the E.C. bags containing registered letters will be forwarded to the G.P.O.

Arrangements for Saturday and Monday, May 17th and 19th.

The same force will attend on the above days at 10 A.M. The postmen will make hourly collections from pillar boxes and private posting boxes.

The correspondence should be faced, stamped, sorted, and despatched. Corresponding bags will be made up for the district offices and forwarded to the E.C. Office, for inclusion in the despatches thence to the districts.

Separate bags should be made up for the E.C. Office. The vehicles running from the E.C. Office to the districts will start from the Guildhall for this purpose. Foreign letters in bundles to be enclosed in the E.C. bags, and the country correspondence should be forwarded in bags for the Inland Branch.

Parcel Post Business.

Arrangements for Friday the 16th May.

Mr. Hunt, overseer, and Sorter Douglas will attend the Guildhall from 6 P.M. till the close of the special duty.

Road-borne parcels for Brighton should be despatched from Mount Pleasant Depôt to Guildhall Post-Office at 6.30 P.M., 7.30 P.M., and 8 P.M.

Only as many parcels as will fill the above baskets should be included in the despatches, and the greatest care should be exercised in the packing of the parcels.

The remainder of the parcels, and those coming to hand after 8 P.M., should be sent in the ordinary coach despatch from Mount Pleasant to Brighton at 8.40 P.M.

On the nights of the 16th, 17th, and 19th instant the London to Brighton parcel coach will be despatched from the Guildhall Jubilee Office at 9 P.M.

Three baskets of parcels for Brighton, labelled "Guildhall Jubilee Post-Office to Brighton," (1), (2), and (3 final) respectively, will be despatched by the coach each night, after which it will proceed direct to the London Bridge Depôt for despatch at 9.45 P.M. as usual.

The Guard is to join the coach at the contractors' yard (Messrs. McNamara and Co., Castle Street, Finsbury), and he will attend there for the purpose not later than 8.30 P.M. He is to take with him, by cab, from the London Bridge depôt, the basket containing the coach horn, weapons, &c., and place it in the coach. When on duty in the coach the Guard must be in full uniform and wearing the belt with the revolver (unloaded), sword bayonet, &c. attached. He should take care to see that the horn is hanging on the side of the coach, ready for use, in the basket provided for it, when the coach starts from the contractors' yard. The Guard should blow the horn both on the arrival and departure of the coach at Guildhall.

Special time bills and bag lists have been provided for use in the coach each night.

JUBILEE CONVERSAZIONE AND EXHIBITION AT THE GUILDHALL, 16TH, 17TH, AND 19TH MAY, 1890.

REPORT OF THE CONTROLLER OF THE LONDON POSTAL SERVICE.

IN the belief that the celebration of the Uniform Penny Postage Jubilee at the Guildhall, under the kindly auspices of the Lord Mayor and Corporation of the City of London, will not be a mere nine days' wonder, and that any particulars concerning it will be of historical interest, at all events to those connected with the great Post-Office service of the country, I venture to submit a short report with respect to the postal branch of the exhibition, which it was my privilege to organize and conduct.

The arrangements made for exemplifying to the citizens of London the methods adopted in dealing with their letters in the post, and of demonstrating to them the modes in which money order, savings bank, postal order, and other branches of business are carried on, are set forth in the pamphlet of instructions to the staff, and need not therefore be recapitulated here.

The pressure of business at the Guildhall Post-Office, 1890, specially opened for the occasion; the rapidity with which the sorting work had to be performed in the postal sorting office; and the crowds surging round the barriers, likened the exhibition, from a post-office point of view, to the busy scenes which are enacted at the General Post-Office in St. Martin's-le-Grand on Christmas Eve.

Telegrams kept reaching me from the Guildhall during the

short time that I could attend at the General Post-Office, such as: "Immense crowd here. Work very heavy but going on satisfactorily." "Run on post-card, money order, and savings bank business very great." "Another long table placed in passage for public to write upon," thus vividly reminding me of the shower of telegraph messages received at the Christmas season.

Giving, in these remarks, the place of honour to the Guildhall Post-Office, 1890, and not wishing thereby in any way to detract from the prestige of the neighbouring picturesque representation of postal antiquity—the Post-Office of 1790—I shall be but echoing the opinions expressed by the visitors, private and official, when I say that no part of the entertainment gave greater satisfaction or was more extensively patronized than the Jubilee Post-Office.

The office was literally besieged from first to last, but the beleaguered staff were enabled to keep up communication with the head-quarters staff in the postal sorting office by means of a speaking tube, and thus to get their wants attended to.

At the Office about 5,000 of the Jubilee post-cards were disposed of on the night of the conversazione, the remainder having been sold at four other points in the building.

When it was announced at 10 p.m. that these cards were sold out, a run immediately took place on ordinary post-cards. In all 20,508 were sold. Of these 19,300 were inland cards, and 1,208 such as are used for the foreign service.

These cards were chiefly sold singly, and it can be imagined, therefore, how quick the staff had to be in giving them out.

As the visitors are said to have been 20,000, each person on the average must have bought one post-card for the purpose of getting an impression of the special Guildhall Jubilee obliterating and post-marking stamp.

As the stock of post-cards, inland and foreign, became exhausted, notwithstanding that all the branch post-offices in the neighbourhood were requisitioned for further supplies, a demand set in for embossed envelopes and registered letter envelopes, of which 452 were sold.

Penny Postage Jubilee-1890.
Guildhall, London.

The excitement was further sustained by the numerous purchases of postage stamps, 1,140 at a halfpenny, 1,920 at a penny, and, amongst others, one at 1*l.* and one at 5*l.* having been sold. The number of stamps vended reached a total of 3,845.

Postal orders were also in great demand. Of these 180 were taken; 134 of them representing amounts of 1*s.*, 1*s.* 6*d.*, and 2*s.* Probably few of these will reach the Receiver and Accountant-General's postal order branch.

Then 365 money orders were issued, the majority being for 1*d.*

The exhibition did good in the way of encouraging thrift, for actually 200 new accounts were opened and 134 deposits effected. Evidently the visitors were in funds, for only two withdrawals were made.

The catalogue of business is not yet exhausted, for I have to add that thirty-eight letters and post-cards were registered. Receipts were refused in some cases by the senders of the registered articles. Three licences were issued, twelve parcels posted, and, what was not anticipated, 400 letters and cards were received for delivery from the Poste Restante.

A reply card, addressed to the Guildhall Post-Office, came to hand, inscribed, "Have come many miles, cannot get in. Please post reply half of card, and oblige—Disappointed."

To end the account, there were 422 telegraph messages sent, and 37 delivered. That was exclusive of 207 official messages. Between 8 p.m. and midnight on the 16th, 135 private telegrams passed over the wires.

In addition to all the actual business transactions I have enumerated, the staff had to answer very numerous questions, and even to serve people, who could not get near the counter, over the heads of others.

They did their best to please the public by impressing their Jubilee Stamp on catalogues, envelopes, address cards, pieces of paper, telegraph forms—a penny per impression, for the benefit of the Rowland Hill Fund, was frequently offered. In this connection, a humorous incident occurred. A young gentleman begged that he might have, for his accompanying lady to keep, an impression of the stamp, and on handing in a paper for the impression, he was horrified to find he had presented his unpaid tailor's bill. He retired somewhat abashed. A young lady was extremely anxious to get an impression of the stamp on two pocket handkerchiefs. She was obliged, and when told the ink would wash out, said, rather than lose the impressions she would never use the handkerchiefs again.

Overwhelmed as the staff was, one old lady, having affixed a 10d. stamp to a card, returned to the counter, saying she had lost the card, and asked that the card drawer might be gone through, with a view to its being found. Another asked that a telegram might be written out for her.

I am very pleased indeed to be able to state that, notwithstanding all the confusion, bustle, and turmoil which attended the transaction of the postal public business, the accounts have been accurately balanced, there being several losses—such, for instance, as the sale, by a postal assistant hurriedly summoned for duty and not properly instructed, of many of the Jubilee cards at 1d. instead of 6d.; the sale of ordinary post-cards at $\frac{1}{2}d$. each by a telegraphist; and from many other causes. Yet these losses were covered by the sale of ordinary best post-cards singly at 1d. each, instead of 6d. for ten.

On the whole account there is a surplus of 2s. 4d. This I submit reflects the highest credit on Miss Parsons, of the Regent Street Post-Office, who was in charge of the account, and on Miss Turner, of the North-Western District Office, who partly shared the responsibility.

So numerous were the transactions, and so many the coins to count—the silver forming a huge pile—that the check occupied these two accountants the whole of the 20th instant up to 10 p.m. The other counter officers whose names are mentioned in the instructions deserve every praise for their able and zealous co-operation.

I will now speak of the postal sorting office, which was carried on under the immediate direction of Assistant Superintendent Mr. Bray.

Great interest was manifested in the stamping, sortation, and despatching of letters.

Not only was this the case as regards the general public, but our sorters and postmen took great delight in explaining the several processes to their wives and children. The red collar of the postman's coat, and the new uniform of the mail cart drivers, were more in evidence at this section of the exhibition than elsewhere.

The records indicate that letters, &c., to the number of 190,000 in all, were stamped, sorted, and despatched from the postal sorting office in the three days. Of these 40,000 were actually written and posted in the Guildhall itself.

From a special observation which was kept it can be said that 10,000 letters and cards thus written were posted in the four Jubilee boxes in two hours on the 19th instant. Persons who could not gain admission to the Hall sent messages in to inquire in what city boxes they could post so as to secure an impression of the Guildhall stamp.

On the evening of the 16th a person asked one of the officials where he could post the Jubilee card he had in his hand. When asked to where it was addressed, he replied, "Oh! Sir, I quite forgot that." He had written his communication on the obverse side of the card and omitted to address it. The card was then addressed on the reverse side, and no doubt reached its destination in due course.

Said one lady to another, "You observe how busy those men are; they are now sorting letters." The men in question were signing the attendance book and making out their bills. Evidently the guide required a leader herself.

Several letters were noticed in the postal sorting office which had been through the post in the year 1840, and bore the 1d. gummed and cut stamp of that time. Penny stamps as now in use had been placed upon the letters and they were committed to the post for delivery at the old address, thus to form a connection between 1840 and 1890 by means of the respective dated stamps of the two periods.

A tradesman in Cheapside posted in the Guildhall pillar

letter boxes 250 open envelopes addressed to himself. They bore ½d. postage labels. No doubt the object was, by getting the Guildhall Jubilee Stamp upon them, to render them valuable for the purpose of sale to stamp collectors hereafter.

A visitor, fired with enthusiasm at the postal Jubilee, or with a view to future profit, bought postage stamps of each denomination and stuck them on envelopes addressed to himself at the West End. Even the 5l. stamp was not omitted.

Another visitor was very persistent in a demand for a sight of the first London Post-Office which, he stoutly maintained, was a bag said to have been the only receptacle for the posting of letters in Westminster during the reign of King Charles I. He had read in the *Daily Telegraph* that such a bag was in existence. I had great difficulty in making him believe that it was not on show in the exhibition.

It was intimated to me that several cards posted at the Guildhall did not reach their destination, but I heard afterwards that one gentleman who complained of having lost five cards subsequently found he had not posted them! On the other hand, to show what care is taken in some instances by the Post-Office, it may be mentioned that a Jubilee card posted in the western central district with a piece of blotting-paper round it, to keep it clean, reached its destination at Derby with the blotting-paper still round it, and was thus delivered. On the sender reaching Derby he asked whether the card had been received, and was told "No;" but on instituting inquiry it turned out that the card, enclosed in the blotting-paper, was delivered into the box with letters, and was not looked into until the sender's inquiry was made.

A considerable number of Jubilee cards were addressed to places abroad, principally to France and Germany. About a dozen were addressed to Australia on the evening of the 16th instant.

The old Post-Office of 1790 came in for a good share of the visitors' appreciation and surprise. Their interest was increased when it was found that the old and curious notices exhibited were *original*. Many assumed that the notices were, like the erection itself, only prepared for the occasion. The sight of the two Post-Offices—1790 and 1890—side by side attracted much attention and gave a point to postal progress.

In the Art Galleries the mail bag apparatus excited absorbing interest and astonishment amongst the public. Visitors seemed most anxious to thoroughly master the details of the arrangement, and many and various were the questions asked respecting it.

The models of Travelling Post-Office carriages and the apparatus attached thereto were worked many hundreds of times, so great was the interest taken in these exhibits, and so anxious were the visitors to know how mail bags could be taken in and put out of a train going at the rate of fifty miles an hour. Mr. Garrett, the supervisor in charge of this section, literally had a warm time of it, for he was constantly at work, invariably surrounded by crowds, and the temperature of the Gallery was very high. No words of mine can praise him too highly for his exertions and cheerful endurance of a most fatiguing and trying exposition.

The Book of Curious Addresses which was exhibited in the Art Gallery proved to be a source of great interest. It contains a certain penny postage label, bearing an address on its reverse side, which had once safely circulated through the post. The effect of the exhibition of this stamp was that persons tried the experiment by posting addressed postage stamps at the Exhibition and elsewhere. The use of postage stamps in this way is much deprecated by the Department.

Outside the building the "Wonder" coach attracted much attention. It was supposed by not a few that a service of coaches had been re-established between London and Edinburgh.

The postal branch exhibits, except the Travelling Post-Offices, were cleared out of the Guildhall by 6 P.M. on the 20th May.

The officers in attendance with the Post-Office Ambulance had little call upon them. There were eight cases of faintness and one of blistered feet.

K

I cannot speak too well of the postal staff connected with this great Jubilee Guildhall celebration. One and all worked with praiseworthy diligence throughout, and contributed in no small degree to make the Exhibition a decided success.

The Dissolving Views attracted large and appreciative audiences on the nights of the 17th and 19th instant.

The wonderful approbation the Exhibition met with on all hands from Royalty downward seems, I think, to indicate that if the more ambitious scheme of an International Post-Office Exhibition were attempted in London in the near future, it would prove successful, mightily please the public, and be of great benefit to the Post-Office world as a means of interchange of ideas and comparison of processes, methods, and appliances.

R. C. TOMBS.

GENERAL POST-OFFICE,
27th May, 1890.

Report of the Electrician.

THE celebration of the Penny Postage Jubilee at the Guildhall having come to a termination, the secretary would probably like to have, as a record, a report of the work done in providing apparatus and arranging the Exhibition, and also of the subsequent proceedings.

The exhibits consisted of both ancient and modern apparatus, and, as far as possible, they were shown actually at work.

A selection of instruments, which it was thought would be appropriate to the occasion, was made from the Historical Collection at the South Kensington Museum. This consisted of specimens of the earliest forms of Telegraph Instruments, invented by Cooke and Wheatstone, Bright, Highton, Varley, and others. To these were added a large number of historical instruments and cable specimens collected from various rooms in this building.

From the stores at Gloucester Road some early forms of insulators were selected, and these were mounted on a model telegraph pole and exhibited side by side with a second pole

upon which was mounted a set of the modern insulators now used by the Department.

Specimen coils of iron and copper wire as used for aerial lines and of gutta-percha covered wire as used for underground work were also shown.

The modern apparatus consisted of every form of instrument adopted by the Department for telegraphic purposes, and, where working wires could be obtained, communication was actually established.

The Hughes was worked to Paris and Berlin.

The Multiplex (six ways) to Birmingham.

The Quadruplex (four ways) to Bristol.

The Duplex to Manchester.

The Simplex Sounder to Aberdeen and Penzance.

Communication was also established with Brighton.

In addition to the above-mentioned circuits, which were used for asking questions and obtaining answers and for the transmission of dummy telegrams, special wires were connected to the *City Press* and *Citizen* newspaper offices for actual business.

The Guildhall was also connected, by means of a news wire, with Birmingham, Manchester, and Liverpool, for the transmission of news handed in at the counter.

To enable these connections to be made, thirteen spare wires existing between the General Post-Office and Aldermanbury were temporarily extended into the Guildhall by means of a cable passing over the roofs of the adjoining buildings. The working apparatus required 980 battery cells, which had to be put together and charged with acid, bichromate, and sal-ammoniac after delivery at the Guildhall.

A separate room was set apart in the crypt for the batteries, and a cable of sixty wires was run between that room and the instrument tables.

In the case of all cables the wires were cut of such a length as to be afterwards available for ordinary purposes without waste. The working of the simpler apparatus, such as the A. B. C. Single Needle, Double Sounder, Direct Inker, and Direct Inker Duplex, was illustrated by their being connected locally from one part of the table to another. A local Wheatstone news circuit, composed of the transmitting and three Receiving Offices, representing London (transmitting) and Birmingham, Manchester, and Liverpool (receiving), was fitted up complete to demonstrate the method of working such circuits. This circuit and the Multiplex and Hughes were most popular; the latter instruments being type printers, combined with the additional novelty of being in direct communication with Paris and Berlin, were particularly interesting to the visitors.

The Exchange Telegraph Company was kind enough to fit up one of their latest "Column Type" printing instruments, and to provide clerks to work it. A complete set of my "Railway Block Signalling" instruments, as used by the department in Ireland, and by the London and South-Western Railway Company in England, was supplied by Mr. Goldstone, the telegraph superintendent of the London and South-Western Railway, and Mr. Wyles, his inspector, was good enough to attend to illustrate the method of working.

A set of Fire Alarm Call Posts and Indicators used at a Central Fire Station was shown in operation.

A small Telephone Exchange was established with three telephone circuits running from it to different parts of the Guildhall, to demonstrate the method of automatically indicating the completion of communication as used in the Departmental Exchanges when two renters have finished a conversation.

A Pneumatic Tube was established between the temporary Post-Office and the News Wire in the Telegraph Section for actual traffic on the opening day, but it was kept in operation during the three days of the Exhibition.

A piece of an old telegraph pole in which a hole had been nearly pecked through by woodpeckers was exhibited, with a stuffed green woodpecker mounted as if at work.

A descriptive catalogue of all the exhibits was prepared. Each exhibit was labelled and numbered upon the tables in large characters.

The whole technical staff of this office, assisted by Mr. Fischer's supervising officers, was assiduously and zealously engaged in explaining the history and working of the various systems.

The Exhibition was apparently very popular and interesting to the visitors, who crowded round every portion of it during the whole time it was open.

W. H. PREECE.

GENERAL POST-OFFICE,
  28th *May*, 1890.

EXTRACTS FROM THE REPORT
OF THE
PENNY POST JUBILEE COMMITTEE APPOINTED BY THE CORPORATION.

To the Right Honourable the LORD MAYOR, ALDERMEN, *and* COMMONS *of the City of London, in Common Council assembled.*

WE, whose names are hereunto subscribed, of your Penny Postage Jubilee Committee, to whom, on the seventeenth day of April, 1890, it was referred to carry into execution our Report, then presented, upon the Letter of Sir Stevenson Arthur Blackwood, K.C.B., Secretary of H.M. Post-Office, by direction of the Postmaster-General, on the subject of the proposed celebration of the Jubilee of the establishment of Uniform Penny Postage, wherein we recommended that a Conversazione should be given in the Guildhall, on Friday, the 16th day of May, 1890, and that the illustrations to be then given of the working and progress of the Postal Service be repeated on the following Saturday and Monday, and for authority to carry out the necessary arrangements, at an expense not exceeding Two thousand Guineas, DO CERTIFY, that we duly proceeded therein, and appointed Alderman Sir James Whitehead, Bart., the Mover of the original Resolution in your Honourable Court, to be our Chairman. We were attended by Mr. F. E. Baines, C.B., one of the Assistant Secretaries, Mr. R. C. Tombs, the Controller of the London Postal Service, and Mr. Preece, the Chief Electrician of the Post-Office, whom, together with Major Cardin and Colonel Raffles Thompson—with Mr. W. G. Gates, Mr. Sydney Beckley, and Mr. G. A. Aitken as Honorary Secretaries —we appointed, with their concurrence, to act with us as a

Committee of Co-operation, and we received from them the most hearty and unstinting assistance throughout our proceedings, more especially in the planning and arrangement of the numerous and interesting postal illustrations, which were minutely set forth in an official pamphlet published on the occasion.

It may, however, be here generally stated that the Guildhall itself was thoroughly fitted, and used, during the whole period of the three days' exhibition, as a Post-Office, in which was transacted every species of postal and telegraphic business. Postcards were printed of a special pattern appropriate to the occasion, to the number of 10,000, and these were all quickly disposed of to the public at an agreed price of sixpence each, for the benefit of the Rowland Hill Memorial and Benevolent Fund.

During the evening of Friday, the 16th of May, not only were Telegrams sent to and Replies received from various parts of the Country and the Continent by H.R.H. the Prince of Wales, the Lord Mayor and others; but we desire to mention as an especial feature of interest that many telegrams of warm and hearty congratulation were received in Guildhall by the Right Hon. the Lord Mayor from various, some being the most distant, Municipalities, and from other public Bodies in England, Scotland, Ireland, and Wales, every one of which was replied to on behalf of his Lordship and the Corporation, by the Town Clerk, the same evening.

These facts, we venture to think, point conclusively to the extraordinary interest taken by the public, not merely of London, but in the provinces, in the absolutely unique proceedings.

A most appropriate card, submitted by Messrs. Blades, East and Blades, having been selected and approved by us, we issued Invitations for the evening of Friday, the 16th May, to the number in all of 3,645.

We had already been gratified to learn that His Royal Highness the Prince of Wales proposed to honour the occasion by his presence.

With reference to Saturday, the 17th, and Monday the 19th of May, we resolved, as the safest and most convenient course,

THE CONVERSAZIONE AT THE GUILDHALL. 137

that there should be three periods of admission to Guildhall on each of those days, viz. :—from 10 a.m. to 1 p.m., from 2 to 5 p.m., and from 6 to 10 p.m., and that distinctive tickets should be printed for each of these periods, amounting, in the whole, to 21,000. Of these, we sent 4,750 to the Post-Office Authorities for distribution at their discretion, and the remainder, after compliance with written applications that reached us in considerable numbers, were sent to the several Members of your Honourable Court for appropriation among the citizens and the public generally.

We further resolved that *employés* of Her Majesty's Post Office, in uniform, should be admitted without tickets throughout the appointed hours of the Saturday and Monday, a privilege of which, we are glad to say, those for whom it was intended largely availed themselves.

The Guard of Honour on the Friday evening was supplied by the Post-Office Volunteers.

The Instrumental musical arrangements on the same evening consisted of the Band of the Coldstream Guards in Guildhall, and Willoughby's String Band in the Art Gallery.

Vocal Concerts of great excellence were given in the New Council Chamber at various periods of the exhibition by the Post-Office Choir, under Mr. Sydney Beckley, and by the Guildhall School of Music, under Mr. Boulcott Newth.

We have received on all hands the most gratifying testimony of the success of the proceedings undertaken by us on the Reference from your Honourable Court, and we especially congratulate ourselves that the whole has been carried out considerably within the amount voted for the purpose.

We have audited the various bills and accounts, which we have the satisfaction to report amount in the total to 1,675*l*. 4*s*.

We have specially recorded our thanks to the Postmaster-General, to the Secretary of the Post-Office, and to those acting under him, and we feel we cannot speak too warmly of the services rendered by Mr. F. E. Baines, C.B., and those of his colleagues who heartily co-operated with us in the performance of our duties.

We have also expressed our sense of the excellence of the police arrangements, which were admirably carried out by Colonel Sir James Fraser, K.C.B., assisted by Lieutenant-Colonel Henry Smith, and the Superintendents of the force.

We are equally sensible of the great assistance afforded us by the Town Clerk, who, with the Principal Clerk of his department and those acting under him, heartily seconded our efforts in every possible way.

In conclusion, we desire to add the following Resolution, unanimously passed by us in recognition of the manner in which our Chairman presided over our deliberations and proceedings :—

"That the very sincere thanks of this Committee be presented to Alderman Sir James Whitehead, Bart., Chairman, for the admirable manner in which he has discharged the important duties devolving upon him.

"The success attending the Conversazione is doubtless to him a full satisfaction for his work ; at the same time the Members generally feel it a personal pleasure to acknowledge their great indebtedness for the manner in which he presided over them throughout their labours."

All which we submit to the judgment of this Honourable Court. Dated this eleventh day of June, 1890.

JAMES WHITEHEAD.	WILLIAM LAWRENCE.
J. E. SLY.	W. J. R. COTTON.
STUART KNILL.	WM. H. PANNELL.
CHAS. E. SMITH.	FRANCIS MCCARTHY.
HENRY CLARKE.	SAML. PRICE.
A. PURSSELL.	W. R. PRYKE.
THOMAS SANGSTER.	J. T. HEPBURN.
G. H. EDMONDS.	LEWIS M. MYERS.
ARTHUR B. HUDSON.	CHAS. J. CUTHBERTSON.
JAMES CLOUDSLEY.	THOS. H. ELLIS.
R. C. HALSE.	JAMES BASTOW.
CORNELIUS BARHAM.	J. L. SAYER.
THOMAS WILDASH.	DAVID BURNETT.
M. WALLACE.	GEORGE FISHER.
J. TICKLE.	

THE CONVERSAZIONE AT THE GUILDHALL. 139

Copies of Telegrams of Congratulation received on Friday Evening, the 16th May, 1890, and acknowledged by the Town Clerk, on behalf of the Lord Mayor:—

MAYORS AND PROVOSTS OF THE UNITED KINGDOM.

From the LORD PROVOST OF ABERDEEN.

The Lord Provost of Aberdeen sends hearty congratulations on the occasion of the celebration of the Jubilee of the Penny Post, one of the most valuable of modern institutions, and hopes it may soon be extended to reach all our Colonies and dependencies.

From the MAYOR OF BATH.

Britain's gratitude, and the pattern given to the world, is the best recognition of the Postal Jubilee.

From the MAYOR OF BELFAST.

On behalf of the City of Belfast, I beg to transmit very hearty congratulations on the occasion of your celebration of the Jubilee of the Penny Post, and wish you every success. May the Post-Office continue to keep pace with the times.

From the MAYOR OF BIRMINGHAM.

Sincere congratulations on occasion of Jubilee of Penny Post—look upon the past as a stimulus for an Ocean Penny Post in near future.

From the MAYOR OF BRADFORD.

Allow me the pleasure, on behalf of the inhabitants of this Borough, to offer my hearty congratulations in reference to your meeting for celebrating the Jubilee of the Penny Postage, which has conferred a great blessing on all classes of the community.

From the MAYOR OF BRIGHTON.

The Mayor of Brighton sends congratulations to the Lord Mayor of London on the Jubilee of the Penny Postage.

From the MAYOR OF BRISTOL.

Congratulations on the celebration of the Postal Jubilee—hope your Conversazione will be a great success.

From the MAYOR OF CAMBRIDGE.

Hearty congratulations on the Postal Jubilee.

From the MAYOR OF CARDIFF.

Many congratulations on the Jubilee of Penny Postage. I trust that soon it will be world-wide.

From the MAYOR OF CARNARVON.

The Mayor of Carnarvon sends hearty congratulations on the celebration of the Jubilee of the Penny Postage.

From the MAYOR OF CHELTENHAM.

The Mayor of Cheltenham sends congratulations on occasion of Penny Postage Jubilee—hopes next Jubilee may witness Universal Penny Postage.

From the MAYOR OF CHESTER.

Celebration of Jubilee of Penny Post. The Mayor of Chester desires his hearty congratulations.

From the MAYOR OF CHIPPENHAM.

Accept congratulations from the Borough of Chippenham on the celebration of the Jubilee of the Penny Postage. One of the greatest boons conferred on the nation during Her Majesty's Reign.

From the MAYOR OF CORK.

Accept hearty congratulations on Jubilee of Penny Post. I earnestly trust its application may soon become universal.

From the LORD PROVOST OF DUNDEE.

The Lord Provost of Dundee sends congratulations on Postal Jubilee.

From the MAYOR OF DOVER.

The Mayor and inhabitants of Dover congratulate your Lordship on this interesting celebration and the reduction lately made in Foreign Postage rates.

From the LORD PROVOST OF EDINBURGH.

The Lord Provost of Edinburgh congratulates the Lord Mayor of London on his celebration of the Jubilee of the Penny Post and on the presence of His Royal Highness the Prince of Wales.

From the MAYOR OF EXETER.

The Mayor of Exeter, as representing the Citizens, sends congratulations on the Jubilee of the Penny Postage, to which is largely due the unsurpassed progress and enterprise of the country.

From the LORD PROVOST OF GLASGOW.

The Lord Provost, Magistrates, and Town Council of Glasgow send hearty congratulations to the Lord Mayor and Company at the Guildhall assembled to celebrate the Jubilee of the Penny Postage.

From PROVOST RODGER OF GREENOCK.

The Corporation of Greenock send hearty congratulations on the celebration of the Jubilee of the Penny Postage. Robert Wallace, the first member for this Burgh, by his casting vote as Chairman of the Parliamentary Committee, carried a recommendation in favour of a uniform cheap postage, and materially assisted the great Reformer, Rowland Hill, in passing the measure which has proved such a boon to this country.

From the MAYOR OF HASTINGS.

The Mayor and Corporation of Hastings send most hearty greetings and congratulations on this Postal Jubilee Anniversary.

From the PROVOST OF INVERNESS.

I beg to offer congratulations on the Jubilee of the Penny Post, which has been of inestimable benefit to the people of Great Britain. This part of the Empire has benefited in an especial degree since Rowland Hill's great scheme, perfected by a Scotsman, was carried into effect.

From the MAYOR OF IPSWICH.

The Mayor of Ipswich tenders his warmest congratulations on the attainment of the Penny Postal Jubilee.

From the MAYOR OF KINGSTON-UPON-HULL.

The Mayor of Kingston-upon-Hull sends hearty congratulations on the celebration of the Postal Jubilee.

From the MAYOR OF LEAMINGTON.

May your reception to-night be as successful as the Institution whose Jubilee you are now celebrating.

From the MAYOR OF LEICESTER.

The Mayor of Leicester, on behalf of the Inhabitants, begs to convey hearty congratulations on the celebration of the Jubilee of the Penny Post, the establishment of which has proved so great a national benefit.

From the MAYOR OF LIMERICK.

William Joseph O'Donnell, Mayor of Limerick, sends his congratulations to the Lord Mayor of London on the celebration of the Post Office Jubilee, at this moment being held in the Guildhall.

From the MAYOR OF LINCOLN.

The Citizens of Lincoln heartily join your assembly in celebrating the Jubilee of the Penny Postage system, and in acknowledging the inestimable boon it conferred on the nation.

From the MAYOR OF LIVERPOOL.

Accept the congratulations which, on behalf of this City, I have pleasure in sending you, and the cordial and hearty wishes of the Citizens for the success of the Jubilee festival, which you are inaugurating this evening at the Guildhall, to commemorate the great work of Rowland Hill in the establishment of the Penny Postage system.

From the MAYOR OF LONDONDERRY.

The Mayor of the historic City of Londonderry sends his congratulations and best wishes for the success of the Postal Jubilee.

From the MAYOR OF MANCHESTER.

On behalf of the Citizens of Manchester, I desire heartily to congratulate your Lordship, and all assembled, on the celebration of the Postal Jubilee, an event which marks an enormous advance in commercial prosperity and social convenience.

From the MAYOR OF NEWCASTLE-UPON-TYNE.

The Mayor, on behalf of the City of Newcastle-upon-Tyne, sends hearty congratulations upon the celebration of the Postal Jubilee.

From the MAYOR OF NORTHAMPTON.

The Mayor of Northampton begs to offer his congratulations to the Lord Mayor of London on the celebration of the Jubilee of the Penny Postal system, which has conferred such great advantages on this country.

From the MAYOR OF NOTTINGHAM.

The Mayor of Nottingham wishes to express hearty congratulations at the success which has attended the introduction of the Penny Postage.

From the MAYOR OF OXFORD.

I have much pleasure in offering to your Lordship and your guests my very hearty congratulations on the Postage Jubilee. I am old enough to remember the time when the postage on letters from London was eightpence—what would the present generation feel if they had now to pay eightpence for each letter? All honour to the great man, Rowland Hill, who proposed and carried out so great a work.

From the MAYOR OF PENZANCE.

The Mayor of Penzance, as the representative of the Civic Authorities and the inhabitants of this ancient and loyal Borough, sends congratulations to your Lordship on the happy event now being celebrated under your Lordship's auspices at the Guildhall. The introduction of Penny Postage marks an epoch in our history, and is intimately associated with our commercial advancement and prosperity; it is therefore most fitting and appropriate that the premier city of the world should keep its Jubilee with the distinguished company gathered around your Lordship to-night. May its centenary in 1940 witness its universal adoption. God save the Queen and bless our own Duke of Cornwall, to whom the Mayor of Penzance sends his respectful and loyal duty and obeisance.

From the LORD PROVOST OF PERTH.

The Lord Provost of Perth offers his hearty congratulations on the celebration of the Jubilee of Penny Postage Stamps, and wishes the Exhibition all success.

From the MAYOR OF PLYMOUTH.

Plymouth sends through me its earnest congratulations to yourself on the occasion of present happy Postal Jubilee.

From the MAYOR OF PORTSMOUTH.

Hearty congratulations on this memorable occasion from the Corporation of Portsmouth.

From the MAYOR OF PRESTON.

The Mayor of Preston greets the Lord Mayor upon the Postal Jubilee now being held. Hearty congratulations.

From the MAYOR OF READING.

The Mayor of Reading, on behalf of the town, sends hearty congratulations on the celebration of the Jubilee of the Penny Postage, which has proved an incalculable blessing to the people of this country.

From GEORGE NODDER, ESQ., MAYOR OF SALISBURY.

Accept congratulations of this city on commemoration of the Jubilee of Penny Postage.

From the MAYOR OF SHEFFIELD.

The Mayor of Sheffield desires to congratulate the Lord Mayor on the auspicious occasion of the gathering in celebration of the Jubilee of Penny Postage.

From the MAYOR OF SHREWSBURY.

The Mayor of Shrewsbury sends his congratulations to the Lord Mayor on the celebration of the Jubilee of the institution of the Penny Post.

From the MAYOR OF STOCKPORT.

The Mayor of Stockport sends hearty congratulations to the Penny Postage Jubilee celebration.

From the MAYOR OF SWANSEA.

The Mayor of Swansea sends his congratulations on the celebration of the Postal Jubilee; the Penny Postage system has conduced in no small degree to the marked progress of the last fifty years.

From the MAYOR OF WINCHESTER.

The Mayor of Winchester, premier Mayor of England, sends greeting to the Lord Mayor of London and congratulates his Lordship that the Jubilee of the adoption of the Postage Stamp falls in his auspicious year of office. All Her Majesty's subjects carry in their hearts loyal love, and it is in the happy fitness of things that her head should frank their letters everywhere, —it was a felicitous idea, has achieved mighty results, and is capable of extension. May joy pervade your celebration to-night and your year's possession of the authority of the historic office of Lord Mayor of the capital of England and of the world.

CHAMBERS OF COMMERCE.

From the CARDIFF CHAMBER OF COMMERCE.

Hope you will have a pleasant gathering in connection with the Penny Postage Jubilee.

From the CHAMBER OF COMMERCE, EXETER.

The Exeter Chamber of Commerce desire to record their high appreciation of the advantages of the Penny Postal system, shown in a remarkable degree by the development of the trade of this country.

From PRESIDENT HIDE, CHAMBER OF COMMERCE, PORTSMOUTH.

Hearty congratulations upon Jubilee Penny Postage celebration.

OTHER PUBLIC BODIES, &c.

From the CARDIFF SHIPOWNERS' ASSOCIATION.

Wish every success to the gathering in connection with the Penny Postage Jubilee.

From the EXETER CONSTITUTIONAL CLUB.

The members of the Exeter Constitutional Club send their hearty congratulations on the Jubilee of the Penny Postage, which has done so much to develop the trade and commerce of this country, and conferred such untold benefits on the world at large.

From the VICE-CHANCELLOR OF OXFORD UNIVERSITY.

The Vice-Chancellor of Oxford University begs to transmit to the Worshipful the Lord Mayor his hearty congratulations on the occasion of his presiding over the celebration of the fiftieth anniversary of the introduction of the system of Penny Postage.

From SIR MORGAN MORGAN, CARDIFF.

Congratulations on the celebration of the Penny Postage Jubilee, which I hope will be as successful as the great undertaking itself.

From SIR ALBERT SASSOON.

Sir Albert Sassoon begs to send hearty congratulations on Jubilee of Penny Postage, which your Lordship celebrates to-night.

AN ACCOUNT OF THE CONVERSAZIONE AT GUILDHALL.

(From the *City Press*, May 17, 1890.)

THE brilliant assembly at the Guildhall last evening in celebration of the Jubilee Anniversary of the Introduction of Inland Uniform Penny Postage was certainly one of the most successful entertainments ever given by the Corporation of London. The occasion was one which was sympathetic to the hearts of citizens, for the marvellous growth of wealth and the wide extension of London are almost coeval with the penny postage.

In 1839 few Londoners who had city business slept beyond the bills of mortality, while nowadays not only do we have half-a-dozen deliveries a-day, but the telegraph is not quick enough for some of us, and we have flown to the telephone. What number of letters passed through the Post Office in 1839, when Rowland Hill—then a schoolmaster—wrote his pamphlet on postal reform, the manuscript of which is displayed in the exhibition, has been recorded, but the numbers of last year almost transcend imagination. No less than 850 million letters were posted out of London last year, and 690 million delivered from the country; while the actual local post amounts to over 330 millions. Of mail bags passing between office and office in London there are 4,750,000, to and from the provinces 4,250,000, to and from foreign parts 450,000. The figures as announced in total by Mr. Raikes, amazed the distinguished assembly which crowded the library. When the doors were opened there was abundant occupation for early arrivals in viewing the complete post-offices on the west side of the hall—with examples of

SIR S. ARTHUR BLACKWOOD, K.C.B.
(Secretary of the Post-Office.)
(*From a photograph by Messrs. Elliott and Fry.*)

pillar boxes from the original square ones of 1855, through the tall elaborate edifice with crown and cushion, which formerly stood on London Bridge, to the modern useful pillar with its wire interior.

On the east side was the Telegraph department, where every system from Cooke and Wheatstone's four-needle machine, requiring four wires, to the present single wire and almost instantaneous machine, was exhibited. Several offices were in direct communication with Aberdeen, Bristol, Brighton, Penzance, and other distant places, to which congratulatory telegrams were sent, and the replies returned during the few minutes that spectators waited—one sent to Penzance ran " Gog and Magog are enjoying the fun," to which the Penzance postmaster replied, " I should like to be there also." This was done in three and a half minutes. On the arrival of the Prince of Wales, the following rhymes were sent to every office on the system, and though their lines are crooked, their sentiment is excellent :—

> " England's Prince is with us,
> All honour to his name ;
> May his life continue joyous,
> And crown'd with lasting fame ; "

and from fifty-seven towns in the United Kingdom came answers of congratulation.

The Lord Mayor arrived about eight o'clock and was received by the Committee, who preceded him to the chair of state on the daïs of the Library. Truth to say, the reception, which lasted nearly an hour and a half, was rather slow, and among the multitude of distinguished guests invited only few put in an early appearance. Indeed, for some time the Library was scarcely half full—for the wise ones, knowing how late the Prince was coming, discreetly examined the exhibition during the interval. In the great hall they had the advantage of the music of the Coldstream's band, under Mr. C. Thomas, and in the Council Chamber the Post-Office Choir, conducted by Mr. Beckley, gave two concerts, at eight and ten. The Aldermen's

Room was the home of the phonograph, and in the old Council Chamber was a series of dissolving views. But still the guests poured through the Library, and among the first distinguished arrivals was Sir Stevenson A. Blackwood, K.C.B., Secretary of the Post Office, in Windsor uniform. To him succeeded Sir Thomas Chambers and his daughters; then came Sir Pope Hennessey, looking naturally thinner and grayer than when, nearly twenty-seven years ago, he led the "Pope's Brass Band" in the House of Commons, and struggled in the cause of Poland. Mr. Henniker Heaton, satisfied with his half-way house of $2\frac{1}{2}d.$ postage to the Colonies, and Mr. Shaw-Lefevre, an old Postmaster-General, were quickly followed by an interesting group —Mr. Rowland Hill and Mr. Pearson Hill, sons of the reformer, with various other members of their family, to the number of about fifteen, including Miss Rosamond Davenport Hill, who, to the surprise of Mr. Lobb, had not brought any knitting.

The first Alderman to arrive was Lieut.-Colonel Cowan. The Rev. J. R. Diggle, M.A., chairman of the School Board, was received with cheers, as was General Sir Daniel Lysons, G.C.B. the new Constable of the Tower. After him came Mr. C. Fielding, the new Master of the Turners' Company, only elected on Thursday, in succession to Mr. Burdett-Coutts, M.P. The new Treasurer of St. Thomas's Hospital, and Mrs. Wainwright, were warmly received, as were the Master of the Butchers' Company and Mr. Arthur A'Beckett, in military guise. Sir John Coode, G.C.M.G., soon followed, and then came Mr. George Spicer and Mr. Alderman Newton. Lord and Lady Meath were present, but did not go up to the daïs, nor did Mr. Staveley Hill, Q.C., M.P. But Mr. Austin, who moves that "the question be now put" in the County Council, came up by himself. Then arrived Mr. and Mrs. Russell and Mr. Washington Lyon with Mrs. John Scott (niece of Sir Rowland Hill and wife of Mr. Justice Scott, lately appointed by the Government to supervise the judicial system of Egypt). Dr. McGeagh (as surgeon of the H.A.C.), Dr. Westmacott (as army surgeon-general), and Mr Edwin Freshfield arrived almost together, and Mr. George Sims —introduced as Sir George, amid applause—succeeded. Then came the Master of the Girdlers' Company and Mr. and Mrs. "Tam" Read, Mr. and Mrs. Pennefeather, Sir Edmund Hertzlet, Mr. H. G. Reid (president of the Institute of Journalists), and amid a flourish of trumpets, Mr. Cecil Raikes himself, the great head of the Post Office.

The LORD MAYOR, who was received with cheers said: My Lords, Ladies, and Gentlemen,—The committee entrusted with the arrangements for to-day's celebration were good enough to ask me to make a speech. You will doubtless be pleased to hear that I had sufficient fortitude and self-denial to resist that very great temptation. My reasons were various; firstly, I thought that there were very many in this assembly who have heard at least enough of my voice during the current week; then I thought of the many ladies who are amongst this audience; and, lastly, I thought it would be wrong of me to stand between this assembly and the two distinguished speakers who will presently address you, in the persons of the Right Hon. Mr. Raikes, the Postmaster-General, and my excellent friend and predecessor the late Lord Mayor, who was, as you are aware, the founder of the Rowland Hill Benevolent Fund. Ladies and Gentlemen,—You will, perhaps, be asking yourselves why, if I am not going to make a speech, I must detain you. I will answer that question for you in a moment. I thought if I had contented myself with setting before you the mere fact that I had been able to resist that temptation to make a speech my silence might be open to misconstruction. There might be some doubt whether my heart is in this celebration, and I venture, therefore, to tell you that it is, and that if I resisted the temptation it was for the consideration that I have given you, and I desire to assure you that no one in this assembly, or in this country appreciates more than I do the eminent services of the late Sir Rowland Hill. I cannot think of him but as the greatest benefactor of his time—a man who did more than any other in his time in the interest of civilization. I have now the privilege to introduce to you the Postmaster-General.

The POSTMASTER-GENERAL said: My Lord Mayor, my Lords,

Ladies, and Gentlemen,—The Lord Mayor, who has shown on this occasion no less than his usual sympathy with all good works and useful institutions, has almost too modestly restricted his right to make a speech to-night. And yet he has said enough, I think, to satisfy this great and influential audience how warmly he sympathizes both with the triumphs and the progress of the great institution, the Imperial Post Office, and also how sincerely he feels for the objects of the Rowland Hill Benevolent Fund, which I trust and believe must be greatly benefited by assemblies like this.

We are collected in this ancient and historic hall—connected as it is with so many of the greatest and most interesting events of our history—to celebrate the jubilee of quite a modern institution, but of an institution which may be said to have done more for the cause of universal civilization than almost any other political or social discovery. The memory of Sir Rowland Hill, associated as it will always be with the introduction of the penny post, will, I think, be dear, not only to his own country, and not only to those who speak the English language in other and distant Continents, but also to all those who speak in other tongues and inhabit other countries, and who are able to appreciate the greatness of that peaceful revolution of which he was the prime mover. It is almost impossible at this time of day for us to realize the greatness of the change which has been brought about by the establishment of the penny post. Although I would not to-night weary an assemblage like this with tedious and tiresome figures, it may be at least permitted to me to remind you that, whereas in the year immediately preceding the establishment of the penny postage, the number of letters delivered in the United Kingdom amounted to seventy-six millions (and I have no doubt that was at the time considered an enormous number), the number of letters delivered in this country last year was nearly sixteen hundred millions—twenty times the number of letters which passed through the post fifty years ago; to these letters must be added the six hundred and fifty-two millions of postcards and other communications by the halfpenny post, and the enormous number of newspapers, which bring the total number of communications passing through the post to considerably above two billion. I venture to say that this is the most stupendous result of any administrative change which the world has witnessed.

If you estimate the effect of that upon our daily life, if you pause for a moment to consider how trade and business have been facilitated and developed, how finally relations have been maintained and kept together, if you for a moment allow your mind to dwell upon this change which is implied in that great fact to which I have just called attention, I think you will see that the establishment of the penny post has done more to change—and change for the better—the face of Old England, than almost any other political or social project which has received the sanction of the Legislature within our history. I cannot forget, speaking here to you to-night, that Her Majesty's Government has found in this jubilee year of the penny post a suitable occasion for establishing a uniform postage from this country to our Colonies, together with those many great nations who are, like ourselves, the members of the Postal Union. I am happy, indeed, that the honour has been reserved for myself during my tenure of office to be the Minister specially charged with the carrying out of this great, and, as I believe, beneficial measure.

I do not know whether it is possible for us to-day to forecast what may happen in the distant future in the way of drawing closer those family ties which bind the mother country to her daughter colonies, but if the result of the change which is taking place—as I hope it will take place—this year should be in any degree commensurate with the change which has occurred in England since the penny post was established, I think that this humble department, whose first duty is to carry your letters, to convey your telegrams, and to take care of your savings-bank deposits, may claim to have done more and to have laid a deeper and wider basis for the great British Empire of the future than might have been achieved by the most daring or brilliant statesmanship, or by the most successful and triumphant war.

We are here to celebrate a jubilee which nearly coincides with that of the reign of our most gracious Majesty, who had only occupied the throne of these realms for less than three years when the Ministry of that day found it possible to introduce that great change which Sir Rowland Hill had so powerfully and disinterestedly advocated. Therefore, it is but natural that the Royal House of Britain should take particular interest in this great triumph of peace. I am glad to think that not only you, my Lord Mayor, have placed the traditional hospitality of the Corporation of this great City on this occasion at the disposal of those who desire to celebrate the event in a fitting manner, but that this assembly is to be graced to-night by the presence of the Heir to the Throne.

I ought not to detain you by reference to those other branches of the work which have grown up around the Post Office in the course of the last quarter of a century. It would be enough for me to remind you how, in 1861, the Post-Office, not contented with its duty of being the letter-carrier for all classes, undertook to be also the bankers of the poor; how nine years later it accepted the responsibility of the telegraphic communication of the United Kingdom; how, ten years after that, it dared to enter the field as carrier of parcels for the public generally, and how it has been constantly on the watch to extend the scope of its usefulness and bring to bear on the national life that nervous organization which it has perfected. So much has been done for the public, that while some ladies and gentlemen here may say that too much almost has been done, at least those of you who think that the present posts a-day are more than the most voracious appetite could desire—while so much has been done, and is being done, and has still to be done by the Post Office in the interest of the public, we hope that the public will not forget those—the humblest class of the servants of the Post Office—who form the basis of this great superstructure, and by whose labour the great benefits of civilization are carried to every corner of the globe.

Those of you who may have studied the pamphlet which has been circulated this evening, or who may have looked at the first pages of the catalogue which your committee kindly placed in my hand, may realize how much there is still to be done to ameliorate the lot of our working postmen, to comfort them in their anticipation of the future, and to console their declining years. The State is bound to be just before it can be generous. The public can afford to be generous before it considers whether it will be just, and I for one am certain that there can be no juster cause for unloosing the purse strings of that benevolence which has such high tone in the City of London than to ameliorate the condition of those servants of the public, for whom the State has not found it possible to make a sufficient provision. As you know, there are pensions and superannuation funds by which servants of the public may expect to receive a very moderate amount of subsistence when they have served their full time and have passed out of the sphere of active usefulness; but there are cases in which a man breaks down, perhaps in the middle of his career, or a man has served the public without being actually and technically in the service of the State, and who finds when he is incapacitated from further public service that no provision exists for his necessities, and those of his family.

All honour to those who, like Sir James Whitehead, not enlisted in the actual service of the department, have conceived that the great name of Rowland Hill, and the magnificent services rendered by him to his country may best be ameliorated and assisted by inviting the sympathy and kind consideration of the public at large on behalf of those servants of the public whose labours have been so greatly increased by this reform. I think, my Lord Mayor, that you, as the Lord High Almoner of your countrymen, have never more worthily discharged that important function of your great office than in presiding over this meeting to-night; and I am satisfied that, however feebly and imperfectly I have attempted to connect in your minds those immense benefits and conveniences which have become part of our daily lives with the services of a most laborious, of a most honest, and a most dutiful class of public servants, the fact that you have been brought here to-night, under the presidency of the Lord

Mayor, and upon this most interesting and important occasion will have sufficiently brought home to you the duty, if I may say it, or at least the wish, which must pervade every generous breast in this country, to improve the condition, to meet the necessities of those to whom we are so greatly indebted for the benefits which we all in common enjoy.

The LORD MAYOR, again rising, said: I have the honour to call upon Sir James Whitehead.

Alderman Sir JAMES WHITEHEAD said: My Lord Mayor, my Lords, Ladies and Gentlemen,—I feel somewhat in a difficulty in being called upon to address you on this occasion, inasmuch as I have been preceded by the Postmaster-General, who has, to a very great extent, said what I myself was going to say. I had been asked, and I hope without any vanity I may add, not inappropriately asked, to say something this evening on behalf of the Rowland Hill Benevolent Fund.

It may be in the recollection of some who are here to-night, that about eight or ten years ago I took part, along with others, in what we felt to be a due recognition of the great work that had been done by Rowland Hill, and starting from the point that we desired to erect a statue to his memory and a monument to record his good work in Westminster Abbey, we found ourselves in course of time in possession of a larger amount of money than we had at first anticipated. With a surplus of something like £15,000, it occurred to us that we might possibly perpetuate the memory of a great man, to whom we owe the introduction of the uniform system of penny postage, in a manner that would be in accordance with what we believed to have been the spirit of his life, and in what we believed to be the desire of his family, and also the desire of a large number of the present officials of the Post Office, who desire to keep his virtues and his good deeds green in the recollection of the present generation.

Well, now, the Corporation have given this conversazione just as they always, as I conceive, do the right thing at the right moment, and they have opened their hand, and opened their purse in a manner which, I believe, will be well appreciated, not only by the citizens of London, not only by the people of the metropolis, but by the great bulk of the English-speaking people throughout the entire empire. Now it is not in accordance with the usual custom of the Corporation that there should be any charge for admission, or that there should be any collection within the precincts of this Guildhall. But while that is the rule which obtains amongst us, we are bound, as we feel, to respect the desire and the wishes of those officials who are connected with the Post Office, and to whom we owe such an exhibition of ancient and modern postal arrangements and postal facilities as has probably never been gathered together at any time under one roof. Well, we know that the postal leaders, the leading officials of the Post Office, desire nothing for their own services, but they do desire that some good should arise out of this great gathering on this occasion, for the benefit of an institution—the Rowland Hill Benevolent Fund—which has been referred to in such eloquent and kindly terms by the Postmaster-General.

But you may very reasonably ask, What is the Rowland Hill Benevolent Fund—what is its object and what is its aim? The Rowland Hill Benevolent Fund was established in the first instance by a few friends and myself, and it is to-day doing an enormous amount of good in proportion to the funds at its disposal—an amount of good that could not, in all probability, be exceeded by any other institution or association possessing so small an amount of money for the purpose of its usefulness. Now the pamphlet which has been placed in the hands of a large number of those who are here to-night does convey in clear and concise language what is the object of this fund, and at the risk of being what the Postmaster-General desired to avoid, at the risk of being tedious and tiresome, I fear I shall be obliged to give you some statistics. The fund, according to the book which has been put into your hands, is available for the relief of every class of officers employed by the Post Office, whether in receipt of a pension or not, the only condition being that there shall be actual distress on the part of the person relieved, or on the part of the widow or children.

Aged persons past work and with very small means, or none at all, and widows with young children, and few or no resources, are the chief recipients of this fund.

I know the public will ask, and perhaps not unreasonably ask, why there is a necessity for this. I know the public run away sometimes with the impression that the great public departments ought to provide for everybody engaged in the department, and for all who belong either directly or indirectly to it. But it is perfectly impossible that that can be so, looking at it from a national point of view, and while I am prepared to say that the amount of remuneration given to the servants of the Post Office is not too high, I am bound to admit that the Postmaster-General and those who act under him do at all times, so far as I am able to ascertain, pay the full market price for the value of the labour they employ in each district where they require servants. Of course we are aware that the servants of the Post Office are some of them in the receipt of pensions, through what is called the Superannuation Act, but even if a servant of the Post Office is on the staff, it is well known that no pension is given until a servant has been in the service of the department for ten years. If he has been there for less than ten years, and he is unfortunately obliged to retire from the service, he is granted a gratuity, which is equal to one month's salary for every year he has served his country. Of course, if he has served for eight years, and his salary has been at the rate of £6 per month, when he retires from the service he receives a gratuity of £48, and every one who has had any experience of family life must know that there is the possibility that such a sum as that may be swallowed up either by the doctor's bill, or by the funeral expenses, or by the two put together.

The Rowland Hill Benevolent Fund comes in under circumstances such as these, to give aid to the person who has received the pension, and to the widow and children of the man who may be taken away. Then again, if a servant of the Post Office has served for more than ten years, he is entitled to one-sixtieth part of his income for every year he has served. I may give you an example: Supposing he has £120 a year, and has served the Post Office for fifteen years, and is obliged to retire, his pension would be £30. If he had served twenty years it would be £40. Now, we know a great many men are obliged to retire because of delicate health, and it may be the man has a sick wife and a large family, and that he is called upon to look to other and extraneous aid for the support of those who are near and dear to him. There, again, the Rowland Hill Benevolent Fund steps in and gives assistance. Then again, if he dies his pension dies with him, and the widow not infrequently has a very hard struggle, and then, again, the Rowland Hill Benevolent Fund gives such aid as it is able to give in accordance with the funds at its disposal.

I will not trouble you either with a long dissertation on the wants of the servants, or with more figures to illustrate the object I have in view, but I do desire to bring home to you this evening that there is another object—there is a claim upon us which those of us who come here this evening ought, to some extent at least, to recognize. We know that the servants of the Post Office are among the most trustworthy of all labouring for the public good. We know that they convey missives which are of vital importance in commerce, that they convey missives which are of an affectionate and endearing character, and we know therefore that the penny postage service introduced by Sir Rowland Hill, apart altogether from the good that has been realized by us as a mercantile nation, has tended to knit and hold together whole families, who, except for that system, would have been very largely divided from each other.

We ought, too, as it seems to me, to show our gratitude to the memory of Sir Rowland Hill for the services of those who act so well for us, and I am satisfied that if we who are here to-night decide that, from this time, we will contribute more largely to the Rowland Hill Fund than we have done hitherto, we shall not only be showing our gratitude to those who have given us this marvellous entertainment to-night, but we shall be doing a great service for the public at large. We shall also be doing something which will stimulate the servants of the public, who are not in the service of the Post Office, to perform their duties with as much zeal and as much desire to benefit the general community at large as those in the service.

The speeches being over, the civic party, with the principal guests, retired to the Library Committee Room for refreshments, and were only summoned thence about twenty-five minutes past ten, when the telegraphist had announced the Prince's departure from Marlborough House. The Lord Mayor and Sheriffs met His Royal Highness at the porch of Guildhall, and conducted him to the daïs, the Lord Mayor having on his arm Mrs. Raikes, while the Prince conducted the Lady Mayoress. Arrived on the daïs the Lord Mayor addressed the Prince, and presented him with a catalogue of the exhibition. He then presented Sir James Whitehead and Mr. J. E. Sly, C.C., mover and seconder of the entertainment; Sir J. Whittaker Ellis, the senior Alderman present; Mr. Baines, C.B., Assistant Secretary General Post Office, and Chairman of the Committee; Mr. Tombs, Controller, London Postal Service; and Mr. Preece, F.R.S., Chief Electrician. Immediately the party rose and proceeded through the building.

The first visit was paid to the Art Gallery, where the Prince was greatly interested in the collection of artistic, quaint, and ignorant addresses found on letters. When a letter is addressed "Esser Quinstaxes, Ldn." it requires some skill to discover that it means "Assessor, Queen's Taxes." When one arrives from Italy with a couple of pears drawn on it, "England," it is only our knowledge of the great advertising firm that leads us to identify it. Then came the pistols and blunderbusses formerly carried by the guards of the coaches; placards announcing rewards for mail robbers; franks of C. J. Fox, W. Pitt, and others of later date, all of which the Prince carefully examined. He also looked at the old accounts of one T. Randolphe, master of the posts, 1566, and another Stephen Lily, 1695. Then at Sir Rowland Hill's portrait and his wonderful pamphlet which changed the old system, but so slowly that there was exhibited the portrait of the sole letter-carrier in Wolverhampton in 1854.

In Wolverhampton of to-day there are over one hundred Post-Office employés. The tent of the Post-Office Volunteers, as used by them in the Soudan, detained the Prince, and he entered into conversation with the decorated sentries who were with the Volunteers the first time they received their baptism of fire.

After admiring the models and pictures of coaches and mail stations, the Prince entered the Great Hall, in which was a machine he used to play with forty years ago. He sent off a message to France by the Hughes system, and waited some minutes for the reply. Again he stopped at the desk whence ran the special wire to the *City Press*, and accepted a copy of the proofs as sent down. One other machine attracted his attention, and then he proceeded to the Council Chamber, where, after the National Anthem, he heard a part song. After traversing the Old Chamber, he retired to the Committee Room, where he remained for nearly half an hour in conversation with the principal guests, among whom was the Duke of Teck, who arrived at the last moment. It was not until half-past eleven that the Prince left, expressing himself interested and delighted with the whole entertainment—as did all those privileged to be present.

The Lord Mayor informed the Prince of Wales that messages of congratulation had been received from all the principal municipalities of the United Kingdom, and that replies had been forwarded. During the evening a number of more or less humorous messages were despatched by the officials at Guildhall to Aberdeen, Penzance, and other towns with which there was direct connection. The Prince of Wales telegraphed an acknowledgment of a "kind message" to Penzance.

The badge worn by the members of the committee is a *replica* of the penny postage stamp at present in use, enamelled on silver, and with a cross bar in red colour bearing the words "Penny Postage Jubilee, 1890."

The design of the admission ticket is entirely in black and tint. In the centre of the top portion is a portrait of Rowland Hill, the City Arms being in the lower part of the card; underneath

THE "CITY PRESS" WIRE AT GUILDHALL.
(By permission of the proprietors of the *City Press*.)

the portrait is a facsimile of the penny adhesive stamp issued by the Post-Office, bearing the letters V. R. in the top corners, with the dates 1840–1890 on either side, and flanked right and left by the two hemispheres. Rays of light proceeding from the portrait of Rowland Hill towards the hemispheres, bear the names of the chief countries of the world. The whole is surrounded by an artistically engraved border, and has been designed and printed by Messrs. Blades, East, and Blades, of Abchurch Lane.

THE "CITY PRESS" EXHIBIT.

The following, printed as *City Press* Extras, was distributed during the proceedings to the company present at the Guildhall :—

Exhibitions are usually at least a month behind, and the first day is simple chaos. There is no rule, however, without an exception, and the Guildhall to-night is a brilliant exception to the rule to which I have referred. The Postmaster-General and Sir James Whitehead are up to time, and the Exhibition to celebrate the Jubilee anniversary of the introduction of Inland Uniform Penny Postage is a marvellous example of postal punctuality and electric speed. As far as one may judge from a hasty and cursory survey of the entire building, everything is ready, every machine is in working order, and every man at his post. Visitors are pouring in by the hundred, and it is expected that within an hour or so over three thousand persons will have assembled beneath the roof of the Guildhall.

The first object which strikes the eye of the visitor as he passes the strong cordon of police under Superintendent Foster, is a mail coach, with passengers on top and bags of letters loaded up ready to start for some distant and unknown destination. The awning outside the Guildhall is distinguished by a Royal Standard in company with two ensigns. A magnificent crush-room has been erected, about three times as large as the one in use at Mr. Stanley's reception. Everything proceeds smoothly, and there is no crushing or crowding at the windows where the hats are received and deposited. The walls of the crush-room are tastefully hung with tapestry and Indian drapery, while the floor is covered with crimson carpet, and piled up with the most lovely of summer flowers, having a fine background of tropical palms.

A hundred men of the 24th Middlesex form a guard of honour in the vestibule under Captain Ogilvie. Along the corridor leading to the Library are stationed, in military order, about seventy postmen and messengers in uniform under Overseer Barnes and Inspector Howard. Beyond these and in the same line are a number of telegraph boys, some of them looking remarkably like girls, attired as Elizabethan pages, whose duty it is to distribute programmes to the passers-by. Leaving the Library, which is the reception-room for the evening, on the left we pass to the Art Galleries, which, strangely enough, contain anything but pictures. There are, indeed, on the walls a few splendid specimens of mail packets, which are even better represented in models under glass cases. There are an electric engine, which works whenever a penny is dropped into the slot, also a model travelling post-office, with apparatus for receiving and despatching mail-bags, and a model of the Liverpool and London mail coach. There are some grim rusty old blunderbusses, such as were probably used to frighten our grandmothers or protect the pockets of our grandfathers as they travelled north or south, while close by are notices offering rewards, varying from £50 to £200, for the apprehension of miscreants who had waylaid hapless post-boys and the benighted mails. The facsimiles of certain letters which have passed through the Post-Office form a curious feature. There is a specimen penned with an artistic border, "Sacred to the memory of the fine weather, which departed from this land June, 1888."

Perhaps the most interesting object in this department is the Army Post-Office. The interior of the tent has a somewhat gloomy appearance, and one might almost imagine that the men inside were laying some deadly mine for the destruction of Arabi's devoted followers, rather than about to engage in the innocent work of flashing home the news of Wolseley's victory.

The men dressed in canvas suits and white helmets are those who served on the sands of Egypt a few years ago. The large hall is brilliantly lighted and in full working order, telegraphy at one end and post-office business at the other. The decorations are much the same as at the Stanley reception. The Congo flags have been removed, but there remain trophies, representing England, America, Germany, Italy, Belgium, and other nations. A large temporary gallery at the east end is draped with crimson cloth and gold fringe, and in the opposite gallery the band of the Coldstream Guards is discoursing most excellent music.

The Guildhall Post-Office is doing a roaring trade, not to be equalled at St. Martin's-le-Grand a few minutes before post time. There is an extraordinary demand for the Jubilee penny post-card, for which sixpence is charged, and which, owing to the limited supply, will, it is rumoured, be worth at least five or ten guineas in a few years' time. I hope this information will not have the effect of increasing the rush, and causing anything like a disaster at the Guildhall. All the telegraphic machines, which extend along two parallel lines down one-half of the hall are clicking, and messages are being flashed to distant parts of the world. The *City Press* instrument, through which this report is being dispatched, is the centre of a small crowd of interested observers. Lower down scores of postmen are actively engaged receiving, sorting, and despatching letters to different towns of the country, and far beyond its borders.

At the present moment the chief interest centres in the Library, which has been transformed into a magnificent reception-room; curiously enough, books are conspicuously absent, being closed in by a mass of crimson drapery. All the bays of the two galleries are filled with fair forms and faces, while the body of the Library is crowded to such a degree that the temperature is anything but agreeable. At the far end a large daïs has been erected, with a background of flowers of almost every colour and variety, red and white—the Corporation colours—naturally predominating.

In front of the gilded chairs stand the Lord Mayor—in his

State robes—and the Lady Mayoress—in a beautiful dress of golden hue, and wearing a magnificent necklace of diamonds—receiving the guests as the names are announced by the masters of the ceremonies. Close by are the Sword and Mace Bearers and the Sergeant-at-Arms, with the symbol of civic authority, Mr. Alderman and Sheriff Knill, and Mr. Sheriff Harris, in their scarlet robes and chains, Alderman Sir James Whitehead, Bart., in black velvet Court dress, with the chain of a past Lord Mayor, and Sir Stevenson Blackwood, in Court dress, with a mass of gold braid.

Since nine o'clock the company in the reception-room has been gradually dwindling away, and not even the music of Willoughby's string band, and a superabundance of the most brilliant diamonds and jewels on the loveliest of dress which presents almost every variety of colour, can stop the exodus. At last the Postmaster-General, the Right Hon. Cecil Raikes, has arrived, and the speech-making begins before a comparatively meagre audience, the four heralds, in scarlet coats, blowing a preliminary blast on their silver trumpets. The Lord Mayor, stepping to the front of the daïs, starts the flood of oratory, standing on his right being the Postmaster-General, and on his left Sir James Whitehead, both ready to take their turn.

The following message was sent by the Prince of Wales to the Emperor of Germany at 11.4 p.m.: " We are celebrating the Jubilee of Uniform Penny Postage at Guildhall, London, and I send you my warmest greetings on the 50th anniversary of an invention which has had such a marvellous influence for good in every country of the world."

THE JUBILEE OF THE PENNY POSTAGE.

THE COLLECTION OF HISTORICAL EXHIBITS AT THE GUILDHALL.

(From the *City Press*, May 17, 1890.)

Of all the departments of Government work, that which comes closest to the greatest number of Her Majesty's subjects is the Post-Office. Difficult as it would be to conceive of the limitations which surrounded the collection, transmission, and delivery of the mails fifty years ago, even within the confines of the United Kingdom, how impossible of realization the far more primitive methods of a century and two centuries ago! We have only to go back a little more than 250 years to find nearly every merchant who transacted business by correspondence to any extent his own postmaster, dispatching and receiving his letters by private carriers; and when Charles I. attempted to put a stop to this practice by proclamation, the system of posts he established was little to the taste of the mercantile community, and scarcely less costly than the private post. With the great mass of the community the receiving or sending of a letter was a rare, almost an unknown, sensation, and the public news conveyed by one such epistle trickled like a refreshing shower through numberless rills, till it watered the parched minds of the remotest neighbours of the recipient.

It was, in fact, exactly 250 years ago that the King's posts may be considered to have been fairly established as a settled institution of the country, for then the establishment was placed in the hands of Philip Burlamachy, to be exercised under the authority of the Chief Secretary of State, though "Chief Postmaster of England" is the term bestowed by Camden on one Thomas Randolph, in the days of Elizabeth. In these early days, and up till as late as 1784, the mails appear to have been carried entirely by mounted couriers, or post-boys, furnished with relays of horses. In this latter year, however, the coach was first utilized by the Post-Office, the idea having been suggested, it seems, by the custom of tradesmen to send letters by these conveyances, for the sake of the greater speed and safety thus ensured. The post-boy had fallen into condign disgrace with the public, and Mr. John Palmer, who made the suggestion of the change, characterized the post as then carried on as "about the slowest conveyance in the country!" There is a singular parallel between the experiences of Mr. Palmer and of Sir Rowland some fifty years later. Both proposed to the department radical reforms; each encountered the hostility of the establishment, and gained the ear of the public, and each was afterwards appointed to inaugurate and carry out the reforms proposed and urged by him. Sixty years ago, in 1830, the first mails were conveyed by railway.

From conditions like these to those of to-day, what a leap! It is stating a truism, but one which, after all, few realize, to say that nothing so plainly indicates our commercial and intellectual progress as the development of our postal facilities, and at the same time, nothing has had so great an influence on our material progress as that particular line of development. Of course, increasing facilities of transportation, both by land and water, have gone hand-in-hand with this development, and the total progress is the sum of many units and influences, but we might have had the steam-boat and the railway without the modern machinery of the Post-Office; and what we venture to say is, that the enormous economical stride of the last fifty years is due more to the cheapening and rapidity of communication by post, telegraph, and telephone than by any other single agency.

To-day, scarcely a household is so poor and friendless and insignificant as never to receive a Government messenger, bearing to its very door some welcome message from friend or relative at home or abroad. The postman's knock is in a very real and true sense the most significant evidence of nineteenth century progress. It is a daily announcement to every one of us that the whole world is knit together by a system at once complex and simple, a piece of human machinery, stretching over six continents and isles of the sea innumerable, working with marvellous precision, certainty and dispatch, making minds a thousand miles apart beat to the same rhythm at the same time. It is just this close relationship which the Postal Department bears to every man and woman that makes its operations, even its stupendous statistics, of absorbing interest to all. And it is just this absorbing interest which gives to the present exhibition at the Guildhall a claim upon general attention which probably no other collection of objects could command.

In the Great Hall has been erected a counterfeit presentment of the Post-Office of 100 years ago, with its inquiry window and a hanging sign, bearing the Royal Arms, suspended above. The sign is a genuine relic. Genuine, too, is a notice board to prevent loitering before the Post-Office. "Every hawker," so it reads, "newsvendor, idle, or disorderly person who shall loiter on the pavement opposite the General Post-Office, or in any part thereof, will be liable to a penalty of five pounds."

Other genuine and interesting announcements, furnished by the archives of the Post-Office, are posted up in the front of this ancient structure. Here is an "Account of the Days and Hours that the Post sets out from the Post-Office in Oxford," from which we learn that the mail coach left for Bath, Bristol, and "all parts of the West" three days in the week "at two o'clock at noon"; to London every day except Saturday, and came in from London every day except Monday. One post a day, and that on five days in the week only, between London and Oxford! This notice, though it bears no date, was earlier than the days of pre-paying stamps, for it contains the information that when any letters are put into the office marked "pre-paid," but the money not handed in at the same time they will not be sent. It is supposed to date from about 1790. A copy of the printed "Notice of Special Instructions to all Letter Receivers," being

A POST-OFFICE IN 1790.
By permission of the Proprietors of the *City Press*.

the announcement of the reduction of postage, and bearing date January 2nd, 1840, is also shown, as well as a proclamation of an award of £1,000 for the discovery of the person who stole certain bank-notes from the Ipswich mail on its way from London on the night of September 11th, the year not being given.

Contrasted with this early and primitive post-office is shown by its side the arrangement of a counter in a modern post-office, with which we are all so familiar; the high brass railing surmounted with the signs which testify to the multifarious functions of the Department to-day, the "Parcel Post," the "Insurance and Annuity" department, the Money Order, Postal Order, and Savings' Bank, Registered Letters, Inland Revenue Stamps and Licences, and Telegrams. In the Great Hall, too, are other exhibits of now obsolete appliances, such as a singularly uncouth-looking and cumbersome Pillar Box of the date of 1855, but the display here is chiefly of apparatus now in actual use. The process of sorting letters at large receiving offices, so deftly and quickly performed by trained hands, is one of the chiefest of mysteries to the uninformed. Much light will be gained, especially as to the appliances for facilitating that operation, by an intelligent study of a group of exhibits at the west end of the large hall. Here, for example, is a large stand illustrating the work performed at ten principal district and 100 sub-district sorting offices in the London area; and another stand exhibits the appliances for parcel sorting, large baskets, appropriately labelled, standing upon a three-tier frame work. Packet and newspaper sorting requires a still different form of construction, the baskets being arranged in long rows and tiers, each labelled, and each pivoted at the lower back edge so that it may be tipped back and its contents discharged without removal from the rack. In fact, all the appliances for cancelling stamps, sorting every species of matter which passes through the post, modern pillar-boxes of the improved style now in use, are shown here, and form an object lesson to the uninitiated of the whole process of receiving and dispatching postal matter. One of the latest improvements shown is a large model, half full size, showing a combined lamp-post, letter-box, and fire alarm.

In this section, though on a relatively diminished scale, all the operations of a modern post-office are being actually carried on. Letters, papers, parcels, are being received, stamped, sorted, and despatched to their several destinations. Telegrams are received and delivered, postal and money orders issued and paid, stamps are sold, letters registered, and, in fact, the Guildhall Post-Office, by special dispensation established and maintained for such brief space of time as the exigencies of the occasion demand, is to all practical purposes a genuine branch of the department to which the public are invited, and where they may, so to speak, get behind the scenes and study the manipulation of postal matter in all its stages. Finally, the modern mail coach stands in Guildhall yard, and once a day starts with its burden to the sound of the post-horn, while Post-Office vans come and go much as though St. Martin's-le-Grand had suddenly changed places with the abode of Gog and Magog.

The process of sorting is too confusing to the outsider to be adequately described in the limits of such an article as this, but the confusion is only in the uninitiated mind. Order, system, and the perfection of routine machinery mark the actual operation. The following extract from a description written by a postmaster at one of the largest offices, will best convey a suggestion of the nature of the work which has to be done: "The letters when posted are of course found all mixed together, and bearing addresses of every kind. They are first arranged with the postage-stamps all in one direction, then they are stamped (the labels, that is the postage stamp, being defaced in the process), and thereafter the letters are ready to be sorted. They are conveyed to sorting frames (or tables) where a first division is carried out, the letters being divided into about twenty lots, representing roads or despatching divisions, and a few large towns. Then at these divisions the final sortation takes place, to accord with the bags in which the letters will be enclosed when the proper hour of despatch arrives. This seems very simple, does it not? But before a sorter is competent to do this work, he must learn 'circulation,' which is the technical name for this system under which correspondence flows to its destination, as the blood courses through the body by means of the arteries and veins."

The east-end of the Great Hall is devoted to the display of telegraphic apparatus. This exhibit comprises specimens of almost every known form of telegraph instrument. It may be divided into two classes, those of historical interest—showing the earliest inventions of Wheatstone and Cooke, with subsequent improvements by them, together with the productions of rival inventors—and the working apparatus of all kinds as actually now used in carrying on the telegraphic intercourse of the country. Close to the entrance two model telegraph-poles have been erected for the purpose of illustrating the ancient and modern methods of insulating aerial lines. The first pole supports no fewer than sixteen contrivances formerly in use, but now discarded in favour of more effective means. They include a lip insulator with a zinc cap in use about 1850, several specimens of glass insulators, Walker's double cone device, an ebonite insulator, and a few made of earthenware. The other pole is equipped with specimens of insulators for aerial lines as now used by the Post-Office. First comes a double-shed porcelain screw insulator, which is fixed by screwing to the bolt an indiarubber washer that serves as a cushion between the insulator and the shoulder of the bolt. Other examples include a single shed porcelain insulator used for unimportant and short wires, a post-office terminal, and several earthenware insulators. Arranged behind these poles is the *City Press* wire. The instrument is a direct-writing Morse inker. Its advantage over the Morse "embosser" lies in the greater legibility of the signals, which can be read in any light, and it at the same time requires much less power to work it. This form of instrument, which is fitted with a signalling key and galvanometer, is generally used on lines of moderate length, where the direct current is sufficient for all purposes. Passing up the right-hand side of the hall, a curious example of the woodpecker's determination and power is shown. This pole was removed from Shipston-on-Stour last autumn. It had been erected only three years. The perforations which eventually resulted in a large hole, were made by the common green woodpecker, of which a stuffed specimen is shown upon the pole. It is supposed that the birds were attracted by the humming of the wires produced by the wind, and were under the impression that insects were concealed in the interior of the pole. The farther end of the hall is given up to the display of early forms of the telegraph instrument. There are several needle telegraphs of the Cooke and Wheatstone type. One dated 1838 is fitted with four needles. In this instrument some of the letters are indicated by the convergence of two needles, while other letters are indicated by the deflection of one needle only. Four-line wires are required, and the signals are transmitted by the simultaneous depression of two out of ten finger keys. Another instrument dated 1844 is fitted with crutch handles and supplied with two needles. Two-line wires are used, and letters indicated by the movements of one or both needles. An alarm bell was originally used for calling attention, but it was afterwards found that the "click" of the needles acted sufficiently well, and the alarm bell was abandoned. In the case of Highton's single needle instrument, shown here, the letters are indicated by the movement of the needle from side to side. Certain letters are formed by one or more movements of the needle to either side, other letters requiring combinations of movements to both sides. Two tapper "keys" are used to transmit the signals. A Dering's single needle telegraph, as used by the Electric and International Company, forms the adjoining exhibit. This instrument differs from the Highton and the Cooke and Wheatstone instrument, inasmuch as the movement of the needle is effected by means of an electro-magnet instead of a coil. A Bright's bell telegraph, as used by the British and Irish Magnetic Telegraph Company, is exhibited. It is worked with a relay. The single needle alphabet is produced in this case by striking two bells of different tones, the hammers being actuated by electro-magnets, each worked by a relay and local battery. The relay consists of two electro-magnetic bobbins placed side by side, their ends being furnished with pole pieces turned inwards. Other instruments shown in this division include Henley's magneto-electric single needle, Cooke and Wheatstone's A B C telegraph receiver, several Cooke and Wheatstone's A B C transmitters, Siemens' A B C transmitter, 1858, a Morse embosser, and Wheatstone's automatic telegraph transmitter. In this last apparatus, the transmission of the electrical current is regulated by the action of three vertical rods, which are caused to move up and down by the rotation of a wheel worked by hand. A slip of paper punched with holes corresponding to the signals to be transmitted passes over the upper end of the rod and through it the ends of the rods can pass. Near this exhibit are two old forms of Wheatstone's automatic telegraph receiver and also a telegraphic puncher.

Coming now to the modern apparatus at work, there is seen opposite to the entrance a pneumatic tube as used for sending messages from a counter in the Post-Office to an instrument or to another room where the rooms are situated apart from each other. The messages in bulk are forced through the brass tube by air power, and are received in the cage as shown.

Near at hand is a model telephone exchange, with a handsomely-fitted Gower-Bell loud speaking telephone. The next stand contains an exhibit illustrating the working and mechanism of Preece's railway block system. Diagrams of the down and up signals are shown on the operator's instrument. Two levers are provided to turn "off," and switches are placed in front to "open" or "close" the line. In the same annexe are shown the multiplex system of transmitting six messages over one wire at the same time as working to Birmingham, and the Hughes' type-printing telegraph. The Hughes' machine is mainly mechanical, the electrical action being confined to sending a single short pulsation of current at the instant the type wheel is in the proper position. Only one wave of current is needed to produce a letter. The transmitter and receiver are combined in one apparatus. The signals are dispatched by working keys similar in appearance to those of a piano. This instrument is extensively used for continental messages, for which it is especially suitable. Several forms of acoustic or "sounder" telegraphs are shown. These machines are widely used, and over long distances. A special exhibit is made of the Wheatstone automatic system, so largely used for press telegrams. The messages have first to be prepared on a slip of paper. This takes the form of perforating the Morse characters along the slip. The slip is next passed on to the transmitter, and the message is received at the distant station in the ordinary dots and dashes of the Morse code. Enormous speed may be obtained with this instrument, ranging from 100 to 400 words per minute; indeed, a speed of over 600 words per minute has been obtained between London and Bristol. To illustrate the connection of the Press with the telegraph, an apparatus is arranged showing a complete news circuit. It consists of a transmitting instrument and three receivers, representing offices, say, in London (sending office), Newcastle, Edinburgh, and Glasgow (receiving offices). Along the farthest stand are placed cases containing specimens of different submarine cables. The most interesting is the piece of the first cable laid between Dover and Calais in 1850. The gutta-percha was not protected. It was sunk by means of lead weights attached at intervals throughout its length. The cable worked for one day only, and the specimen shown was picked up in 1875. A portion is also shown of the first sheathed submarine cable laid between Dover and Calais the year after the laying of the before-mentioned failure. Other specimens include portions of the seven-wire Irish cable, and of the first cable to Holland. In connection with the cables is shown a piece of rock removed from a cable off Portland. The groove shows the outline of the sheathing of the cable, and has probably been cut into the rock by the continued friction of the cable. Portions of aerial wires fused by lightning are also shown, together with the old and new methods of making joints in the air lines. The Exchange Telegraph Company show one of their recently-invented column printing telegraph, with transmitter and receiver in operation. There is also a model electric locomotive, lent by the North London Railway Company.

If we were to notice the exhibits in the order substantially as visitors are directed to progress through the several apartments, we should be led first to the Art Galleries. Here the walls are covered with engravings, photographs, and paintings, chiefly illustrative of the now obsolete features of mail carriages before the introduction of railways. A strong sentiment, for which our novelists are largely responsible, still exists for the old mail coach, and it must be admitted that these views suggest a picturesqueness in travel by high road which is sadly lacking in journeyings by rail. The starting of the Royal mail coaches, the scenes at the relay stations, the adventures of the road, midnight travel—these and many more, here brought together in profusion, present a singularly vivid *ensemble* of the varied experiences of those whose lot it was to travel by mail coach, when they travelled at all, at the not very exhilarating rate of ten miles an hour, though even that was considered a marvel of speed when macadamized roads first enabled it to be done, in the earlier part of this century.

These pictures exhibit, we should say, about every form which the mail coach has taken, and by arranging them in chronological order a fairly true view of the evolution of the modern mail-coach could be obtained. In connection with the pictured coaches we should not overlook a model, enclosed in a glass case, of the Liverpool and London mail-coach, and a model of the Indian post-cart from the collection of the South Kensington Museum. A special interest may be said to attach to a painting representing the last of the four-horse Royal Mail-coaches leaving Newcastle-on-Tyne for Edinburgh, July 5th, 1847. The coach bears the Union Jack, but at half-mast, thus pathetically announcing its own death before the steady advance of the iron horse.

Amongst the pictures is a small painting which will attract no little attention. It is a portrait of the last of the mail guards, Mr. James Nobbs, who is still retained in the service of the Post-Office. Possibly his whip-hand has parted with some of its strength, if not its cunning, or his should be the post of responsibility on the box of the Royal Mail four-horse parcel coach, which, in memory of old days, starts nightly (for a brief time only), at nine o'clock, from Guildhall Yard for Brighton, carrying parcels mail made up in the Guildhall.

The glass cases lining the Art Gallery contain a great variety of *ana* in connection with the history of the Post-Office, far too numerous for special mention, but all deserving the attention of visitors. The postage stamp collector may here revel in the contemplation of many a coveted addition to his stock, one album containing no less than 8,000 stamps.

A full collection of English adhesive stamps, from 1840 to 1890, is shown in Case 1, and in connection with the system of prepaying letters with the adhesive stamp is shown the famous Mulready envelope of 1840, with an assortment of the caricatures which this ornate affair called forth from the light-minded humorists of a caricature-loving people. In other cases are collections of both foreign and English stamps, specimens of "franks," and dated stamps used in connection with them, printed notices issued by the Post-Office; one, amongst the earliest, being in reference to undelivered letters, directing the length of time they shall be retained, depending upon whether they be refused, or the person to whom sent be dead or "gone away, not known where," whether "not to be found," or "not called for." The Post-Office, too, it seems, has not escaped the honour paid to most distinguished persons and institutions in having been the victim of the joint muse and musical composer, though the song here shown, entitled "The Post-Office," is that doubtful honour bestowed by the comic poet and his sympathetic collaborateur. It appears to have been composed by Mr. J. Sanderson, written by Mr. Lawler, and published by Messrs. Munro & May, Holborn Bars, but bears no date, though it is placed at about the year 1840.

Those who are most interested in the curiosities of Post-Office working will linger over the books of curious addresses; the envelope of the letter which was twelve long years in reaching its destination; the print of the dormouse which was entrusted to the tender mercies of the post; the time-bill of the London and Edinburgh mail coach, which made the journey in forty-two hours in 1836; the nest of the tom-tit that was built inside a letter-box, and the famous bird itself, now preserved in a glass case; a copy of the second edition of the *Post-Office Directory* issued in 1801, in which it is stated that 5,000 copies of the first issue had been sold; *Mr. Punch's* cartoon, representing Britannia crowning Sir Rowland Hill with a wreath of laurel, and *Punch's* famous joke thereon, in which he applauds Sir Rowland's act of sticking on the head of a good Queen as more meritorious than Cromwell's cutting off the head of a bad king.

Another case on the north side of the gallery contains a particularly interesting collection of objects. Among them is the original Treasury warrant for regulating the rates of postage (245) dated November 22nd, 1839, and signed by Lord Melbourne, Sir F. Baring, and Mr. Tuffnell. This warrant directed that all letters should, after December 5th, be charged by weight, and not according to sheets of paper or enclosures, which calls attention to the practice formerly prevailing, when even the use of an envelope or cover doubled the postage on the letter, and two enclosures required treble postage. The previous rates, high though they were, only carried a single sheet of paper, which gave rise to the use of the large square sheets, folded in four, and then secured with a seal, the direction being written on the letter back. The introduction of the gummed envelope is comparatively modern, but the first envelopes were invariably sealed with wax, and the use of wafers is well within the memory of men still young.

In the same case which encloses the Treasury warrant referred to is a diary of Sir Rowland Hill. It is opened at a page on which appears the following significant entry: "January 10 Rose at 8.30. Penny postage extended to the whole kingdom this day. Very able articles on the subject in the *Chron., Advertiser,* and *Globe.*"

Thus modestly did the originator of the penny post record the accomplishment of his task, but we can imagine that he had looked forward to this tenth day of January with an emotion which, if it finds no expression in his diary, was not the less real and intense. Something of the anxiety which he must have felt as to the ultimate success of his scheme, however great his confidence, is shadowed in the preceding entry, which deals with the then recent rapid increase in the number of letters posted in the United Kingdom. An illuminated copy of the resolution presenting the freedom of the City of London to Sir Rowland Hill, forms another interesting object in the same case.

It is consonant with this Jubilee celebration that very much of the documentary and printed matter embraced in the collection should bear upon the introduction of penny postage, its inception, the literature of the subject, Treasury and Post-Office Minutes, Royal proclamations, instructions to officials and servants of the Department, and explanatory matter, officially issued for the information of the public.

The curious in such matters will find in the several cases devoted to this branch of the subject abundant matter to arrest attention and reward scrutiny. Besides the collections furnished by the Government, many private possessors of curious fragments bearing upon the history of the Reform have sent their possessions to swell the lists of exhibits, and there can be no doubt but that the present collection is, at least in this feature, the most complete that has been, or for a long time will be, gathered together.

In this connection a very fine portrait in oils of Sir Rowland Hill, painted by J. A. Vintner, should be mentioned. It hangs near the centre of the north wall of the art gallery. A fine, strong, intellectual face; the head well set on an apparently robust body; just the type of man to carry a reform sturdily, and yet with fine forbearance and patience, through to the end, if he had set his heart upon it; a man to meet obstacles unflinchingly, to turn them aside graciously, if possible, but to turn them aside effectually. It is a genuinely English face in feature and complexion, and few who realize what benefits he conferred by his far-sighted intuition and judgment and self-confidence and persistence, will pass this portrait by without an inward acknowledgment of the debt we owe him.

In still other cases arranged around the sides of the Art Galleries we find abundant evidence of the perils of the road in the times of the post-courier and the mail coach. A pair of flint pistols, carried by the guard of the mail coach running between Clapham and Lancaster in 1835; a blunderbuss used by a guard in about the year 1780, and another, which belongs to a much later time, 1830, are fair specimens of the uncouth weapons with which the carriers of the Royal mails occasionally had to fight their way over lonely moors and along forest roads, to the no small peril and discomfiture of their passengers. Even now the guards to parcel coaches require to be well armed, as witness the revolver and the sword-bayonet, which form the defensive weapons of to-day. Comparing this modern sword-bayonet with the cutlass used by a mail-coach guard in 1800, we are able to say that, though humanity is still unpurged of its dangerous classes, we are able to arm our protectors rather more efficiently than our ancestors ninety years ago. A curious survival from a theft perpetrated upon a post-boy running between Selby and York, which occurred in 1798, is the mail-bag of which he was robbed. It was found in 1876, hidden away in the roof of an old public-house, when the latter was pulled down to make room for improvements. One would like to dower that old leather bag with a tongue and other vocal organs, and get its story. As an evidence of specially perilous times, we are shown an ugly-looking bludgeon or baton, such as were issued to the letter-carriers and others in the employ of the Post-Office in 1848, during the prevalence of the Chartist riots.

Curious, too, is an original bell as used even so late as 1840 by the bellmen who collected letters. From the itinerant bellman to the pillar-box involves a reconstruction of street scenes as striking as the growth of correspondence which had crowded the former out of existence as an altogether obsolete and inadequate piece of machinery. A battered post-horn, which saw service in the earlier years of this century, has also been preserved and contributed by a private collector to the Exhibition; and a postman's leather pouch, used in 1837, is equally interesting by way of comparison.

One of the most attractive features in these old prints of the mail-coach days, especially to the Londoner, is the series of glimpses many of them afford of the appearance of old London streets and buildings, as, for example, the views of the Bull and Mouth Inn, with exterior and interior, at St. Martin's-le-Grand, with the despatch of the mails; the Bull and Mouth, Regent Circus, Piccadilly, and the Brighton Coach; the "Peacock" at Islington, with the North-country mails; and others which are scattered here and there on the walls of the room.

Deserving of especial note as a grimly humorous illustration of the abuse of the franking system is one view of the Edinburgh coach. This coach is represented as bearing 354 lbs. of postal matter, but note the disproportion between the quantities and weights which go free and those which pay postage. Of newspapers, there is a parcel of 2,496, weighing 273 lbs., which pay nothing. There are 454 franked letters, weighing 47 lbs., and these go free. As a set-off we have from the general public 1,555 letters, weighing but 34 lbs., and paying the sum of £93 in postage. What a commentary upon the system which came to an end with the advent of the days this jubilee anniversary so fitly celebrates! The 1,555 letters, which averaged less than half an ounce in weight, paid an average of upwards of a shilling each.

Fashions in uniforms, if not quite so ephemeral as those which regulate the ordinary attire of civilians, evidently change from time to time, and a water-colour drawing, exhibiting eleven different styles of uniforms for postmen, will be scanned with as much amusement as interest. These uniforms all belong to the last fifty years, and do not represent among them that now worn by postmen, so that the average duration of any one style of dress is but little more than four years. Another, and earlier fashion, is shown in the sketch of the postman (but one was required for the work) of Newcastle-on-Tyne in 1824, who is represented in a tall hat of remarkable proportions, and in the act of delivering a letter at the open door of a residence.

Two small pictures, which will be found in the cases, illustrate phases of post-office working that always have an attraction for the public. One is a drawing, and represents six gentlemen bending over a table, whereon lie the contents of a "dangerous parcel" in the Returned Letter Office. In this case the "dangerous parcel" appears to have contained nothing more perilous than a collection of forbidding looking crustaceans, which invite to biological and, possibly, to piscatory studies. Post-Office officials, we may presume, are not above enjoying the pleasures of a lobster salad, even though the post is the fishing ground. Much more delectable, however, is the view given us in a small photograph of the "Returned Letter Office Larder" at Christmas time. Here is a display of game and poultry which would do credit to any poulterer's shop. What becomes of these returned delicacies? and how comes it that those for whom they were intended have departed like an Arab who folds his tents in the night time and leaves no trace behind him?

The omissions, mistakes, and blunders of every sort, which make a large part of the business of the Returned Letter Office, are often amusing as well as perplexing. Large sums of money are frequently sent under cover, upon which the sender has failed to put any address whatever. Curious addresses are by no means uncommon, and the greatest ingenuity is often displayed in deciphering some of the more remarkable specimens of ill-spelled and ignorantly-written addresses. Who, for example, but a trained hand at the business would have ever discovered that "2, 3 Adne Edle Street," was really meant for "2 Threadneedle Street," or that "hat the ole oke Otchut, 10 Bury," stood for "The Old Oak Orchard, Tenbury"?

One gentleman—or could it have been a lady?—who was in grave doubt as to an address, and was resolved not to be baulked by any lack of knowledge on the part of the Post-Office authorities, wrote the following instructions upon the envelope:—

"For a gentleman residing in a street out of the —— Road, London. He is a shopkeeper, sells newspapers and periodicals to the trade, and supplies hawkers and others with cheap prints, some of which are sold by men in the street. He has for years bought the waste of the Illustrated ——, their prints printed in colours particularly. He is well-known in the locality—being wholesale. Postman will oblige if he can find this."

The letter was delivered.

These curiosities of the Office lead us by a natural connection to those remarkable evidences of childlike confidence in the ability of the postal department to furnish all sorts of information, much as though it had the power of omniscience. Long-lost relatives appear to be, in the minds of some simple folk, always within the eye of the Postmaster-General and his subordinates, as witness the following naïve requests :—

"I write to ask you some information about persons that are missing. I want to find out my mother and sisters who are in Melbourne, in Australia, I believe —if you would find them out for me please let me know by return of post, and also your charge at the lowest."

"We heard in the paper about 12 or 14 months back Mary Ann ——, the servant girl at London was dead. Please send it to the Printer's office by return of post, whether there was a small fortune left for —— "

Others appear to have regarded the Post-Office as a general inquiry or detection department. And among letters asking for information of this sort the following may be cited as a fair illustration : "I have just been hearing of 3 men that was drowned about 9 months ago. I hear there was one of the men went under the name of John ——. Could the manager of the office give any particulars about that man ——, what he was like, or if there was such a name, or if he had any friend. He just went amissing about that time. I here enclose a stamp and address to ——," &c.

Of the attempts made by the unscrupulous to defraud the Post-Office in one way or another volumes might be written, but the most curious of the attempts are those which seek to avoid the payment of proper charges for articles of value by concealing them in the folds of newspapers, books, and the like. Loose gold pieces are occasionally found thus enclosed in a newspaper, or a hole is cut in the leaves of a book, valuable jewellery inserted therein, and then sent for a small rate, in the hope of escaping the vigilance of the Office. Perhaps the most valuable open letter ever sent was a five-pound note, simply folded and stamped, with the address written on the back, and thus consigned without cover to the care of the post.

No one outside the Department hears of the isolated complaints, threats, anathemas, which are hurled by private individuals with real or fancied grievances. They are neither few nor always framed in very courteous form, however. One or two specimens of this class are worth giving as samples. One individual, who seems to have had a previous tussle with the authorities, wrote :—

"I got no redress before, but I trust I shall on this occasion, or else there must be something rotten in the State of Denmark. Judas Iscariot was a thief, and carried the bag, and it will be a pity and a great scandal if he has found a successor in some branch of the Post-Office."

And another shows a very inflamed state of mind on the subject of a bullfinch :—

"Not having received the live bullfinch mentioned by you as having arrived at the Returned Letter Office two days ago, having been posted as a letter contrary to the regulations of the postal system, I now write to ask you to have the bird fed, and forwarded at once to ——; and to apply for all fines and expenses to ——. If this is not done, and I do not receive the bird by the end of the week, I shall write to the Postmaster-General, who is a very intimate friend of my father, and ask him to see that measures are taken against you for neglect. This is not an idle threat, so you will oblige by following the above instructions."

Undoubtedly a very large proportion of the complaints which are addressed to the Post-Office authorities have no other genuine basis than in the fancies or vagrant humours of those who make them. A capital illustration of this truth is afforded in the account given by Mr. Anthony Trollope of a bit of his own experience. The complaint came from a gentleman in County Cavan, who conceived himself, to judge by his letters, most grievously injured by some postal arrangement. Trollope was sent to have a personal interview and appease the old gentleman's wrath, if possible. He arrived at the squire's country seat on a jaunting car, wet through and chilled to the bone. We will let Mr. Trollope describe his reception in his own words :

"I was admitted by a butler, but the gentleman himself hurried into the hall. I at once began to explain my business. 'God bless me!' he said, 'you are wet through. John, get Mr. Trollope some brandy and water—very hot!' I was beginning my story about the post again, when he himself took off my coat, and suggested that I should go up to my bedroom before I troubled myself with business.

"'Bed-room!' I exclaimed. Then he assured me that he would not turn a dog out on such a night as that, and into a bed-room I was shown, having first drank the brandy and water standing at the drawing-room fire. When I came down I was introduced to his daughter, and the three of us went in to dinner. I shall never forget his righteous indignation when I again brought up the postal question on the departure of the young lady. Was I such a Goth as to contaminate wine with business! So I drank my wine and then heard the young lady sing, while her father slept in his arm-chair. I spent a very pleasant evening, but my host was too sleepy to hear anything about the Post-Office that night. It was absolutely necessary that I should go away the next morning after breakfast, and I explained that the matter must be discussed then. He shook his head and wrung his hands in unmistakable disgust—almost in despair. 'But what am I to say in my report?' I asked. 'Anything you please,' he said. 'Don't spare me if you want an excuse for yourself. Here I sit all day, with nothing to do, and I like writing letters!' I did report that he was now quite satisfied with the postal arrangements of the district; and I felt a soft regret that I should have robbed my friend of his occupation."

Scattered throughout the larger gallery and in the two small rooms reached by the stairs, are numerous models of mail steamers, some of great size, and all most beautifully made and finished. The largest of all the models is that of the *Umbria*, of the Cunard Line, which stands in the entrance lobby to the Guildhall, but scarcely inferior in size is the splendid model of the *Occana*, of the Peninsular and Oriental Steam Navigation Company, which stands in the centre of the large Art Gallery. This ship is 465 feet long, 52 feet broad, and 34 feet deep, and contrasted with these proportions is a model close by of the packet *William Fawcett*, the first vessel employed in the Contract Mail Service to the Peninsular ports in 1837. She was a paddle-wheel steamer, and her dimensions were 74 feet 3 inches by 15 feet 1 inch by 8 feet 4 inches, with a tonnage of 206, and developing 60 horse-power; whereas the *Oceana* has a tonnage of 6,362, and her engines a capacity of 7,000 horse-power. Other models of steamers are those of the *Ireland*, the City of Dublin Company's Royal Mail steamer, built by Messrs. Laird Brothers, and one of the *Scotia*, belonging to the British and North America Royal Mail Steam Packet Company. From the South Kensington Museum comes a working model of Crampton's engine and a beautiful model of the marine steam boiler. A very curious model is that of a Red Sea Dhow, from the same collection.

Ascending now to the smaller galleries, south of the main picture gallery, we find some of the most interesting exhibits of the collection. The larger tent illustrates the Army Post-Office, and this tent, with most of its contents, is a true veteran, having seen actual service in the field in the last Egyptian campaign. Here are sorting boxes and all the appliances, though on a necessarily small scale, for carrying on postal operations in the field.

Besides this very modern development of the postal service, the room we are now in is almost entirely devoted to exemplifying in models, pictures, and full-size structures, the highest advance in the direction of saving time in the distribution of postal matter. We mean the postal train service and its appliances. A drawing hanging upon the walls shows us the new postal train which runs every night from Euston to Glasgow and Aberdeen, starting at 8.30, distributing and collecting while *en route*, and without stopping the mail bags from and for the several stations it is intended to serve. The train is made up of seven postal carriages, each forty-two feet long, and of two guards' vans. Communication is continuous throughout five of these seven carriages.

Now let us turn to the model postal carriages on the other

side of the room. These models are constructed on a scale of three inches to the foot, and through the open doorways it is easy to see their internal construction. The sides are lined with boxes labelled with the names of towns and postal districts, and here sorting goes on all the night long, while the train is rushing on its way to the north. The postal train is in itself a marvellous instrument for economizing time, and, even if stops had to be made to deliver the bags made up for different points and collect those which contained matter for points still further ahead, it would be esteemed an invaluable adjunct to the rapid working of the Department. But what is no doubt the most interesting feature has yet to be noticed. This is the apparatus for collecting and delivering the letter bags while the train is in motion. This apparatus is shown in full size, and a small working model, constructed on a scale of one inch to the foot, is also displayed. Briefly, the appliances consist of a net and a hook, or support, for the bag to be caught. Beside the line is constructed a stout framework of iron and wood, and this supports a network of rope strengthened with chains. A wrought-iron frame attached to the side of the railway carriage supports a traductor and a delivery arm. The stout mail-bag, filled with its complement of letters, is hung upon the delivery arm, and, as the train flies past the network we have already described, the bag is unhooked by the contact, tumbles into the net whence it is removed, and taken to the local post-office. The delivery arm is then automatically returned to an upright position. The operation thus described is exactly reversed in the process of collecting the mail bags. An iron standard is erected by the side of the line. This is furnished with delivery arms, the counterpart of those used in the postal cars. Nets supported by iron frames stoutly secured to the side of the carriage are thrown out as the delivery station is approached and the suspended bags are caught, detached by the concussion, and safely landed in the net, whence they are removed, opened, and their contents arranged, sorted, fresh mail bags made up, and so the operation continues until the journey's end is reached and the last bags despatched to their destination. This mechanical collection and delivery can be safely made at any speed up to seventy-five miles an hour, and at a trial recently carried out with all the improved appliances a train was run four miles in three minutes thirty-seven seconds and collected four packages, each weighing fifty-five pounds. In fact it is rare that a bag is missed or dropped.

Improvements are being made from time to time in the details of the mechanism employed, the latest being in the construction of the traductor which supports the delivery arm where the strain chiefly comes. The newest system is being gradually introduced on all lines in the United Kingdom. A small model is shown of the style of net used for many years before the adoption of the present one. It will be noticed that the net work of ropes was so arranged as to allow the bag to fall to the ground. In wet weather this was objectionable, and at all times the wear and tear of the bag was greatly increased by that cause. The modern net does not permit the bags to touch the ground.

Such is, in brief, the travelling post-office and way-side delivery system of 1890, and we may very fitly conclude this review of the postal advance of fifty years by comparing the present mode of operations with that shown in one of the coloured prints hanging on the walls of the large gallery below. The mail-coach is represented as rattling through the deserted streets of a sleeping village. Dawn seems to be just breaking along the sky line in the distance, and one of the box passengers is stretching his arms and yawning after the broken slumbers of the night. The coach is just passing the village post-office, and the postmaster, in nightcap and robe, is handing out of an upper window a meagre-looking post bag to the guard.

THE GUILDHALL CONVERSAZIONE.

(From *Punch*, May 31, 1890.)

Everybody, from the Prince of Wales hisself, down to the werry 'umblest postman or sorter, left that nobel old Hall, estonished, and dilited, and 'appy.

And no wunder, for, by the combined efforts of the hole Copperashun and its werry numerus staff, and the hole army of postmen, and tellacram men, and all manner of sorters and stampers, St. Martin's-le-Grand was removed boddily to Gildall, and everything that was ever done in the one place was dun in the other before the estonished eyes of sum two thousand of us, even includin' four-horse male coaches, with sacks of letters, and reel gards with reel horns, which they blowed most butifully. It was a gloreous Jewbelee ! I'm that bizzy I hardly noes wich way to turn first, so no more at pressant, from yores trewly,

ROBERT.

THE CONVERSAZIONE

AT THE

SOUTH KENSINGTON MUSEUM,

JULY 2, 1890.

THE POST OFFICE COMMITTEE.

CONVERSAZIONE

AT THE SOUTH KENSINGTON MUSEUM.

Under the
Most Gracious Patronage of HER MAJESTY THE QUEEN.

Their Royal Highnesses the DUKE *and* DUCHESS OF EDINBURGH *have graciously intimated their intention of being present.*

President of the Conversazione—
HIS ROYAL HIGHNESS THE DUKE OF EDINBURGH, K.G.

Vice-Presidents—
THE RIGHT HON. HENRY CECIL RAIKES, M.P.
Her Majesty's Postmaster-General.
THE MOST HON. THE MARQUIS OF SALISBURY, K.G.
THE RIGHT HON. W. H. SMITH, M.P.
THE RIGHT HON. G. J. GOSCHEN, M.P.

And the following ex-Postmasters-General—
HIS GRACE THE DUKE OF ARGYLL, K.G., K.T.
HIS GRACE THE DUKE OF RUTLAND, G.C.B.
THE RIGHT HON. LORD EMLY.
THE RIGHT HON. THE MARQUIS OF HARTINGTON, M.P.
THE RIGHT HON. G. J. SHAW-LEFEVRE, M.P.
THE RIGHT HON. SIR LYON PLAYFAIR, K.C.B., M.P.

Also

His Grace The DUKE OF ABERCORN, C.B.	The EARL GREY, K.G.
His Grace The DUKE OF MARLBOROUGH.	The EARL OF JERSEY.
His Grace The DUKE OF PORTLAND.	The EARL SPENCER, K.G.
His Grace The DUKE OF WELLINGTON.	The EARL STANHOPE.
The MARQUIS OF RIPON, K.G.	The EARL OF STRAFFORD.
The MARQUIS OF BREADALBANE.	The EARL WALDEGRAVE.
The EARL OF ASHBURNHAM.	The EARL OF WINCHELSEA AND NOTTINGHAM.
The EARL OF BRADFORD.	
The EARL OF CLARENDON.	SIR JAMES WHITEHEAD, BART., D.L.
The EARL OF DERBY, K.G.	SIR ARTHUR BLACKWOOD, K.C.B.
The EARL OF GAINSBOROUGH.	PEARSON HILL, ESQ.

PROGRAMME.

THE doors of the Museum will be open at 7 p.m.

The usual Cloak Room accommodation will be afforded at the entrance to the Museum in Cromwell Road.

Royal Mail Vans, horsed and the lamps alight, will be stationed at various points between the Museum and Cromwell Road.

A Guard of Honour of the 24th Middlesex (Post-Office) Rifle Volunteers, with the band of the Regiment, will, with the kind permission of the Colonel commanding, be mounted.

The sale of the Jubilee Envelope (price 1s.) will take place at the General Post-Offices in the Architectural Court and Art Library; and at the branch Post-Offices which will be found in various parts of the building. At the General Post-Offices, all kinds of business—postal and telegraphic—will be transacted.

In the Architectural Court too will be established the sorting and stamping processes, and the stampers will be prepared to impress dated stamps of unique design on the special envelope, or on postal cards presented with that object.

In the Textile Gallery there may possibly be met with a Telegraph Office of 1990, where special facilities for the transaction of new developments of Post-Office business will be provided, and where, by means of contrivances which are certainly not as yet publicly known, the expectation will be held out of instantaneous communications passing between London and all parts of the world by sight and speech, and not by the old-world contrivances of the nineteenth century, and its so-called Electric Telegraph. Moreover the greatest invention of the age—the Electrophonoscope—will be shown there for the first time.

In the Science Library a variety of Post-Offices will be established. Those of 1790 and 1990, with a branch of 1890, will be conducted by a specially selected staff (the members of which have generously given their services), composed of:—Mrs. Dion Boucicault (the original "Colleen Bawn"), Miss Patrice Boucicault, Mrs. Charles Lamb Kenney, Miss Rose Kenney, Mrs. Conyers d'Arcy, Miss Grace Winall, Mr. Conyers d'Arcy, Mr. Edwin Gilbert, Mr. Egginton, and Master Conyers d'Arcy.

A full Post-Office of 1890, with ample writing accommodation, will also be provided in the same Library.

The bands of the Grenadier Guards (conducted by Lieut. Dan Godfrey), by permission of Colonel Trotter; and of the

WALTER G. GATES, ESQ.

SYDNEY BECKLEY, ESQ.

G. A. AITKEN, ESQ.

S. WILSON, ESQ.

THE HONORARY SECRETARIES TO THE POST OFFICE COMMITTEE

Royal Artillery (conducted by Cavalier Zavertal), by permission of the Regimental Band Committee, will play during the evening.

The Quadrangle will be lighted by the electric light.

The Committee have the pleasure of announcing that with great liberality and kindness the following distinguished artistes have generously given their services for the occasion:—Madame Valleria, Madame Annie Marriott, Miss Alice Gomez, Miss Nellie Levey, Mr. Sims Reeves, Mr. Percy Palmer, Mr. Fredk. King, Mr. Sydney Beckley, Mr. J. E. Payne (Violin), Mr. Leo Stern (Violoncello), Madame Frickenhaus (Piano), Mr. Alfred J. Caldicott (Mus. Bac.), and Mr. Arthur Fagge.

Part songs will be sung by the Post-Office choir, under the direction of Mr. Sydney Beckley.

The line of procession, and order generally, will be maintained by the Gentlemen Marshals, who will be distinguished by wands of office and rosettes.

At 8.30 p.m. the Royal Parcel Mail Coach for Brighton will be despatched; at 8.40 the coach for Watford and at 8.50 the coach for Oxford.

An extensive collection of British stamps, kindly lent by the Board of Inland Revenue, will be shown in the Cruikshank's Gallery. The collection belonging to the Government of New South Wales has also been kindly lent for the occasion; and the Post-Office collection will likewise be shown.

Telegraphic communication with the Continent will be maintained, as at the Jubilee at the Guildhall, under the eyes of the visitors.

Her Royal and Imperial Highness the Duchess of Edinburgh, accompanied by the President of the Conversazione, His Royal Highness the Duke of Edinburgh, will arrive at the Royal entrance. The Guard of Honour will give a Royal Salute, and the band will play the National Anthem.

The Royal and distinguished party will be received by the Postmaster-General, the Vice-Presidents of the Conversazione, and by the Executive Committee.

A bouquet will be presented to Her Royal and Imperial Highness by Miss Raikes.

Some presentations will be made to Her Royal and Imperial Highness by His Royal Highness the President.

A procession will then be formed: A Gentleman Usher, followed by Four City Trumpeters (by special permission) in scarlet uniforms, with silver trumpets, will lead the way.

Her Royal and Imperial Highness the Duchess of Edinburgh will be conducted by the Postmaster-General, and Mrs. Raikes by His Royal Highness the President.

On the signal being given for the procession to start, the Trumpeters will sound a Fanfare, and the procession will move slowly along the line of march indicated by a crimson carpet.

On the Fanfare being concluded, the Band of the Guards will play. The trumpets, on the procession entering the South Court, will again sound a Fanfare. On the procession reaching the Southern Arch of the Italian Court, the Band of the Royal Artillery will play the National Anthem.

On reaching the daïs at the end of the main avenue, the Postmaster-General and the Secretary of the Post-Office will take up a position right and left of the daïs; the remaining gentlemen ranging themselves right and left of the open space.

Their Royal Highnesses being seated, a letter will be delivered to Her Royal and Imperial Highness, containing a respectful welcome and appreciation of Her Royal and Imperial Highness's kindness, signed by old officers of the Post-Office—the first signature being that of Mr. Frederic Hill, the sole surviving brother of the late Sir Rowland Hill, K.C.B.

An officer of the Post-Office will then deliver a letter. This letter is from present servants of the Post-Office, expressing their thanks to Her Royal and Imperial Highness; signed on their behalf by the Postmaster-General and the Secretary of the Post-Office.

A telegraph-wire and apparatus will then be brought on to the daïs, and on Her Royal and Imperial Highness touching the key, an electric signal will be sent inviting Post-Office officials in various parts of the British Isles to unite with their colleagues assembled at South Kensington in giving simultaneously three cheers for Her Majesty The Queen.

Her Royal and Imperial Highness will probably visit the Music Room and then proceed to the Quadrangle. The Guards' Band will play a selection of airs.

There will be a Reception from 7 to 9 p.m., and carriages may be ordered for 12 o'clock.

Light Refreshments will be provided.

Uniform, Levee, or Evening dress will be worn.

The South Kensington Museum.

Few people who have not visited South Kensington Museum can be aware of the beautiful spectacle its interior presents, when lighted up by the electric light, and filled with company. The building, which contains many splendid collections illustrative of science and art, stands on twelve acres of land. The first portion of the building was opened in June, 1857, and during the thirty-three years which have since elapsed vast numbers of rare and valuable objects have been added to the collections.

The Architectural Court, where the Chief Postal Sorting Office will be established, is the largest of the three principal courts. It is 133 feet long, and sixty feet wide. The height from floor to ceiling is eighty-three feet. The width of the central passage, along a portion of which the royal procession will be conducted, is seventeen feet; so affording ample space for spectacular effect. In this court are full-sized reproductions of many remarkable and beautiful architectural works, the most magnificent of all perhaps being a carved chimney-piece, A.D. 1529, which is probably one of the finest and largest specimens of oak carving ever seen. Scarcely second to this, however, are the casts of two portions of Trajan's column erected in Rome, A.D. 106—114. The base of the column is twenty-one feet square, and the total height must have been at least 150 feet. Both portions stand in the Architectural Court, not far from the Reception chamber.

The visitor will enter the Museum through a spacious cloakroom, constructed (with the permission of the Lords of the Committee of Privy Council for Education) by the Post-Office for the occasion, and which measures about 100 feet in width by forty-eight feet in depth. Turning to the right hand, he will pass through a collection of very beautiful specimens of textile fabrics—some hanging on the wall as tapestry, others protected in glass cases—and will enter the Ancient Sculpture Room. Here there will be a Reception from 7 p.m. until 9 p.m. The visitor will pass on to the Architectural Court already mentioned, and then into the South Court, which is divided into two parts by a gallery, known as the Prince Consort's Gallery. On the west side are ivory carvings, gold and silver work, and loan collections of a similar character. There are here innumerable articles of beauty and value. On the east side is a fine collection of bronzes and Chinese porcelain. To the east of the South Court are the Oriental Courts, where are shown examples of the art workmanship of China and Japan.

The North Court is entered from the South Court under an archway, described in the programme as the Southern Arch, and which reproduces the form of an Italian music gallery. This spacious hall is specially appropriated to the exhibition of examples of Italian art workmanship. It is 107 feet long, 106 feet wide, and 33 feet high. The roof is of a single span, without pillars. Around the cornice is a broad band of blue and gold.

The Saracenic and Persian Courts speak for themselves. In the galleries will be found the Keramic or pottery collection, which is of great variety and splendour. In the Prince Consort's Gallery are placed many of the most interesting and costly possessions of the Museum; while in the Western Galleries, in five rooms, are the famous Dyce and Forster collections.

In the North Gallery are the Raphael Cartoons, and in the Sheepshanks' Gallery the valuable collection of oil paintings, the gift of the late Mr. John Sheepshanks.

Near at hand is the Jones collection, which is of great interest and variety; and in the gallery which contains specimens of the water colours and drawings of the late Mr. George

Cruikshank will be temporarily placed the fine collection of postage stamps lent by the Commissioners of Inland Revenue, another beautiful collection lent to the Post-Office by the Government of New South Wales, and a collection which the Post-Office itself exhibits.

This account, however brief and imperfect, will give the reader some idea of the varied and costly collections which will be on view on the night of the Conversazione; but it will fail to convey any idea of the beauty of the interior of the building, when it and its sparkling contents are lighted up by the electric light, and the galleries are crowded with a numerous and agreeable company.

The Royal Procession will enter the building beneath a magnificent Rood Loft, erected in 1625 at Bois-le-Duc, in North Brabant.

A full programme and plan of the building will be presented to each visitor who expresses a wish for one. It will include a programme of the songs which will be sung by some of the most eminent vocalists of the day, and by the Post-Office choir, which has already sung with great success before His Royal Highness the Prince of Wales. The bands of the Grenadier Guards and the Royal Artillery are amongst the finest in the United Kingdom.

INSTRUCTIONS FOR POSTAL DUTY

AT

SOUTH KENSINGTON MUSEUM.

Museum Yard.

Royal Mail Vans, horsed and lamps lighted, will be stationed from 6.30 p.m. to 10 p.m. in the middle road usually serving as a carriage entrance, and near the Cloak Room at the side road in the direction of Exhibition Road.

A Royal Mail Four-Horse Parcel Coach will leave the Yard at 8.30 p.m. for Brighton; at 8.40 p.m. another will leave for Chelmsford and Ipswich; and a third Coach for Oxford at 8.50 p.m. They will carry Parcel Mails made up in the Museum.

A Mail Coach, to illustrate a Royal Mail Coach of the past, drawn by four grey horses, and carrying Mails, Passengers, an Luggage, will arrive with Sir A. Blackwood and party at 8 p.m., and another Coach, with a team of bays, at 9 p.m. with the Postmaster-General and party.

The Coachmen and Guards of the Coaches, and the Post-Office Servants who look after the Vans which will be stationed in the Yard, must implicitly act upon the instructions they receive from the Police entrusted with the duty of regulating the traffic.

Entrances.

Eight Officers, in Scarlet Coats, will be on duty at the Royal or Turnstile Entrance; at the Office Entrance; at the General Entrance; in the Textile Gallery, and Reception Room. At

9 p.m. all will repair to the Italian Court to aid in keeping line, except two, who will remain at their posts. The Tickets of Admission will be taken by the Museum authorities.

Six Boy Messengers will be stationed at the General Entrance to hand Catalogues to Visitors as they enter the Museum.

"Hand" Notices indicating routes will be put up.

A model of a Travelling Post-Office will be exhibited in a Gallery. The working of it will be explained by Mr. Supervisor Garrett.

Public Post-Office Business.

A General Post-Office will be established for the occasion. It will be situated in the Architectural Court, and will be designated the "South Kensington (Penny Postage Jubilee) Post-Office."

In order to illustrate the postal system in operation at the present day, public business of all kinds will be transacted at this Jubilee Office, thus :—

Special Jubilee Envelopes sold.
Registered Letter Covers for enclosure of Jubilee Envelopes sold.
Postage Stamps of all denominations sold.
Inland and Foreign Post-Cards sold.
Letters registered and insured.
Parcels (Inland and Foreign) accepted and insured.
Postal Orders and Money Orders issued and paid.
Savings Bank Deposits received, Withdrawals cashed, and new Accounts opened.
Licenses issued.
Life Insurance and Annuities business transacted.
Telegrams accepted for transmission, and received for delivery

There will be a Poste-Restante at one corner of the Post-Office, where letters may be called for by the Addressees.

Telegrams for Visitors should be placed on the Notice Board near the Post-Office.

Posting Boxes will be placed at the Post-Office Counter for the reception of letters and cards, which will be accepted and impressed with the Jubilee Marking Stamp. These boxes will be cleared every half hour up to midnight, and more frequently if necessary.

A Pneumatic Tube Post will be established at the Post-Office, and letters and cards handed over the counter there will be stamped and forwarded by tube to a Poste-Restante in the Postal Sorting Office.

It will thus be possible for visitors to see their letters or cards stamped and sent by Pneumatic Tube for delivery at another point of the Architectural Court.

The charge will be 1d. per letter or card. If replies are given the charge will be 3d. per letter or card. The cash should be kept apart from other moneys.

The special envelopes, in commemoration of the Jubilee event, which will be sold in the Museum, will have a white ground In the left-hand corner will appear a crown, with the letters "V.R." and a rose, shamrock, and thistle beneath. In the centre the words "Penny Postage Jubilee, 1890"; and in the right-hand corner an impression of a penny stamp similar to that used for foreign post-cards. The printing of the whole will be of blue colour. The Envelopes will be made up in packets of ten and one hundred. They can be sold singly or in larger quantities, at 1s. per Envelope. They will each contain an appropriate correspondence card.

Registered Letter official covers, with cards enclosed in them, for the safe transmission of the Jubilee Special Envelopes through the Post, will be on sale, price 3d. each, and ordinary covers with card, price 1d. each.

Ordinary covers for visitors to place the Jubilee Envelopes in to carry in the pocket can be given away. A stock of such covers will be supplied to the staff.

The Public Office business will be conducted from 7.0 p.m. to midnight by Miss Parsons of the Regent Street B.O., who will be in charge; Miss Seaton Brown, Broad Sanctuary B.O.; Miss Turner of the North-Western District Office; Miss Girton,

Regent Street B.O.; and Miss Fletcher, Westbourne Grove B.O.

The Telegraph business will be undertaken by Mr. Bolton, Inspecting Telegraphist of the Controller's Office, and the Pneumatic Tube work by Mr. Gilbert.

A long table for writing purposes will be placed between the Public Office and Postal Sorting Office.

Mr. Angell will arrange for six Telegraph Messengers to be in attendance near the Post-Office.

Science Library Post-Office.

In the Science Library there will be a long counter at which full Post and Telegraph business will be transacted. The counter will be improvised out of the desks and tables ordinarily in use, which will be covered with red baize for the occasion.

The reading tables in the Library will be used by the Public for addressing the Envelopes.

This Office will be conducted by Miss Coombes, Lambeth B.O., in charge; Mrs. Taplin, Broad Sanctuary B.O.; Miss Martin, Blackheath; Miss Townsend, Holloway; and Miss Martin, Eastcheap.

Four Telegraph Messengers from South Kensington B.O. will act as attendants.

Two Letter Boxes, painted red, will be placed on the counter, from which special collections will be made quarter hourly, or more frequently if necessary.

Two quick Boy Messengers will be engaged in carrying, at express speed, bags from the 1990 Post-Office to the Poste-Restante in Architectural Court.

Branch Post-Offices.

A Stall will be opened in the Writing Room near Cruikshank Gallery, and will be conducted by Miss Adeney, Holloway, and Miss Bean, Queen Victoria Street. Another Stall will be conducted by Mrs. and Miss Blewitt at left of Royal Entrance where catalogues and photographs are usually sold.

A Posting Box will be placed near each Sale Table, from which collections will be made at frequent intervals.

Two Telegraph Messengers from the S. K. Branch Office will act as attendants, one at each Stall.

Cruikshank Gallery.

The Curious Address Books of the Inland Branch, Albums of Christmas Cards, and a collection of Postage Stamps, &c., will be exhibited, in charge of Mr. W. Matthews, Inland Branch, assisted by Mr. Thomas, Controller's Office.

Impression of Jubilee Stamp.

The Special Jubilee Date and Obliterating Stamp can be impressed on letters and post-cards not intended for transmission by post at a charge of 1d. per impression. This stamping can be undertaken at the two central Post-Offices, and at the Branch tables where the Jubilee Envelopes will be sold. The pence thus received should be kept in bowls apart from the Official and Jubilee Envelope cash.

The Jubilee Envelopes can be impressed with the stamp free of charge, though not intended to be posted.

The india-rubber Jubilee Stamps require inking before each impression. The lower part of the Stamp is indicated by the brass plate as a guide.

Tables of Inland and Foreign Rates will be on sale; price, impressed with Jubilee Stamp, 2d. each.

Local Telegraph Circuit.

There will be a Circuit between the Post-Office in the Architectural Court and that in the Science Library whereby Public and Official Messages can be transmitted. The charge to the public will be 1d. for the impression of the Jubilee Stamp on the Message form.

Arrangements for the Performance of Postal Sorting Work.

This branch of business will be carried on in the Architectural Court.

Fittings as follows will be supplied from the Wimbledon Post-Office :—

    1 Bag opening, facing, and stamping table.
    1 Sorting table.
    8 Roads for despatches, &c.
    1 Rack for parcel duty.
    1 Collapsible packet sorting table.

A "Pearson Hill" stamping machine will be affixed to the stamping table, and hand stamps will also be available for use on packets, newspapers, &c.

A supply of bags, string, sealing-wax, sealing-lamp, oil, and other necessaries for the conduct of the postal duty will be at hand.

In the Postal Sorting Office will be placed two pillar letter-boxes for the reception of letters enclosed in the Jubilee Envelopes, cards, or any ordinary correspondence. The boxes will be cleared at intervals of half-an-hour, or more frequently if necessary.

All letters, &c., posted in these boxes must be impressed with the special Jubilee Stamp.

The letters, &c., posted in the boxes in the Museum itself must be stamped with the Jubilee Stamps separately from those brought in from outside boxes by the postmen, and a very careful account should be kept of the numbers. The letters, &c., from outside need not be counted. They should be impressed with the ordinary stamp—not with the Jubilee Stamp.

The Jubilee Envelopes are to be selected from other letters. They must be very carefully stamped and counted by the officer deputed to undertake that part of the duty. On despatch they should, as far as may be found practicable, be tied up in the middle of the bundles of letters, so as to secure them against injury in transit.

Particular care should be taken that ink of one kind only should be used for impressing the Jubilee dated stamp.

The ink provided is black, and is supplied with special pads for use with india-rubber stamps.

All concerned must exercise the utmost care in using the stamps, so that the impressions may be perfect, and placed in the proper position on the envelopes.

Parcel Post Business.

Mr. Hunt, Overseer, and Sorter Douglas from Mount Pleasant, will attend the Museum from 6.0 p.m. till the close of the special duty.

Parcels for the places served by the Brighton and Ipswich Coaches should be selected at the Chelsea (Cale Street), West Brompton, and Earl's Court Sorting Offices at the 6.0 p.m. and 7.0 p.m. collections, and sent to the S.K. Sorting Office for transfer thence with S.K. Parcels to Museum in bag protectors.

Parcels for despatch by the coaches should be forwarded from the S.W.D.O. to the Museum by special carts. The unloading must be smartly done, so that the entrance may not be blocked.

The parcels on receipt at the Museum will be sorted at the rack provided for the purpose, and will be made up in receptacles for the S.W.D.O., Brighton, Brighton Coach (Unsorted), Colchester, and Ipswich Coach (Unsorted).

The receptacles will be labelled "South Kensington Museum Jubilee Post-Office to ————." Those for the S.W.D.O. will be conveyed by the carts mentioned above.

The coach-borne receptacles will be forwarded by the respective coaches which will start from the Museum as under:—

London to Brighton Parcel Coach at 8.30 p.m.
London to Chelmsford Parcel Coach at 8.40 p.m.

A properly equipped coach marked specially "London to Oxford" will start from the Museum at 8.50 p.m. This coach will carry dummy receptacles which must be made up for it, and after leaving the Museum will return to Mount Pleasant Depôt to deliver its load of dummies.

The Brighton and Chelmsford Coaches will proceed direct to the London Bridge and Mount Pleasant Depôts respectively to take up the rest of the mails and to be despatched as usual.

Special time bills and bag lists have been provided for use in the coaches.

The guards must join the coaches at the contractors' yards (Brighton Coach—Messrs. McNamara and Co., Castle Street, Finsbury; Chelmsford Coach—Mr. Webster, Laycock's Yard, Upper Street, Islington) at 7.0 p.m. The coaches must reach the Museum at the appointed times and be loaded at once, so as not to interfere with the traffic.

The Brighton and Chelmsford Coach Guards must take with them, by cab, from the depôts the baskets containing the coachhorns, weapons, &c., and place them in the coaches. Each guard must be in full uniform and wear the belt with revolver (unloaded) and sword bayonet attached. The horns should be placed in the baskets hung outside the coach, and the guards must blow the horns both on the arrival at and departure from the Museum.

The Oxford Coach will call at Mount Pleasant Depôt at 7.0 p.m. on the way to the Museum to be loaded with empty receptacles labelled for towns on the road between London and Oxford.

Local Telegraph Circuit.

The Local Telegraph Circuit, from the Science and Art Library to the Branch Office in the Architectural Court, should be worked as follows:—

Visitors should be invited to address communications to themselves or friends, to be telegraphed from the Office in the Architectural Court to the Office in the Science and Art Library, or *vice versâ*. No charge is to be made for telegraphing, but each received copy must be impressed with the special Jubilee dated stamp, and for this impression one penny should be charged on each telegram on delivery.

Money received on account of local telegrams should be kept separate from any other moneys received, and should be handed to the Officer in charge of the Branch Office at the close of the duty.

Visitors inquiring, should have the work of the circuit explained to them, and be allowed to make verbal inquiries and receive replies over the circuit, free of charge.

Local official inquiries and Service telegrams will pass over the wire, which will also be used for the transmission of ordinary public telegrams from the Science Library, the Branch Office acting as transmitting station.

All telegrams must be written neatly, in a clear legible hand.

There will be a message circuit from the Central Telegraph Office to the South Kensington Post-Office, over which public messages, and, in short, all messages sent by the public from South Kensington, or addressed to their Royal Highnesses, to the Postmaster-General, or to the public at the Museum, will be forwarded.

Certain special messages from India, Canada, and the far North of Scotland will be received probably very early in the evening for delivery to their Royal Highnesses, and these messages must be carefully written out on the large foolscap Government Message Form, with envelopes to match. These telegrams must be held in reserve by the Officer in charge of the telegraph duty until close upon 9.30 p.m., when he must take them to Mr. Bundy, who will be the Marshal in charge at the southern arch.

Certain telegrams, original and duplicate, such as that alluded to as coming from Canada, must be exhibited on a Notice Board placed near the daïs.

Tube Post.

Visitors should be invited to patronize this mode of postal communication, now brought into use for the first time.

Cards, Jubilee Envelopes, communications written on the form specially provided for the purpose, or anything that can be safely transmitted through the tube, will be accepted, stamped with the proper date stamp, tubed to the other end, and delivered to callers. The charge will be one penny for transmission in either direction.

Visitors should also be invited to address questions either to the officials or to their friends, and prepay the reply. The charge for a reply card or letter will be 3*d*.

The replies should be short, to the point, and facetious where the question admits. They will be written by Mr. Powell, of the Controller's Office, who will attend for the purpose.

Money received on this account should be kept in a separate receptacle which will be provided for the purpose at either end, and handed to the Officer in charge of the Branch Office in the Architectural Court at the close, with a slip showing the amount.

1890 *Postman.*—The Postman W. Stewart of the S.W. district will act as 1890 Postman to deliver letter to Her Royal and Imperial Highness the Duchess of Edinburgh.

Savings Bank Books.—It should be understood that frequent communication by local wire should be held between the two officers in charge of the Branch Post-Offices in the Museum as to the issue of new Savings Bank Books so that at the termination of the duty the numbers of the books may run consecutively instead of there being any break.

Ambulance.—The ambulance, attended by Sergeants Hone, Carney, and Payne, will be located in the Cloak Room at the front entrance.

Cards for Jubilee Impressions.—A supply of plain blue cards will be distributed to each of the Post-Offices. These cards can be impressed with the Jubilee Stamp and be sold for a penny.

Mr. Howson will make the necessary arrangements for the conveyance of the Counter Staff to their homes after the Conversazione.

DESCRIPTION OF THE POST-OFFICE OF 1990.

Business on entirely new Principles.

Letters of all kinds sent by New Patent Electrotubular Lightning Express.

Write to any part of the world; post here (fee 6*d*.—the smallest coin of the realm) and you will find a reply from your correspondent awaiting you on applying at the "Poste Restante," Architectural Court.

Thus a lady—say Miss Jones—who has posted a letter at the 1990 Post-Office will presently appear at the office marked "Poste Restante" in the Architectural Court and say, "Have you got a letter for me?" "What name, if you please?" "Jenny Jones." The Poste Restante officer will then look into the box of "J" letters and will find one addressed at the 1990 Office for Miss or Miss J. Jones, and this he will duly deliver. The 1990 and 1890 Delivery Stamps will be impressed on the letters before despatch to the Poste Restante.

R. C. TOMBS,
Controller.

LONDON POSTAL SERVICE,
June 28th, 1890.

SUBSEQUENT REPORT OF THE CONTROLLER OF THE LONDON POSTAL SERVICE.

Conversazione at South Kensington.

The work of preparation for the commemoration of Uniform Penny Postage in the United Kingdom by a grand Conversazione at South Kensington Museum was, so far as regards the Postal Section, of a somewhat difficult character, as the fittings to be used for the illustration of Postal work had to be brought from the new Wimbledon Post-Office (just about to be opened) to South Kensington by road, a distance of about seven miles. The fitting up of the Sorting Office and the two Post-Offices had to be done under most adverse circumstances. The time allowed to do the work was very limited, and great care had to be exercised in carrying the large sorting-tables and the long and cumbrous counter through the Museum, crowded as it is with glass cases and extremely fragile articles.

Two plain desks in the Science Library were transformed into a bijou Post-Office, decorated with the colours for the day—blue and white—within two hours.

The force employed had to be drawn partly from the city, partly from the Buckingham Gate Office, whilst the directing arrangements had to be carried on from St. Martin's-le-Grand.

As, however, on many other occasions, the Post-Office axe was able to clear a way through the whole forest of difficulties; but its edge would been considerably blunted but for the clearance of heavy exhibits effected by order of Mr. Thompson, the acting Director of the Museum, whose kindness, courtesy, and ready assistance evoked the admiration and gratitude of all concerned in the Postal part of the entertainment who came in contact with him.

Outside the Museum it might have been supposed that St. Martin's-le-Grand had temporarily removed to the West end, for the postmen flitting to and fro, the stationary mail vans and carts with lamps lighted, the mail coaches typical of a bygone time, and the parcel coaches starting for Brighton, for Ipswich, and for Oxford, lent a realistic character to the scene, and suggested the idea that perhaps fifty years hence it would be necessary to have in the immediate vicinity of the Museum a Post-Office equal in size to the old building at St. Martin's-le-Grand.

The teams turned out on the occasion by Messrs. Birch, Webster, and McNamara and Co. were greatly admired by the lovers of horseflesh present.

As regards the interior of the building, I will begin my narrative with the Postal Sorting Office, as that was the first object of interest which came under the notice of the Royal visitors in the line of procession. It was situated in the Architectural Court, and measured 27 feet by 22 feet. In this small space the letters, &c., faced, stamped, sorted, and despatched, consisted of collections from thirteen receiving houses, thirty-two pillar boxes, and three wall boxes outside the Museum.

There were seven posting boxes within the Museum walls, and visitors during the Conversazione used them freely. Indeed, there could have been few persons present who did not consider their mailing arrangements one of the features of the evening.

Altogether 23,200 Jubilee envelopes were posted in the Museum and dealt with at the Postal Sorting Office, and 5,700 ordinary letters, and 6,700 ordinary post-cards.

Many persons retained the Jubilee envelopes and posted the inside corresponding cards, which in many instances were not prepaid, and had consequently to be surcharged 2d. each, the charges raised in this way amounting to over £5.

POST OFFICE JUBILEE
OF
UNIFORM PENNY POSTAGE
AT SOUTH KENSINGTON MUSEUM, 2ND JULY, 1890.

THE NORTH MAIL MAKING FOR HIGHGATE, 1700 AT 6 MILES AN HOUR.

RATES.
4d.
8d.
1/2
2/6

1840.

1890.
1d.

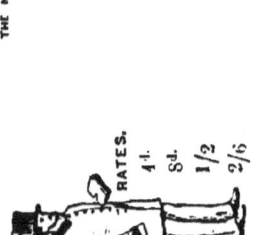

THE NORTH MAIL, 1890, APPROACHING CARLISLE AT 40 MILES AN HOUR.

THE SOUTH KENSINGTON JUBILEE ENVELOPE.

Other of the correspondence cards bore halfpenny instead of penny stamps, and some had stamps of excessive value affixed to them on the front or back.

Many letters, previously posted and bearing ancient dates, several of the year 1839, were, as at the Guildhall, posted again to obtain the impression of the special South Kensington Jubilee stamp. Some of the Guildhall Jubilee cards were used again in this way. Many rare stamps, both adhesive and embossed, were brought for the same purpose. Amongst them were six of the old black stamps, and two of the original Mulready envelopes.

Many inquiries were made as to whether the Jubilee envelopes were available for foreign circulation. It was explained that by the addition of adhesive stamps to the necessary amount the envelopes could be sent to any part of the globe. From the queries put, it was evident that very many of the envelopes would find their way to the United States.

Many of the Jubilee letters were stamped at the counters in the Museum where sold, and when posted such letters had to be carefully selected in order that they might not be spoiled by a second impression of the stamp.

In the Postal Sorting Office, and under a full-sized model of a splendid pulpit, a post by pneumatic tube was carried on, and in connection with it a Poste Restante was established.

Ordinary communications sent through the tube were charged at the rate of 1d. each. For replies, the questions being chiefly on Postal subjects, by tube letter, 3d. each was charged. The latest questions had reference to the Barrow election, which took place on the Conversazione day. Many persons, disappointed at the result, thought the reply dear at the charge of 3d.

The revenue to the Rowland Hill Benevolent Fund accruing directly from the Tube Post was £7 4s. 11d.

At the close of the evening £3 5s. 9d. had been taken at the Tube-Post table for impressions of the Jubilee stamp at 1d. each.

Next in order I come to the Public Post and Telegraph Office.

At the Guildhall Conversazione the Public Office had for its

guardians the grim giants Gog and Magog, but at the South Kensington Museum the young ladies who presided at the Postal counter in the Architectural Court had above them a statue of a more noble kind—that of David.

This office received a larger share of patronage than any other part of the exhibition, and for a time locomotion near it was almost impossible.

The Telegraph duty was conducted under great disadvantages. It had been intended to use "Inker" instruments, but there was only space enough for "Sounders," and reading by sound was a difficult matter owing to distracting noises, especially when the band was playing. The difficulties were, however, surmounted.

The Post-Office of 1890, in the Science Library, conducted by officers of the London Postal Service, was, owing to its remote position, not so well patronized as the office in the Architectural Court.

The counter for the sale of Jubilee envelopes in the Architectural Court South, under the management of Mrs. and Miss Blewitt, came in for a fair share of select patronage, but the counter in the Cruickshank Gallery, presided over by Miss Bean and Miss Adeney, was almost entirely overlooked.

At the two Post-Offices and the two stalls 5,370 of the Jubilee envelopes were disposed of, and, in addition, 2,166 post-cards were sold. Of the latter 1,855 were inland cards, and 311 such as are used for the foreign service.

Each visitor must on the average have bought two envelopes or post-cards, and that probably for the sake of getting impressions of the special South Kensington Jubilee obliterating and post-marking stamp, as the envelopes were procurable throughout the day at all London Post-Offices. Indeed, it is evident that the impression of the stamp was considered a desideratum, for nearly 20,000 more Jubilee envelopes were posted in the Museum than were actually sold in it.

The number of postage stamps sold reached a total of 1,174, amongst them being one at £1 and one at £5.

The demand for postal orders was not so great as at the

Guildhall, only twenty having been issued, and those were for small amounts only. It is probable these orders will be retained as souvenirs and never be cashed. Five orders only were paid.

The total number of money orders issued was 157, the majority being for 1d. None were presented for payment.

New Savings Bank accounts to the number of sixty-two were opened, and 137 deposits made. There were no withdrawals.

Letters and post-cards registered numbered 276, as against thirty-eight at the Guildhall Conversazione.

There were twenty parcels posted.

As regards the sale of Uniform Penny Postage Jubilee envelopes in London. It may be stated that these envelopes —sold at the rate of 1s. each at the head district, branch, and receiving offices in London—numbered 148,830. Of these 21,200 were sold at the counter of this office (G.P.O., East), 6,000 of them being for the officers of the Department, 7,483 at Lombard Street, and 5,370 at the South Kensington Museum.

At each of fifteen offices over 1,000 envelopes were disposed of, and between 500 and 1,000 were sold at each of fourteen offices.

At 9 a.m., on July 2nd, the Public Office here (G.P.O., East) and Lombard Street Office were filled by persons requiring Jubilee envelopes. The first stock of 9,000 supplied to the officer in charge at this office was exhausted at 10.30 a.m.

At 10 a.m. the Jubilee envelopes were seen to be in circulation in the sorting offices.

Many people had resorted to the expedient of taking the correspondence cards out of the envelopes and using them as postal communication cards, in some instances prepaying them by means of halfpenny stamps, and thus rendering the cards liable to surcharge.

To end the account. There were eighty-one telegraph messages sent and fifty-three delivered, thirty-two of the telegrams handed in at the Science Library counter having to be transmitted a second time from the Architectural Court to the Central Telegraph Office.

The impressions of the Jubilee stamp given at the rate of 1d. each, and the sale of Tables of Inland and Foreign Postal Rates and of cards for the protection of the Jubilee envelopes (passing through the post), realized the sum of £14 16s. 0d.

The paper bands round the packets of envelopes were much sought after, and in many cases prized equally with the envelopes.

I am very pleased indeed to be able to state that, notwithstanding all the confusion, bustle, and turmoil which attended the transactions of the Postal public business at the chief Post-Office, the money account has been accurately balanced. Miss Parsons, of the Regent Street Post-Office, was in charge of the account, assisted by Miss Turner of the North-Western District Office, and Miss Coombes, of the Lambeth Branch Office, partly shared the responsibility. These officers where ably seconded by their zealous assistants, viz.:—Misses C. S. Brown, A. E. Bean, L. C. Grimes, A. E. Martin, E. C. Fletcher, A. O. Gurton, E. L. Townsend, E. A. Adeney, A. M. Martin, and L. M. Blewitt, and by Mrs. Blewitt and Mrs. Taplin.

Few people found their way to the Cruickshank Gallery, but considerable interest was taken in the curious address books and the splendid show of foreign postage stamps, which took very many days to prepare. Some of the designs in which the postage stamps had been arranged were much admired by the visitors.

The designs (fifty-eight) for the Jubilee date stamp, which were prepared in response to an invitation issued to the Postmasters and staff of the London Postal Service, were exhibited. I think the designs were all so good as to reflect credit on the officers who submitted them.

The models of the Travelling Post-Offices, which were one of the special features at the Guildhall and gave immense satisfaction there, were almost neglected owing to having been placed upstairs.

Mr. Hone, the ambulance sergeant, reported several cases of faintness and giddiness. Fortunately there was no accident whatever.

I may perhaps add to my report that several country postmen were noticed taking particular interest in everything that was to be seen and heard.

One man, who had been in the service of the department thirty-eight years, travelled all the way from Cornwall to be present, and others came from far-off places such as Morpeth and Durham, bringing their wives with them. An officer travelled to London from a point even so far distant as Lerwick in the Shetland Islands.

Perhaps the most strange visitors were several babies in arms, who were being carried about the Museum. The fond parents hoped that at the Centenary of the Uniform Penny Postage System their children would be able to say they were present at its Jubilee.

It is a somewhat invidious task to laud any of the officers of my Department who were engaged in connection with the Conversazione when all worked so well. I should, however, be wanting in proper appreciation of excellent services rendered if I were not particularly to name Miss Parsons, Miss Turner, and Miss Brown, upon whose shoulders fell the brunt of the business at the Chief Post-Office,—Miss Coombes, who most efficiently managed the Branch Office in the Science Library,—Mr. Eynon, who supervised the Telegraph business of the Public Post-Office, —Mr. Kerans, who managed the Counter and Staff arrangements, and attended to stocks,—Mr. Supervisor Cooper, who was indefatigable in the outside department, in arranging the coaches, mail vans, &c., and seeing to their departure and arrival,—and especially Mr. Bray, who was my chief director from first to last.

The fitting up and taking down of the Post-Offices were processes of a far from light character, and it is most gratifying to record the great kindness and assistance rendered spontaneously by gentlemen attached to the South Kensington Museum.

As I have already mentioned, Mr. R. Thompson, the Assistant-Director of the Museum, was urbanity and kindness itself. We are also greatly indebted to Mr. W. E. Streatfield for the shifting of enormous pieces of statuary and for the supply of various fittings in order to enable us to erect our Post-Offices, and for other most valuable aid.

Inspector Rowlands, of the Police, was also most useful.

Mr. Jones, Mr. Clark, and Mr. How, Clerks of Works under the Office of Works, were exceedingly obliging, and supplied not only the necessary fittings, including the 1790 and 1990 Post-Offices, but also furnished a sufficient force of carpenters and labourers for the rapid erection of the fittings upon the selected site of the Museum.

In my report on the City Jubilee Celebration I ventured to suggest that a Grand Post-Office Exhibition of all nations held in London would probably be a success. The only suggestion I have now to make is that the conversaziones and city exhibition brought together so many articles of great interest in connection with the postal service of the country, that it would be a fitting opportunity to commence the establishment of a permanent Post-Office Museum.

R. C. TOMBS.

LONDON, *July 25th*, 1890.

REPORT OF THE ENTERTAINMENTS COMMITTEE.

Conversazione at South Kensington.

1. We endeavoured to organize some special arrangements in connection with a Post-Office of 1790, one of 1990, and a special 1890 counter in the "Science Library" at the Museum. In the result, we are happy to say that while the public appeared to take a very general interest in the matter, and to derive amusement from the efforts made to that end, the gross receipts taken at the 1790, 1890, and 1990 counters were £43 12s. 3½d.

2. Briefly stated, the arrangements were as follows :—

The Post-Offices and special counter were served by a staff of actresses and two or three actors, who kindly volunteered their services, those at the 1790 Post-Office being dressed in the costume of the period, with powder, the fittings of the office being all of that particular date, including brass candlesticks with dips, snuffers, pounce-boxes, blunderbuss, and several volumes of accounts, &c., drawn, by permission, from the stores of the Department. The 1990 Post-Office was chiefly distinguished by being brilliantly lighted with electricity, and the staff consisted of ladies in suitable evening attire. Here were provided facilities for obtaining almost instantaneous postal communication with all parts of the world by means of the "Electrotubular-lightning Express." At the 1790 and 1990 Post-Offices a large amount of work was performed in the shape chiefly of impressing on the special envelopes provided for the occasion, and on post-cards, &c., purchased for the purpose, impressions of the 1790 and 1990 obliterating stamps, the latter being designed and prepared for the occasion. Some ladies obtained impressions on their pocket-handkerchiefs and other objects.

3. Mrs. Conyers d'Arcy kindly took charge of these arrangement, assisted by Mrs. Dion Boucicault (the original " Colleen Bawn "), Miss Patrice Boucicault, and the husband of Mrs. d'Arcy, Major Conyers d'Arcy. Mrs. Charles Lamb Kenney, Miss Rosa Kenney, Miss Winall, Mr. E. Gilbert, and others formed the staff of the 1790 and 1990 offices. When the Royal personages visited these offices, Master Gordon d'Arcy presented the Duchess of Edinburgh with a letter written in Russian, containing suitable complimentary expressions, which was supposed to have reached the 1790 Post-Office for presentation to Her Royal Highness in anticipation of the event, one hundred years after—*i.e.* 1890 !

4. It should be added that all these ladies and gentlemen, some of whom came as early as half-past four, remained until after midnight, and only left their posts when the last of the public had retired from the " Science Library."

ALAN E. CHAMBRE.

August 7th, 1890.

THE POST-OFFICE JUBILEE CONVERSAZIONE.

(From the *Times*, July 3, 1890.)

In connection with the jubilee of uniform penny postage, which is this year celebrated, a monster conversazione was last night held at the South Kensington Museum, under the patronage of her Majesty the Queen, in aid of the Rowland Hill Benevolent Fund, for the relief and assistance of Post-Office servants or their widows and children. His Royal Highness the Duke of Edinburgh was president of the conversazione, and among the vice-presidents were Mr. Cecil Raikes, M.P., the Postmaster-General, the Marquis of Salisbury, Mr. W. H. Smith, Mr. G. J. Goschen, and the following ex-Postmasters-General:—The Duke of Argyll, the Duke of Rutland, Lord Emly, the Marquis of Hartington, Mr. Shaw-Lefevre, and Sir Lyon Playfair. Among the guests invited were the Duke of Abercorn, the Duke of Marlborough, the Duke of Portland, the Duke of Wellington, the Marquis of Ripon, the Marquis of Breadalbane, the Earl of Ashburnham, the Earl of Bradford, the Earl of Clarendon, the Earl of Derby, the Earl of Gainsborough, Earl Grey, the Earl of Jersey, Earl Spencer, Earl Stanhope, the Earl of Strafford, Earl Waldegrave, the Earl of Winchilsea and Nottingham, and Sir Robert Rawlinson.

The Duke and Duchess of Edinburgh had announced their intention of arriving at the Museum at half-past 9, but between 7 o'clock and that hour ample and varied entertainment was provided for the guests. There was music in plenty; concerts were given at intervals during the course of the evening in the theatre leading out of the galleries of the north cloister, and in these concerts Mme. Valleria, Mme. Anne Marriott, Miss Alice Gomez, Miss Nellie Levey, Messrs. Sims Reeves, Percy Palmer, and Frederick King, Mme. Frickenhaus, Mr. Alfred G. Caldicott, and other well-known artists gave their services. Then the Post Office choir, under the direction of Mr. Sydney Beckley, performed a selection of glees and part-songs. In addition to this the band of the Grenadier Guards, under the direction of Lieutenant Dan Godfrey, played throughout the evening, first in the architectural court, and afterwards in the quadrangle, while the string band of the Royal Artillery, under Cavalier Zavertal, discoursed Gounod and Schubert, Strauss and Verdi, in the Italian court. Apart from the musical programme, which, as has been shown, was extensive, there was much amusement, and even instruction, to be found in entertainments and exhibitions which, in keeping with the special occasion celebrated, were more or less of a postal character. In the architectural court had been established a general post-office, at which all kinds of business, postal and telegraphic, might be transacted. Here, as, indeed, at the branch post-offices, established in various parts of the building, were to be found the commemorative jubilee envelope and Rowland Hill correspondence card. This envelope has already been described in the columns of *The Times*. It will be sufficient, therefore, to recall how it shows in appropriate and artistic design the North Mail in 1790, with four horses and a guard with a blunderbuss, making for Highgate at eight miles an hour, and beneath it the North Mail in 1890, approaching Carlisle at forty-eight miles an hour, with all the perfections of sorting offices, nets for catching mail bags *en route*, and other conveniences nowadays carried on an express train. The correspondence card sold with this envelope bears on it a portrait of Sir Rowland Hill, beneath which is the legend, "He gave us penny postage." The envelope and card, which have been specially produced for this occasion and the die of which has already been broken up, were sold for a shilling; the proceeds of the sale to go to the benevolent fund, in aid of which the conversazione was given.

In the architectural gallery also, and close to the General

Post-Office, was a sorting office, where sorting clerks were actively at work, and where, on payment of a small fee, stamps of a unique design might be impressed on the jubilee cards or envelopes. There were three of these stamps, each of a different design and bearing respectively the dates of July 2, 1790, 1890, and 1990.

In the textile gallery had been placed a telegraph office, in which a great number of instruments were exhibited illustrating the latest improvements and perfections made in the construction of telegraphic machinery. Among these instruments were two which typified the very last developments of telegraphic science. They are the Edison quadruplex instrument, by means of which four messages, two from each end, can be transmitted upon one wire at one and the same time. The other marvel of telegraphy is the synchronous multiplex, an instrument which is the invention of Professor Delaney, and by means of which six messages can be transmitted upon one wire, either all from one station or in opposite directions. This instrument was not fixed for working last night; but by the quadruplex, which was connected with the telegraphic office at Bristol, messages were despatched and received all through the evening.

Close to these scientific exhibits was an entertainment arranged by Mr. W. H. Preece which attracted great crowds of visitors throughout the night. This was a telegraph office of the period 1990, where was to be seen the latest invention of Mr. Preece and Professor Hughes, the electrophonoscope, by means of which the operators at either end of the wire while speaking by means of the telephone are by an electric flash revealed to each other throughout their conversation. In the science library a variety of post offices had been established. One of these represented a post office of a hundred years ago, and, considering the small amount of postal correspondence of the time, was provided with a more than ample staff of specially selected officials, among them being Mrs. Dion Boucicault, well remembered as the original " Colleen Bawn." The officers of this post office were all dressed in the costume of the period, and seemed in the course of the evening to transact a very considerable amount of business. There was also close to the 1790 post office, and only separated from it by a branch post office of the present day, an office of the period of 1990, where, as was announced by a placard, business was conducted on entirely new principles, and letters (open) of all kind sent by the new patent electrotubular-lightning express. Among other amusements was the phonograph, which as usual attracted many admirers, while at various hours in the evening the Royal parcel mail coaches for Brighton, Watford, and Oxford were despatched from the main entrance of the Museum.

Very soon after half-past 9 the band of the guard of honour, formed by the 24th Middlesex (Post Office Corps of Volunteers) announced the arrival of the Royal party. Their Royal Highnesses, who were accompanied by Lady Emma Osborne, Colonel Colville, and Lieutenant-Colonel Poore, were received by the Postmaster-General, the vice-presidents, and the members of the Executive Committee in the architectural court; and, a bouquet having been offered to the Duchess of Edinburgh by Miss Raikes, Mr. F. E. Baines, Mr. J. J. Cardin, Mr. W. H. Preece, Mr. S. Raffles Thompson, and Mr. R. C. Tombs were presented by the Postmaster-General. A procession was then formed, the master of the ceremonies, Mr. Alan Chambre, followed by four City trumpeters, leading the way; and the Duchess of Edinburgh was conducted by the Postmaster-General, and Mrs. Raikes by his Royal Highness the President, to a daïs erected at the end of the north-east cloister. Here a programme, hand-painted on vellum and enriched with a picture of the old General Post Office, St. Martin's-le-Grand, was handed to her Royal Highness; and, the Royal guests being seated, the ex-guard of the London and Exeter mail coach, who began his duties in the year 1836, presented to the Duchess a letter signed by old officers of the Post Office who entered the service more than fifty years ago, the first signature being that of Mr. Frederick Hill, the sole surviving brother of the late Sir Rowland Hill, and another signature being that of an officer of the Post Office, Mr. R. S. White, who entered the service in the year 1818. This letter was as follows:—

"May it please your Royal and Imperial Highness, we, the undersigned, who are old officers of the Post Office, desire to welcome your Royal and Imperial Highness to this, the celebration of the jubilee of uniform penny postage.

"We desire to thank your Royal and Imperial Highness for your condescension in coming amongst the officers of the Post Office and in lending approval to the Rowland Hill Benevolent Fund by your gracious presence."

An officer of the Post Office then delivered a letter of a similar character from present officers of the Post Office, and signed on their behalf by the Postmaster-General and the Secretary of the Post Office.

The Duke of Edinburgh, in reply, expressed, on behalf of the Duchess and himself, his warm thanks for the kind terms in which the old and present officers of the Post Office had addressed the Duchess, and said that he felt very deeply the honour conferred on him by making him the president of this conversazione.

A number of telegrams containing congratulatory addresses were then handed in and read by Mr. Raikes, from the President of the United States, and from the Postmaster-General in Washington, and from the Governors of New South Wales, Victoria, South Australia, Queensland, New Zealand, and Tasmania. Telegrams were also received from the Premier of the Cape of Good Hope, Sir John Gordon Sprigg, from the Postmaster-General of Newfoundland, and, lastly, from the telegraph office at Balta Sound, in the Shetland group, the northernmost point of telegraphic communication in the British Isles, 715 miles distant from London. All these messages having been read, and the Duke of Edinburgh having expressed his satisfaction at their reception, a telegraph wire and apparatus was brought up on to the daïs, and, on her Royal Highness touching a key, a signal was transmitted to the post offices in all parts of the British Isles inviting the Post Office officials to unite with their colleagues at South Kensington in giving simultaneously three cheers for her Majesty the Queen.

The cheers, which in South Kensington were very heartily given, brought the ceremonial of the evening to a close. The

Royal party adjourned to the concert-room, where the Duke and Duchess of Edinburgh heard Mr. Sims Reeves, who was in excellent voice, sing Lindsay Lennox's "Dream Memories," "Tom Bowling," and, as a final *encore*, "Come into the Garden, Maud." Their Royal Highnesses then visited the old post office, and before leaving inspected a number of the other postal exhibits on view. The proceedings terminated soon after midnight.

(From the *Daily Telegraph*, July 3, 1890.)

The conversazione of the Post-Office Penny Postage Jubilee, which was held last evening at the South Kensington Museum, was a highly successful and brilliant event, and was attended by their Royal Highnesses the Duke and Duchess of Edinburgh. About 4,000 guests from all parts of the United Kingdom were present, and were received by Sir S. A. Blackwood, K.C.B., Secretary of the Post-Office, Mr. F. E. Baines, C.B., the Inspector-General of Mails, and chairman of the executive committee, and by other officials. Sir James Whitehead, one of the promoters of the fund, was also present.

Preceded by a gentleman usher, Mr. Chambre, and by four City trumpeters in scarlet uniforms, the Royal guests passed through the Architectural Court, where were stationed some very largely patronized sorting, stamping, and special conversazione Post-Offices, into the South Court, and thence across the Italian Court, which was thronged with people, to the daïs in the north-east cloister. The Duchess of Edinburgh was conducted by the Postmaster-General, and Mrs. Raikes by His Royal Highness the President. On the way the band of the Grenadier Guards played, and the National Anthem was struck up by the band of the Royal Artillery as the procession reached the southern arch of the Italian Court.

At the daïs an interesting ceremony was performed. An old officer, Mr. Nobbs, who has been fifty-four years at the General Post-Office, clad in his red coat, delivered to their Royal Highnesses a letter, which was read. It conveyed a respectful welcome to the Duke and Duchess, and expressed the hearty appreciation of their kindness which was felt by eighty-three old servants of the Post-Office, all of whom had joined between the years 1818—1840, and by Mr. Frederic Hill, the sole surviving brother of the late Sir Rowland Hill, K.C.B. Mr. Stewart, a young postman in the uniform of 1890, next handed in a similar letter, which was also read. It is signed, on behalf of the present servants of the Post-Office, by the Postmaster-General, the Secretary of the Post-Office, and by the Inspector-General of Mails.

The Duke of Edinburgh, in reply, expressed the pleasure which the Duchess had in receiving these letters, and he thanked them in his own behalf for having invited him to attend the conversazione as its president. He added that a telegram had been sent to his house, and it was from the Governor of Cape Colony. He was glad to have received this message early, which conveyed the congratulations of the colonists, from this part of Her Majesty's Empire, for it happened that this colony was the first that he had visited.

A telegraph lad, Morrish, then handed in several telegrams, the first coming from the Postmaster of an office at the extreme northern point of the service, being 700 miles distant from London. A succession of despatches were received and read, amongst them being one from the Postmaster-General at Washington to the Duke, and one from the Governor of Newfoundland addressed to the Duchess, in which the hope was expressed that the Newfoundlanders might soon enjoy the benefits of Penny Postage, a wish which created some laughter. The Viceroy of India, the Postmaster-General of Canada, the Premier of Quebec, and others sent despatches to the Postmaster-General.

The reading of these messages having concluded, the Duchess was requested to touch the key of an electric instrument, by means of which a signal was sent all over the British Isles, as an intimation that all should join with their colleagues assembled at South Kensington in three cheers for Her Majesty the Queen. Hearty cheering thereupon resounded, and the names of the Duke and Duchess were also warmly applauded. The ceremony coming thus to an end, the Royal party was escorted first to the Quadrangle, and then upon a tour of inspection.

In the Textile Gallery, as a part of a highly interesting collection of telegraphic instruments, illustrative of the various systems in use for the last hundred years, there was a most remarkable apparatus on view. It is the joint invention of Professor Hughes, F.R.S., and Mr. Preece, F.R.S. The sender of a message from a distant station appears in person before his correspondent, and with a telephone it is possible, not only to speak to him, but to see him, and to watch the expression of his features. It is a perfect complement to the telephone, and will illustrate what telegraphy is likely to be in 1990. There is hardly any need to say that the liveliest curiosity was manifested to view this electro-phonoscope, as it was called, and the dark rooms were besieged by visitors.

On entering a little cabinet one was confronted with a large dark mirror, having a telephone at the side and a pair of strong lamps overhead. Directly communication was made it was possible to talk over the telephone in the ordinary way; but whilst talking the speaker could observe the expression upon his correspondent's face at the other end of the wire. Like an animated coloured photograph the image of this gentleman was seen perfectly and clearly, and at the same moment this individual, whilst addressed by the speaker, could watch his face as he spoke. The effect was really marvellous, and appeared almost like witchcraft. Of course the two instruments were at no great distance apart—perhaps thirty feet—but they were not in a direct line of vision.

The programme also included the provision of three postal offices in the Science Library—one dated 1790, being a quaint reproduction of the Office of a century ago, attended by bewigged ladies and clerks in full-skirted coats. The modern Office was in the charge of Mrs. Dion Boucicault, the original "Colleen Bawn," and the office of 1990 was typical of electricity, and the ladies behind the counter were attired respectively in black, scarlet, and yellow. Postal Cards were despatched, not by tube, as might be supposed, but by boy messengers to the

Poste-Restante in the Architectural Court, where answers of a jocular kind were forthcoming.

In the concert theatre there was a succession of musical programmes, and Mr. Sims Reeves had an especially hearty reception.

During the evening the stamp collections lent by the Board of Inland Revenue, the Government of New South Wales, and the Post-Office were inspected by many people, and visitors also availed themselves of the opportunity of using the Hughes telegraph instrument, which was in communication with Brussels and also Berlin.

It is expected that the Rowland Hill Benevolent Fund will largely benefit by the proceeds of the conversazione.

TELEGRAMS FROM FOREIGN COUNTRIES AND FROM THE COLONIES.

THE following telegrams were received at the Museum during the Conversazione :—

From the POSTMASTER-GENERAL OF THE UNITED STATES.

I beg to send fraternal greetings and congratulations that the postal service is steadily improving throughout the world. We join in the celebration of the Jubilee of Penny Postage, having for many years enjoyed the equivalent rate of letter postage, and we now look forward to an early reduction to one cent letter postage—JOHN WANAMAKER, Postmaster-General, Washington.

From TELEGRAPHISTS AT BERLIN.

(*Translation.*)

Six hundred telegraph clerks assembled in the Central Telegraph Office in Berlin send His Royal Highness the Duke of Edinburgh respectful greetings.

From the VICEROY OF INDIA.

Wednesday noon.—Please accept my cordial congratulations on the Jubilee of the Penny Post. The Indian Post Office was quick to adopt the principles of Sir Rowland Hill's reform, and notwithstanding the great distances in India, our inland letter postage has long been a uniform rate of half an anna, or little more than a halfpenny. In India as in England, the result has been an increase of correspondence altogether beyond expectation, but education and commerce are not yet sufficiently advanced in this country to give our Post Office a surplus, or to place it in the enviable position which British Post Office now enjoys. I am glad, however, to inform you on this auspicious occasion that we hope to be able to join you in reducing the postage from India to the United Kingdom to two and a half annas, at the same time that the postage from the United Kingdom is reduced to twopence-halfpenny.—VICEROY.

From Sir John A. McDonald, *Premier of the Dominion of Canada.*

Please accept hearty congratulations from Canada.

From the Postmaster-General, *Canada.*

I tender you the hearty congratulations of the Canadian Post Office on celebration of your Jubilee in honour of one of the greatest boons modern civilization has given to humanity.—John Haggart.

From the Lieut.-Governor of the Province of Quebec.

Lieut.-Governor Angers offers his greetings and congratulations to the British Post Office on the occasion of the Penny Postage Jubilee.

From the Hon. Honore Mercier, *Premier of Quebec.*

The Prime Minister of the Province of Quebec sends greetings and congratulations on the occasion of the Penny Postage Jubilee.

From Cardinal Taschereau, *Quebec.*

Congratulations to the British Post Office on the occasion of the Penny Postage Jubilee.

From Sir Alexander Campbell, K.C.M.G., *Lieut.-Governor of Ontario.*

The blessings of Rowland Hill's reform were not confined to England, but offered an example which has stimulated the world. In Canada we rapidly followed, as far as the sparse character of our population admitted, and enjoy many of the advantages. Ontario sends congratulations, and heartily rejoices with you in your Jubilee.

From the Governor of Newfoundland.

I beg to offer the congratulations of Newfoundland on the fiftieth anniversary of the institution of that great instrument of civilization, the Penny Postage, in which the Colony hopes it may soon participate.

From the Governor of New South Wales (Lord Carrington), *the* Governor of Victoria (The Earl of Hopetoun), *and the* Governor of South Australia (The Earl of Kintore).

We send our hearty congratulations on occasion of Jubilee of Penny Postage.

From the Prime Minister of Cape Colony.

Respectfully offer congratulations on celebration of Jubilee of Penny Post, the benefits of which are also gratefully enjoyed in this Colony.

From the Governor of New Zealand.

The Governor of New Zealand presents his duty to Her Royal and Imperial Highness the Duchess of Edinburgh, and begs to tender congratulations on the attainment of the Jubilee of the Penny Postage System.—Onslow.

CELEBRATIONS OF THE JUBILEE IN THE PROVINCES.

JULY 2, 1890.

ABSTRACTS OF REPORTS FROM THE PROVINCES AND FROM OFFICES IN LONDON.

England.

Office.	Present.	National Anthem Sung.	Addresses.	
Aberdare	Staff on duty			
Abergavenny	Meeting of Staff	...		Refreshments to staff
Adamsdown	Ditto	Ditto		
Admiral Street, Liverpool	Ditto	...		Refreshments to staff
Almondsbury	Ditto	Ditto		
Ampthill	Meeting of staff and public	Ditto	Ditto	
Augmering	Ditto	Ditto	...	Fireworks
Andover	Conversazione	Ditto	Ditto	
Ashburton	Meeting of staff and public	Ditto	Ditto	
Ashbourne	Ditto	Ditto	Ditto	Band-Supper
Aspley Guise	Meeting of staff	...	...	Supper
Aylesbury	Ditto	Ditto	Ditto	Supper
Bacup	Ditto	Ditto	Ditto	Tea
Badminton	Ditto	Ditto		
Bangor	Ditto	Ditto		
Barlestone	Meeting of staff and public			
Barley	Meeting of staff			
Barnet	Ditto	Ditto	Ditto	Fireworks, refreshments
Barnsley	Ditto	Ditto	Ditto	
Barnstaple	Ditto	Ditto	Ditto	Refreshments to staff
Bath	Ditto (100 in number)	Ditto	Ditto	Special dinner a few days afterwards
Beaumaris	Ditto	Ditto		
Bedale	Ditto	...	Ditto	Cheers at the Market Cross
Bedford	Ditto	Ditto	Ditto	Decorations, refreshments
Ben Rhydding	Staff on duty			
Berkhampsted	Meeting of staff	Ditto	...	Refreshments
Berwick	Ditto	...	Ditto	Meeting of public outside office

JUBILEE OF PENNY POSTAGE.

Office.	Present.	National Anthem Sung.	Addresses.	
Bildeston	Meeting of staff			
Biddenden	Ditto			
Bilston	Ditto	Ditto	...	Refreshments
Birkenhead	Ditto			
Birmingham	Ditto (150)	Ditto	Ditto	
Blackburn	Ditto (95)	Ditto	Ditto	Ventriloquist entertainment
Blandford	Ditto	...		Decorations and illuminations
Bletchley Station	Ditto	Ditto		
Bolton	Staff on duty			
Bootle	Meeting of staff	Ditto		
Bourne	Ditto	Ditto		Dinner
Boston	Ditto (60)	Ditto		
Bradford	Meeting of staff and public in front of office (6,000)	Ditto		Band. Part of staff returning at 10 P.M. from special duty gave cheers in train
Bridgwater	Meeting of staff			
Brentford	Ditto	...	...	Special supper a few days afterwards
Bridlington Quay	Ditto	Ditto	Ditto	
Brighton	Ditto			
Brighton Station	Ditto			
Bristol	Ditto	Ditto		Band, tea
Briton Ferry	Ditto	Ditto		
Broxbourne	Ditto	...	...	Salute fired
Buckingham	Ditto (44)	Ditto	Ditto	Supper, collection for Benevolent Fund
Buckfastleigh	Ditto	...	...	Convivial meeting
BudleighSalterton	Meeting of staff and public	Ditto	Ditto	Collection for Benevolent Fund, illuminations
Burnley	Ditto			
Bury St. Edmunds	Ditto			Supper, dancing
Campden	Ditto			Music, refreshments Office decorated
Cardiff	Ditto	Ditto		Band, illuminations
Cardiff (Bute Docks)	Ditto			
Carlton Street, Castleford	Ditto			
Canterbury	Ditto			
Carnarvon	Ditto (50)	...		Music, fireworks
Carnforth	Ditto	...		Decorated office
Central Telegraph Office	Staff on duty	Ditto		
Charfield	Meeting of staff	...		Decorations, illuminations
Cheetham Hill, Manchester	Ditto			Supper
Chesterfield	Ditto			
Chorley	Meeting of staff and others		Ditto	

CELEBRATIONS OF THE JUBILEE IN THE PROVINCES.

Office.	Present.	National Anthem Sung.	Addresses.	
Church Stretton	Meeting of staff			
Church Street, Whitby	Staff on duty			
Cirencester	Meeting of staff		...	Supper
Clifden	Ditto	...	...	Refreshments
Collingham	Ditto	...	...	Office decorated
Colne	Ditto	Ditto	Ditto	Supper
Coventry	Ditto			
Crawley	Ditto			
Crondall	Ditto	...	Ditto	
Darlington	Ditto (70)			
Dawlish	Ditto	Ditto	Ditto	
Derby	Staff on duty	Ditto	Ditto	
Dereham	Meeting of staff	Ditto	Ditto	Music, refreshments
Doncaster	Ditto			
Dorking	Ditto			
Downham	Ditto			Social gathering
Downton	Ditto			
Dudley	Ditto	Ditto		
Dulverton	Ditto	Ditto		Music, refreshments
Durham	Ditto	...		Refreshments
Dymchurch	Ditto	...		Office decorated
East Finchley	Staff on duty			
Ebley	Ditto			
Evershot	Meeting of staff			
Exeter	Meeting of staff and public	Ditto		Band, illumination
Emsworth	Meeting of staff	Ditto	Ditto	
Falmouth	Meeting of staff and public	...	Ditto	
Farnworth	Meeting of staff			Salute fired
Filkins	Ditto			
Finsbury Park, N.	Ditto			
Folkestone	Ditto (65)	Ditto		
„ (Tontine Street)	Ditto	Ditto		
Fressingfield	Ditto	Ditto		Excursion to Yarmouth, supper
Gainsborough	Meeting of staff and public	Ditto		Supper, decorations, illumination
Gilesgate	Staff on duty			
Gloucester	Ditto			
Grantham	Meeting of staff and public (6,000)	Ditto	...	Open air concert, supper, decorations, illuminations
Gringley on the Hill	Meeting of staff			
Grosmont	Ditto	Ditto		
Guildford	Ditto	Ditto	Ditto	Decorations, illuminations
Guist	Ditto	Ditto		
Halesworth	Ditto	Ditto		Music
Halstead	Ditto			

JUBILEE OF PENNY POSTAGE.

Office.	Present.	National Anthem Sung.	Addresses.	
Harleston	Meeting of staff			
Hartlepool, West	Ditto	Ditto	Ditto	Music, Refreshments decorations
Harwell	Ditto	Ditto		
Hastings	Ditto	Ditto		Concert
Haverfordwest	Ditto	Ditto		Decorations
Haverhill	Ditto	Ditto		Dinner
Havant	Ditto	...		Refreshments
Hemingford road, N.	Ditto	Ditto	Ditto	Social meeting
Hereford	Meeting of staff and public	Ditto	Ditto	
Highbury, N.	Meeting of staff	Ditto		Supper
Highgate	Ditto			
Hitchin	Ditto	...		Social evening
Hoddesdon	Ditto			
Hogsthorpe	Meeting of staff and public	Ditto		
Holyhead and Kingston Packet	Staff on duty			
Hornsey	Ditto			
Horsham	Ditto			Decorations
Huddersfield	Meeting of staff			
Hull	Ditto	Ditto	Ditto	
Huntingdon	Ditto			
Hyde Park, Leeds	Ditto			
Ideford	Ditto	...		Fireworks
Ilfracombe	Ditto	Ditto		
Intelligence Branch G.P.O.	Staff on duty			
Irthlingboro'	Meeting of staff	Ditto		
Ipswich	Ditto	...	Ditto	
Jersey	Ditto (100)	Ditto	...	Music, refreshments
Keighley	Ditto	Ditto	...	Supper
Kendal	Ditto			
Keswick	Ditto	Ditto	Ditto	
Kettering	Ditto	Ditto	...	Supper, decorations
Kidderminster	Ditto	...	...	Supper, decorations
Kidsgrove	Ditto	...		Supper
Kingsland B.O.	Staff on duty	Ditto		
Kirkbythore	Meeting of staff	Ditto		
Lancaster	Ditto	Ditto		
Lawrence St., Llanelly	Ditto	...	Ditto	
Leeds	Ditto	Ditto		
Leicester	Ditto	Ditto		
Leominster	Ditto	Ditto		Decorations, illuminations, refreshments
Lewannick	Ditto	Ditto		Collection for fund
Lewes	Ditto	Ditto		
Lichfield	Ditto	Ditto		

CELEBRATIONS OF THE JUBILEE IN THE PROVINCES.

Office.	Present.	National Anthem Sung.	Addresses.	
Lincoln	Meeting of staff	Ditto		
Liverpool	Staff on duty	Ditto		
Llanelly	Ditto			
Loughboro'	Ditto			
Lower Edmonton	Ditto			
Ludlow	Meeting of staff	Ditto	Ditto	Decorations, illumination, refreshments
Lytham	Ditto			
Maidstone	Ditto			
Malton	Ditto	Ditto		Decorations
Manchester	Staff on duty			
Margate	Meeting of staff	Ditto	Ditto	Refreshments
Merthyr Tydvil	Ditto			
Mold	Ditto			Supper
Moorgate, Lanc.	Staff on duty			
Mount Pleasant Depôt	Ditto			
N. D. O.	Ditto			
Neath	Meeting of staff	...	...	Supper
Nelson	Ditto	Ditto	Ditto	Dinner
Netherton	Ditto	...	..	Supper
Newcastle-on-Tyne	Ditto	...	Ditto	Music
Newmarket	Meeting of staff and public (100)	Ditto	Ditto	Music
Newport. I.W.	Meeting of staff	Ditto	Ditto	
Newport, Mon.	Ditto	Ditto	...	Music
New Southgate	Meeting of staff	Ditto	...	Decorations, social meeting
Newton Abbot	Ditto	Ditto		
Neyland	Staff on duty			
Normanton	Meeting of staff			
Northampton	Staff on duty			
North Finchley	Meeting of staff		...	Social meeting
North Shields	Ditto		Ditto	
Norwich	Staff on duty			
Norwich Sorting Tender	Ditto			
Nottingham	Ditto			
Nuneaton	Meeting of staff			
Ockbrook	Ditto			
Ormaston Road, Derby	Ditto	Ditto		
Oswestry	Ditto	Ditto		Refreshments
Oxford	Ditto	Ditto		
,, High Street R.O.	Staff on duty			
Palmers Green	Meeting of staff			
Parkhurst road, N.	Staff on duty			
Peterborough	Meeting of staff	Ditto	Ditto	
Pill	Staff on duty			
Pocklington	Meeting of staff			

Office.	Present.	National Anthem Sung.	Addresses.	
Prescot	Meeting of staff	Ditto	Ditto	Refreshments
Preston	Ditto			
Pwllheli	Ditto			
Putney	Ditto			
Radstock	Ditto			
Red Hill	Ditto			
Reigate	Ditto	Ditto		
Ringwood	Ditto			
Ripon	Ditto	Ditto		Supper
Rochdale	Ditto	...		Decorations, refreshments
Romsey	Ditto	Ditto		Social gathering
Rugby	Staff on duty			Collection for fund
Runcorn	Meeting of staff			
Saffron Walden	Ditto			
St. Albans	Ditto			Gratuity to each man
St. Ann's Head	Clerk in charge (alone)			He walked six miles for the purpose
St. Neots	Meeting of staff			Collection
St. Helens	Ditto			
Saltburn	Ditto			Supper
Sandy	Ditto			
Saxmundham	Ditto	Ditto		
Scarborough	Ditto			
Sevenoaks	Ditto			
Sherborne	Ditto			Decorations, Social meeting
Sheffield	Ditto (200)	Ditto		
Shrewsbury	Ditto	Ditto		
Sittingbourne	Ditto			
Sidmouth	Ditto			
Sidbury	Ditto			
Sidford	Ditto			
Silkstone Common	Ditto			
Somerby	Ditto	Ditto		Decorations
Southampton	Ditto			
Southgate	Ditto	Ditto		Fireworks, social meeting
Southport	Ditto			
S. E. D. O.	Ditto			Cheers also at all the Branch Offices, &c. in the district open at 10 P.M.
Sowerby Bridge	Ditto			
Spalding	Meeting of staff and public	Ditto		
Stainboro'	Meeting of staff			
Stalybridge	Ditto	Ditto		
Stevenston	Ditto			
Stockport	Ditto	Ditto		
Stockton	Ditto	...	Ditto	Social meeting
Stoke Newington	Ditto	Ditto	Ditto	
Stoke on Trent	Ditto	Ditto		

CELEBRATIONS OF THE JUBILEE IN THE PROVINCES.

Office.	Present.	National Anthem Sung.	Addresses.	
Stoke Prior	Meeting of staff	...		Decorations
Stourbridge	Ditto	Ditto		Social meeting
Stratford on Avon	Ditto	Ditto		Social meeting, decorations
Street	Ditto			
Strood	Staff on duty			
Sudbury	Meeting of staff			
Sunderland	Ditto (120)		Ditto	Entertainment
Sutton, Surrey	Ditto			
Swansea	Meeting of staff and public			Royal salute, decorations, illuminations, band
Taunton	Meeting of staff (73)	Ditto		
Tavistock	Ditto			
Tenterden	Ditto			Decorations, social meeting
Teignmouth	Meeting of staff and public	Ditto		Illumination, refreshments
Thetford	Meeting of staff			Conversazione
Thornton Heath	Ditto			
Tiverton	Meeting of staff and public	Ditto	Ditto	
Todmorden	Meeting of staff	...		Social meeting
Torquay	Ditto	Ditto		Band
Tooley Street	Ditto			
Tottenham	Ditto	Ditto		Decorations, Illuminations
Torpoint	Ditto			
Tring	Ditto			
Truro	Ditto	Ditto		Decorations, social meeting
Tunbridge	Ditto	Ditto		Decorations, social meeting
Twickenham	Ditto	Ditto		Social meeting
Upper Holloway	Ditto	...	Ditto	
Ventnor	Ditto	Ditto	...	Supper
Wakefield	Ditto (50)	...	Ditto	
Walmer Road, Deal	Ditto			Gratuity to each Postman
Ware	Ditto			
Warrington	Ditto			Social meeting
Wateringbury	Ditto			
Wednesbury	Ditto			
Weeley	Ditto	Ditto		Supper
Wellingboro'	Ditto	...		Decorations
Wells, Norfolk	Ditto			
,, Somerset	Ditto	Ditto		Supper
West Bromwich	Ditto	Ditto		Refreshments
Westbury	Ditto	Ditto		Refreshments
West Woathly	Ditto	Ditto		Refreshments

R

242 JUBILEE OF PENNY POSTAGE.

Office.	Present.	National Anthem Sung.	Addresses.	
Weymouth......	Meeting of staff	...		Refreshments, decorations
Whetstone	Staff on duty			Refreshments
Whitchurch, Salop	Meeting of staff			
Wigan	Staff on duty	Ditto		
Winchester ..	Ditto	Ditto		
Winchmore Hill	Meeting of staff			
Winster..........	Ditto			
Wisbech	Ditto			
Woodbridge ...	Ditto			
Wood Green ...	Ditto			
Woolwich	Ditto	Ditto		Illumination
Worthing.......	Ditto			
Wyndham Park Salisbury	Staff on duty			
Yaxley	Ditto			
York	Meeting of staff		Ditto	
York and Newcastle T.P.O.	Staff on duty			

Scotland.

Office.	Present.	National Anthem Sung.	Addresses.	
Aberdeen	Meeting of staff	...	Ditto	
Abernethy	Ditto			
Auchterarder ..	Ditto			
Brechin	Ditto	...	Ditto	
Campbeltown ..	Ditto	...	Ditto	
Crieff	Ditto	Ditto		
Cupar, Fife.....	Ditto	Ditto	Ditto	Social meeting
Dumbarton	Ditto	...	...	Music
Dumfernline. ..	Ditto	...	...	Illumination and fireworks, music, supper
Dundee	Ditto	Ditto	Ditto	Music, refreshments
Edinburgh	Staff on duty			
Gatehouse	Meeting of staff	...	...	Royal Standard, bells rung, refreshments
Glasgow	Ditto (414)	Ditto	Ditto	Post-Office Band
Greenock	Ditto (100)	Ditto	Ditto	
Invergordon ...	Ditto	...	...	Social meeting
Kelso	Ditto	Ditto	Ditto	
Kirriemuir	Ditto			
Laurencekirk ..	Ditto	...	Ditto	
Lerwick	Ditto	Ditto		
Lochmaddy	Ditto	Ditto		
Lockerbie........	Ditto	...	Ditto	
North Berwick	Ditto	...	Ditto	
Perth	Staff on duty	...	...	Staff off duty also met at hotel

CELEBRATIONS OF THE JUBILEE IN THE PROVINCES.

Office.	Present.	National Anthem Sung.	Addresses.	
Stranraer	Meeting of staff	...		Refreshments
Strichen	Ditto	Ditto		
Torry	Ditto	...	Ditto	
Yetholm	Meeting of staff and public	Ditto		

Ireland.

Office.	Present.	National Anthem Sung.	Addresses.	
Ardaragh	Staff on duty			
Aghmagh	Ditto			
Belfast	Meeting of staff (100)			
Broadford	Staff on duty			
Clare Castle	Meeting of staff			
Clonmel	Staff on duty			
Collinstown	Sub-Postmaster alone			
Curragh Camp	Meeting of staff		Ditto	
Derry	Ditto			
Dominick St., Galway	Staff on duty			
Dublin	Ditto			
Dungarvan	Meeting of staff		Ditto	Supper
Galway	Ditto			
Kingstown	Staff on duty			
Letterpack	Ditto			
Kildysart	Ditto			
Kill	Ditto			
Limerick	Meeting of staff	Ditto		
Miltown Malbay	Ditto			
Mullingar	Ditto			
Newtownards	Ditto			
Philipstown	Staff on duty			
Portaferry	Meeting of staff			
Renoyle	Sub-Postmaster alone			
Roslea	Staff on duty			Illumination
Sligo	Meeting of staff			
Stradone	Ditto			
Tarbert	Ditto	Ditto	Ditto	
Thomastown	Ditto	...	...	Refreshments
Tulla	Ditto	Ditto	...	Music, refreshments
Tullamore	Ditto	...	Ditto	Fireworks, entertainment
Waterford	Ditto			Supper

EXTRACTS FROM TYPICAL REPORTS.

ENGLAND.

LONDON OFFICES.

HIGHBURY.

I BEG to report that at 10 P.M. the officers employed in this sub-district returned to the sorting office, and after giving three hearty cheers for Her Majesty the Queen, sat down to supper, after which they spent a pleasant and sociable time in recitation and singing, accompanied with a harmonium. A very enjoyable meeting was brought to a close by all rising and joining in singing the National Anthem.

TOTTENHAM.

I beg to report that several of the men returned after finishing their 8 P.M. delivery, and gave three cheers for Her Majesty. Also several of the men attached to the band played "God Save the Queen." The outside of the office was decorated with flags and illuminated with lights.

HORNSEY.

The whole of the force on duty at the time raised three hearty loyal cheers for Her Majesty.

UPPER HOLLOWAY.

A goodly number of postmen met here at 9.40 P.M., and at 10 p.m. three ringing cheers were given for Her Majesty.

North Finchley.

I beg to report that the whole of the officers returned from their duty to the office as near to 10 P.M. as possible, and gave three hearty cheers, which were started by the Letter Receiver, who also attended, and very kindly gave us light refreshments. The men enjoyed themselves for a couple of hours with music and singing. Altogether the event passed off most satisfactorily.

New Southgate.

I beg respectfully to report that all the postmen attached to this suburban district met at the office at 10 P.M. and gave three hearty cheers for Her Most Gracious Majesty.

After partaking of a light refreshment a few appropriate songs were rendered. The meeting concluded by all singing the National Anthem. Two large flags were hoisted on the roof of the sorting office.

Southgate.

All duties at this office being completed at 10 P.M., the officers assembled on the green in front of the office, and after a grand fire-work display and a double balloon ascent which was witnessed by a great number of people, three hearty cheers were given for Her Most Gracious Majesty the Queen. The officers afterwards adjourned and a very sociable half hour was spent, which was finished with the singing of the National Anthem.

Winchmore Hill.

I beg to report that all the postmen attached to this office, with two exceptions, met for the purpose of celebrating the Jubilee.

Refreshments in honour of the occasion were kindly provided by Miss Riley. The auspicious hour having arrived, three very hearty cheers were raised for Her Majesty the Queen.

HEMINGFORD ROAD.

On this occasion we invited the messengers, twelve in number, to spend the evening with our own family and a few friends.

At 8 o'clock they all met in the conservatory, where they received some light refreshment; after looking round, they adjourned to the drawing-room, where the Receiver gave an account of his experiences in connection with the Post-Office fifty-three years ago, during the coaching days. Then a paper was read by Mr. T. W. Reader on the Post-Office past and present, illustrated with views shown by Mr. C. E. Reader through the magic lantern. At ten minutes to ten we all assembled in the office to give three cheers for Her Majesty, which we all did heartily when the signal arrived. The messengers and clerks then proposed and gave three cheers for the officers of the Post-Office, Mr. Reader and friends.

They returned to the drawing-room where a memorial card which had been prepared was presented to each of the messengers, and an account given of the postal system in the early days of the Colony of New South Wales by the Rev. H. C. Dunning, late of that Colony, a friend of the Receiver's.

The evening was enlivened by music and singing in which they all took part, and a valuable collection of over 11,000 stamps and post-cards exhibited.

In the course of the evening a few well-chosen words of advice and encouragement were spoken to the boys in a homely way by the Rev. H. C. Dunning and Mr. and Mrs. Reader.

After supper they all dispersed after singing the National Anthem.

SOUTH EASTERN DISTRICT.

In this district at every branch office open, at the Head District Office, the Parcel Post Depots at London Bridge and Waterloo, and at all the sub-district offices at 10 P.M. on the 2nd July, three cheers for the Queen were given by the men loyally and heartily; and I am struck by the fact that at some offices where the men were off duty before 10 P.M., they waited until then, or returned at the moment, to join in the manifestation of loyalty to Her Majesty.

VIGO STREET.

I remembered Her Majesty with hearty good wishes at ten o'clock on the 2nd July, though alone at my office.

PROVINCIAL OFFICES.

ABERGAVENNY.

The ancient and ever loyal town of Abergavenny (or rather that portion of it presided over by the Postmistress) determined to be to the front, and accordingly at the appointed hour of 10 P.M. on July 2nd, 1890, the Postmistress and staff assembled in their office, and as the sonorous tones of the town clock striking the hour burst on the ears of the anxious and breathless listeners, forthwith there arose a three times three to our Sovereign Lady the Queen. The cheers having subsided, the flowing bowl was handed round, and Her Most Gracious Majesty's health drunk in hot coffee.

AMPTHILL.

The inhabitants of the town were considerably mystified on Wednesday morning, on noticing that the whole of the front of the Post-Office was artistically decorated with a profuse display of bunting, supplemented by a handsome crown in the centre of the building.

The mystery was soon solved by large posters in the office windows which announced that it was the Jubilee of the establishment of the Penny Post. The interior of the building was tastefully draped with streamers, Chinese lanterns, &c. The Ampthill brass band played a choice selection of music from 9 to 10 P.M. Shortly before ten o'clock the Postmaster with the clerks, and town and rural postmen, appeared at the office door, where a large crowd had assembled. On the arrival of the signal, three ringing cheers were given, after which the National Anthem was played by the band, the crowd taking up the strain in quite a hearty manner.

ANDOVER.

On July 2nd, 1890, at the invitation of their Postmaster, the staff of this office, to the number of thirty, assembled to express their loyalty to Her Most Gracious Majesty, and to commemorate the Jubilee of the Penny Post. In imitation of their colleagues at South Kensington, this little gathering took the form of an unostentatious conversazione, at which light refreshments were liberally provided by the Postmaster.

Punctually at ten o'clock three ringing cheers were given for Her Majesty.

The office, which was tastefully decorated with flowers by the female staff, presented a pleasing spectacle.

ASHBOURNE.

The Jubilee of the Penny Post was celebrated with great *éclat* at the Post-Office on Wednesday evening. The front of the office had been adorned by the Royal Standard, Union Jack, &c.

The fine band of the Ashbourne Volunteers gave a capital selection of music.

At 8.30 P.M. the town and rural postmen sat down to a splendid supper, which was tastefully set out in the sorting room of the office, which had been decorated for the occasion with flags, &c.

AYLESBURY.

On Wednesday evening, July 2nd, the employés connected with the Aylesbury Post-Office celebrated the Jubilee of the Uniform Penny Postage by supping together in the capacious sorting room and postmen's room, under the chairmanship of Mr. Edwin Payne, the Postmaster. The company numbered between thirty and forty. While the repast was in progress, a brief telegram (sent simultaneously to all the offices in the kingdom) was received from South Kensington, where a Jubilee conversazione was being celebrated, viz., "Cheers for the Queen." It is needless to say it was rapturously received, and a verse of the National Anthem sung.

BARLESTONE (HINCKLEY).

In compliance with the express wish of the Executive Committee, in connection with the Post-Office Jubilee Conversazione at South Kensington, the sub-Postmaster and his wife, in conjunction with the curate of the parish, the resident policeman in the village, and the rector's churchwarden, gave at the hour named, 10 P.M. yesterday, Wednesday, July 2nd, 1890, three hearty cheers for Her Most Gracious Majesty the Queen.

BARNET.

Shortly before 10 P.M. on July 2nd, 1890, the staff of this office (who had previously been invited) assembled to give three cheers for Her Majesty in commemoration of this event.

On a signal being received by telegraph from the Central Office at 10 P.M., the staff marched to the front of the office in the public street, and gave three cheers for Her Majesty Queen Victoria, led by the Postmaster. The same compliment was accorded to the Postmaster, led by a postman.

They at once returned to the office, and after partaking of some refreshment and letting off fireworks at the back, sang the National Anthem.

BATH.

Shortly before ten o'clock over a hundred of the force—postal and telegraph—indoor and outdoor, had assembled in the sorting office.

As ten o'clock was striking three hearty cheers for Her Majesty were enthusiastically given, followed by the singing of the National Anthem.

Those who were on duty then returned to their work, but the controlling officers and first-class clerks secured a few minutes' grace to adjourn to the Chief Clerk's room, when the decision was come to that a postal telegraph dinner within the Jubilee week would be a fitting ending of the celebration.

On the Saturday, therefore, about forty of the staff dined together, the Chief Clerk taking the chair, and the Superintendent of the Telegraph Department the vice-chair. After the usual loyal toasts, the healths of the Postmaster-General and Secretary were enthusiastically drunk, as well as those of the heads of the Bath Office, the company breaking up at midnight.

BEDALE.

In order to fitly celebrate the fiftieth anniversary of the institution of Uniform Penny Postage, a supper was held at the Royal Oak Hotel, which was attended by thirty clerks, assistants, sub-Postmasters, and rural postmen, with their friends. After ample justice had been done to the substantial repast provided the table was cleared, and the toast of "Her Majesty the Queen" was proposed by the chairman and drunk to with great enthusiasm by the company.

Punctually at ten o'clock the whole of the company proceeded to the Market Cross, where three very hearty cheers were raised for Her Majesty the Queen, and afterwards several verses of the National Anthem were sung with great heartiness.

It was a very gratifying feature of the celebration that the inhabitants of the quiet little market town turned out almost literally *en masse* to witness the very interesting ceremony.

BEDFORD.

From an early hour on Wednesday, July 2nd, 1890, the Bedford Post-Office was decorated with flags and streamers in honour of the Jubilee of the Penny Postage. There was a meeting at 9.45 P.M. in the postmen's room of the entire staff; the Postmaster was present and said a few words suitable to the occasion; at 9.57 P.M. the Volunteer band, which was stationed in front of the office, struck up the National Anthem, and exactly at 10 P.M. there went up three ringing cheers for Her Most Gracious Majesty from the clerks and postmen, who took up their places in the front windows of the building; the National Anthem was then sung accompanied by the band, and also by hundreds of people who had assembled in front of the office.

An adjournment was then made to the spacious postmen's room, where each person was supplied with a light refreshment.

Birmingham.

I am glad to be able to report that the cheering here last night was very enthusiastic, and that all the staff on duty (about 150) joined very heartily in it.

Blandford.

The Jubilee of the introduction of the Penny Post was celebrated on Wednesday, July 2nd. Mr. Flacke, the Blandford Postmaster, decorated the front of the Post-Office rather profusely, and a string of flags was also strung across the street; fairy lamps hung on the front windows of the office and house. These were lit up in the evening and presented a pretty appearance, coloured fires being lit also as the evening advanced. At ten o'clock three cheers were given within and without the Post-Office by the employés and spectators for the Queen.

Blackburn.

An enthusiastic meeting was attended by ninety-five officers out of a staff of 101, the remainder being absent from causes not their own.

The assembly took place in the sorting office at 9.30 P.M., the Postmaster presiding. An address to Her Most Gracious Majesty the Queen was submitted to the meeting and carried with acclamation. At 10 P.M. three lusty cheers were given for Her Majesty, followed by the singing of the National Anthem. At about the same time telegraphic messages were exchanged with the meeting at South Kensington.

Some facetious remarks were afterwards made by the Postmaster, who exhibited letters in his possession which had passed between Newcastle and Liverpool in 1836-1839, on which the charges were, for postage, 11*d*., delivery 1*d*., making 1*s*. in all.

A short entertainment by Postman Westwell brought a very happy meeting to a close at 10.30 P.M.

BOURNE.

Mr. J. T. Pearce, the Postmaster of the Bourne district, on Wednesday evening, July 2nd, generously utilized the occasion to entertain all officers engaged in the radius of the Bourne district to dinner at the Willoughby Hotel, South Street. At ten o'clock the signal was flashed from South Kensington. At that preconcerted signal, when the enormous gathering in London were sending forth their tremendous cheer, which was joined in simultaneously by all gatherings north, south, east, and west, those of Bourne gave three lusty cheers, which, if not equal in volume and intensity of sound to those of the larger assemblies, were not one jot behind them either in heartiness or loyalty.

This very pleasant and in every respect thoroughly enjoyable gathering was brought to a conclusion by the singing of the National Anthem.

BRADFORD (YORKS).

At 9 P.M. on July 2nd, 1890, the combined postal and telegraph staff assembled in front of the Post-Office in Forster Square.

The splendid band of twenty-four performers, composed entirely of postmen, were in attendance, and played a capital selection of national music until 9.45 P.M., when the whole force of telegraph messengers were formed into a hollow square. Their drill instructor acted as fugleman, and at 10 P.M., upon a given signal, "Three cheers for the Queen" were given with military precision, and "One cheer more for the Postmaster-General."

The cheers were most heartily responded to by the whole force assembled, and were joined in by the immense crowd of spectators, which numbered about 6,000.

Upon the conclusion of the last hurrah, the band struck up "God Save the Queen," which was sung by all present with great fervour.

A more enthusiastic gathering has never before assembled in Bradford.

BRENTFORD.

Three very hearty and unanimous cheers were given at Brentford for Her Majesty the Queen.

On July 11th, in order to fittingly celebrate the Jubilee, the Postmaster invited his staff to a supper.

BRISTOL.

Immediately after the signal from South Kensington was received, three hearty cheers for Her Majesty were given, the Postmaster leading; the Post-Office band then struck up the National Anthem, and the cheers for the Queen were at once taken up by a body of about 200 postmen, who had assembled in the Post-Office yard.

Some light refreshments were afterwards served out to the men and the staff officers.

BUCKINGHAM.

The Jubilee of Penny Postage was celebrated here by a supper in the White Hart Hotel, at which all the male clerks, postmen, messengers, and several of the sub-Postmasters were present, and presided over by the Mayor of Buckingham.

The ex-Mayor and several friends were present, making a total of forty-four.

BUDLEIGH SALTERTON (DEVON).

At Budleigh Salterton notices were issued by the local Post-Office officials, inviting the public to join in the expression of loyalty to Her Majesty on Wednesday evening. In response a large crowd, numbering several hundred, assembled at the Post-Office (which was very prettily decorated with Chinese lanterns, and had the Union Jack flying) at about ten minutes to ten o'clock. Mr. F. N. Parsons, representing the Post-Office, opened the proceedings with a few appropriate remarks, in the course of which he appealed to the generosity of the assembled crowd on behalf of the Rowland Hill Memorial and Benevolent Fund, saying they would at the close of the proceedings be asked to contribute to its support. The speaker was supported by Colonel Lee, who had kindly consented to take part, and who followed by remarking on the privileges accruing from the establishment of the cheap postage system. He then called for the first verse of the National Anthem, which was sung with great force. The hour of ten having now arrived, Colonel Lee led off the cheering, which was sustained most heartily. Then three cheers to the memory of Sir Rowland Hill were raised, after which the donations were taken, the amount gathered reaching a very fair sum.

BURNLEY.

Exactly at 10 P.M., three hearty cheers were given for Her Majesty the Queen in a most enthusiastic and loyal manner. After supper an entertainment was held consisting of music and recitations.

BURY ST. EDMUNDS.

At 10 P.M. the message "Cheer for the Queen" arrived, and three such hearty cheers were given, that in the still night they were heard over a considerable portion of the town. The staff having partaken of refreshments, one of the most novel and interesting meetings of the officers at Bury St. Edmunds was brought to a close by the singing of the National Anthem.

CARNARVON.

As soon as the office clock indicated the hour (10 P.M.), three ringing cheers were given for the Queen, after which the National Anthem was sung in fine style by the staff, the crowd joining in with vigour.

Squibs and crackers were let off amongst the crowd by several members of the staff, and Mr. Jones superintended the firing off of a number of sky-rockets.

CHARFIELD (GLOS.).

Over the office was a floral device erected by the sub-Postmaster, representing a shield bearing the words " Jubilee Penny Post" surmounted by the Royal Standard, braced on each side with Union Jack flags, &c., and illuminated with Japanese lanterns.

During the evening at the appointed time three hearty cheers were given for Her Majesty by all who were assembled.

DERBY.

Between 9.30 and 10 P.M., is always a specially busy time at the Derby Post-Office, on account of the preparation and dispatch of one of the principal night mails—that to Liverpool and the north-west. This duty having been punctually performed, there was a slight lull, of which the Postmaster took advantage to address a few remarks to his staff.

Just as he ceased speaking the clock struck ten, and the whole staff gave three ringing cheers for Her Majesty, and followed them up with " God Save the Queen." As the last notes of the Anthem were dying away, a vociferous echo burst from the upper stories. The Duchess of Edinburgh's signal " South Kensington Cheers!" had arrived in the instrument room, and was being flashed along all the wires to the neighbouring towns and villages. Then a bugle call was heard, and a crowd of messengers, mail drivers, and others outside the building joined in the rejoicing.

After this the telegraphists trooped down stairs into the postmen's room, and called upon the Postmaster for another speech. This was given; and, stimulated by the remark, that Her Majesty had not anywhere a more loyal and devoted set of servants than the officers of the Derby Post-Office, the men gave three more lusty cheers.

DEREHAM.

The most hearty and loyal feeling prevailed throughout, and the 2nd July, 1890, will long be remembered by the force here as a red-letter day in their experience.

Dymchurch (Folkestone).

I have enclosed you a drawing of my flagstaff as it was on the 2nd July, 1890, in honour of the Jubilee of the Penny Postage.

The flagstaff, as you see it (with the exception of the flags) is always standing, with the postman on it, in my garden. The top flag I made myself for the Jubilee, as you see it.

The small flags were lent to me by Her Majesty's coast-guard officer. They were hoisted at ten A.M., on the 2nd July, 1890, and taken down at six P.M. the same evening. The hoisting of the flags caused great commotion in this small village, the population of which is only 700.

Exeter.

On receipt of the pre-arranged signal from South Kensington, very hearty and sustained cheers were raised by the whole of the telegraph staff for Her Majesty the Queen, conjointly with the like manifestation by an immense crowd assembled outside the building, and with the cheers of the postal staff and the playing of the National Anthem by the Post-Office Band.

Falmouth.

Shortly before ten o'clock P.M., the younger members ascended to the roof where they repeatedly raised cheers for the Queen, the Postmaster-General, the Postal Service, &c., blowing, between the rounds of cheering, a postman's bugle.

The unwonted sounds caused some excitement in the neighbourhood, so that at ten o'clock P.M., when all the before-mentioned had assembled at the front windows of the top-floor of the Post-Office, a crowd had gathered in the street below.

The Chief Clerk having briefly addressed the crowd, explaining the reason of the jubilation, called for three cheers for the Queen, which were at once heartily and repeatedly given.

Fressingfield (Harleston).

The Postmaster and as many of the Staff as could be spared, spent a very enjoyable day at Great Yarmouth. On their arrival home a substantial supper was provided; at 9.55 the National Anthem was sung, and as the clock struck ten, three hearty cheers were given for Her Most Gracious Majesty, Queen Victoria, followed by three cheers for the Postmaster-General.

GAINSBOROUGH.

At one minute past ten came the signal, "Three cheers for the Queen," which was immediately responded to by every member of the Post Office Staff most heartily in front of the Post Office, several residents in the neighbourhood and others uniting in the cheers.

The whole of the employés in the Post Office—clerks, town postmen, rural postmen, and telegraph messengers, were afterwards treated to wine, sandwiches, queen cakes, &c., by Mr. W. Harrison, the Postmaster, and a most convivial evening was spent.

An impromptu song on the Penny Post Jubilee, in which the name of Sir Rowland Hill concluded each stanza, sung by Rural Postman Samuel Spray, was well received.

The following three flags were suspended from the Post Office buildings, viz., "Royal Standard," "Red, White and Blue," and "Union Jack." The Office and Postmaster's residence above also being illuminated.

GRANTHAM.

As shown in accompanying photo the Office was decorated with flags, banners, emblematic devices, flowers, plants, &c. A picture of Her Majesty the Queen, and Sir Rowland Hill will also be observed. The Office was beautifully illuminated with fairy lamps outside, and with Chinese lanterns, lamps, &c , inside, which was exceedingly pretty.

A platform was erected in the ancient market place where over 6,000 people had assembled to honour the Jubilee.

An open air concert under the patronage and in the presence of the Mayor, Aldermen and Councillors of the Corporation was given at eight P.M.

The great concourse was thoroughly representative of all classes of the people.

On receiving the signal, 10 P.M., a special wire rang a bell on the platform, which gave great delight to the assembled thousands, who, in accordance with previous orders uncovered their heads and gave three hearty and tremendous cheers for the Queen.

Over sixty of the officials and friends had supper at the Blue Lion Hotel.

GROSMONT (MON.)

I beg most respectfully to state that last night at ten o'clock, myself and also the Morton letter carrier went into the ruins of Grosmont Castle and sang the first verse of "God save the Queen," and gave three cheers for Her Most Gracious Majesty.

I have been spared to see a great change even in this small Office. In 1858, the date I settled in Grosmont, only a few letters were received and despatched; now it is a Savings Bank and Money-Order Office, and the increase in letters is no doubt tenfold. I think if any place has cause to be thankful for the penny postage it is this out-of-the-way village.

GUILDFORD.

On Wednesday a large flag was displayed from an upper window of the fine office in North-street, and in the evening coloured lights were burned on the parapets outside the office. In accordance with the general arrangements that there should be a simultaneous display of loyalty throughout the country, exactly at the stroke of ten on Wednesday night, hearty cheers were given for the Queen, led off by Mr. J. H. Wiles, the postmaster, and a verse of the National Anthem was sung by about forty employés, who had assembled in the telegraph room.

HASTINGS.

In connection with the Postal Jubilee held in the South Kensington Museum yesterday, a concert was held by a large number of the local postal and telegraph staff and their friends at the Clarence Hotel, when a very enjoyable evening was spent. At ten, the chairman called on all present for three cheers for the Queen, which was heartily responded to. Immediately afterwards a telegram was forwarded to London announcing that the Hastings and St. Leonards officers had carried out this loyal token of respect. The National Anthem was then sung upstanding. The remainder of the evening was spent in music and harmony till eleven, when the proceedings were brought to a close by another ringing cheer for the Queen.

HAVERFORDWEST.

The indoor and outdoor staff attached to this Office, numbering twenty-seven, met at the Office last night, and at ten o'clock precisely, gave three cheers for the Queen, followed by three cheers for the Postmaster-General.

At 10.30 a very pleasant meeting was ended by singing "God save the Queen."

Flags were flying from every window in the building and a line of flags across the street.

HAVERHILL.

Mr. E. W. Griggs, Postmaster, gave his Staff a dinner at the Bell Hotel. The Haverhill brass band was in attendance. At a few minutes to ten P.M., the party adjourned to the Post Office to await the signal from South Kensington. On receiving it three hearty cheers were given for Her Majesty Queen Victoria.

HEREFORD.

At a few minutes before ten o'clock, the members of the Press, Mr. Alderman Maund, J.P., and Mr. A. C. Edwards, arrived at the Post Office, and were courteously welcomed by the Postmaster, who invited them to his private room. A moment later the officials of the office, the clerks—both ladies and gentlemen —the postmen and others connected with the department, were also invited thither, and when the majority of the Staff had assembled the Postmaster addressed them.

The company then adjourned to the front of the Office, and ranging themselves upon the steps, they gave cheers for the Queen, after which they sang three verses of the National

Anthem, led by Mr. W. James, bandmaster of the 4th Batt. K. S. L. I., who played the hymn upon his silver cornet. Mr. Jordan then called for cheers for the Postmaster, which were heartily given, and at the suggestion of Mr. F. Cope a round of cheers was given for the Postmaster-General.

Hitchin.

On July 2nd, the Postmaster of Hitchin, invited the clerks and other attendants connected with the Office, and a few friends to a friendly meeting in connection with the conversazione then being held at South Kensington in commemoration of the Penny Postal Jubilee, and at ten o'clock, on signal given by the Duchess of Edinburgh, all joined in giving three lusty and hearty cheers for the Queen, afterwards spending a very agreeable evening.

Huddersfield.

The whole of the staff both postal and telegraphic with but few exceptions, assembled in the sorting office at a few minutes to ten P.M., and promptly at ten their most hearty and vociferous cheers were given for Her Majesty, after which the National Anthem was as heartily sung.

I don't know that I was ever present at a more enthusiastic meeting of Post Office officials.

Hull.

A very large and enthusiastic gathering of the Staff of the Hull Post Office took place last night in the circulation Office.

Three cheers were most heartily given for Her Majesty the Queen, followed by the singing of the National Anthem.

Ideford (Newton Abbot).

In memory of the "Rowland Hill Benevolent Fund," we, at the hour of ten gave three hearty cheers for Her Majesty the Queen and Royal Family, while fireworks of our own preparation were let off. Several spectators watched the scene.

This being a small village most of the inhabitants retire to their slumbers early.

JERSEY.

On Wednesday evening at 8.30 almost the whole of the staff of the Jersey Post Office and postal telegraph office on the invitation of Mr. E. Blakeney, the Postmaster, assembled in the postmen's room. Communication was established from the postmen's room to the telegraphic department, and precisely at 10.3, Mr. Blakeney, on the signal from South Kensington, given by the Duchess of Edinburgh, called for three cheers for Her Majesty. These were given with every sign of genuine enthusiasm, "God save the Queen" being then sung by all present, accompanied by the newly-organised Post Office Band under the conductorship of Mr. J. Le C. Adams.

An impromptu concert followed.

KETTERING.

In honour of the Jubilee of the institution of the Penny Post there was a display of flags from the windows of this office, and a supper was given to the Staff by the Postmaster (Mr. Woolston).

On the arrival of the signal from South Kensington, the Postmaster called for three cheers for Her Majesty which were heartily responded to.

KIDDERMINSTER.

At this office an appeal was made to the public for flowers and evergreens in order that the statue erected to Sir Rowland Hill outside the Post-Office might be decorated as well as the office itself, and so well was this responded to that the clerks and postmen were enabled to festoon and decorate the Post-Office in a very beautiful manner with roses and flowers of every description. The doors, windows and public office presented a very charming appearance, the statue had a garland of lovely roses over Sir Rowland's shoulders and the base of column was decorated in same manner.

All the postmen wore bouquets when on their deliveries.

At ten P.M. upon receipt of wire from South Kensington all the Staff gave three cheers for the Queen and a congratulatory message was sent to the Postmaster-General from the Mayor of Kidderminster.

Following this the whole of the Staff sat down to a supper, the Postmaster occupying the chair and the chief clerk the vice. The usual loyal toasts were given as also the Postmaster-General, Secretary and permanent Staff, the evening concluding with usual harmony.

LEEDS.

Prompt at ten P.M. the telegram arrived from the Kensington Museum conversazione requesting that three cheers be given for Her Majesty the Queen, in connection with the great and memorable event then being celebrated in London.

The very pleasurable command was most loyally obeyed here by the whole Staff on duty; and the postmen's new band played "God save the Queen" in a splendid manner.

LEOMINSTER.

On Wednesday the 2nd July the Penny Post Jubilee was celebrated by the Leominster Post-Office officials; the exterior of the office being covered with floral decorations carried out by the employés and the Postmaster. The Post-Office is a timber built house erected in the year 1600.

By the kind permission of Captain Gunnell the band of the rifle volunteers assembled at eight o'clock in front of the office, led by Bandmaster J. H. Davis (himself one of the rural postmen) and played a selection of music till after nine o'clock. They then entered the office with the postmen and were regaled by the Postmaster and his wife with a plentiful supply of sandwiches and plum cake, beer and lemonade.

A few minutes before ten they all returned to the street and at the signal given by H.R.H. the Duchess of Edinburgh gave three hearty cheers for Her Majesty the Queen, the band concluding with the National Anthem, which was heartily sung by the whole of the officials.

It is pleasing to record that the whole of the town and rural postmen, without exception, assembled at the office and joined most heartily in the proceedings.

LIVERPOOL.

Immediately the signal reached the instrument room, the telegraphists assembled, cheered lustily and heartily. At ten P.M. the men in the Parcel Post Office stopped work and on receipt of the signal gave three ringing cheers, with "three cheers more."

The Liverpool and Manchester Parcel Mail coach due to leave this office at ten P.M. waited for a minute or two until the cheering of the officers inside the building was heard, when the guard blew his horn vigorously in honour of the occasion and the coach went on its journey.

LUDLOW.

Wednesday, July 2nd, being the day appointed to celebrate the Jubilee of Uniform Penny Postage, the Postmaster of Ludlow, Mr. John Valentine (who is also the Mayor of Ludlow for this year), gave special invitation to every one of the officials to attend at the Post-Office at 9.30 P.M. that day.

Early in the morning the British Ensign and Union Jack flags were hoisted, and the Crown and V.R. beautifully painted on canvas. The windows of the Post-Office were artistically decorated with designs in postage stamps representing—

1840
V. Jubilee R.
1890

At nine P.M. the windows in the post office building were illuminated with candles to every pane, and the Post-Office window tastefully lighted up with fairy lights of all colours.

At 9.30 P.M. the Post-Office officials assembled in the Post-Office in compliance with the invitation they had received; and at ten P.M., when a telegram was received announcing that at that moment, "Three cheers were being given for the Queen," by the assembly at the conversazione in London, the officials gave three very hearty cheers for the Queen in echo and in support of the movement in London.

MALTON.

On Wednesday the Malton Post-Office was decorated with flags, and the men who could be spared from duty were allowed a holiday. Many Post-Offices were in direct telegraphic communication with the soirée at South Kensington and at ten o'clock P.M. a message came to Malton by way of York, calling for three cheers for the Queen, which message was loyally responded to, and the National Anthem heartily joined in.

MANCHESTER.

The officers here, at ten o'clock last night, responded to the suggestion given in an enthusiastic manner,

At ten P.M. three hearty cheers were given for the Queen, and a verse of the National Anthem was sung.

MOLD.

Having partaken of supper, provided by myself, we adjourned to the public office at 9.58 P.M. to await the signal from South Kensington. This being given, we gave three lusty cheers for the Queen, followed by the singing of the National Anthem.

The evening was enlivened by the singing of songs, &c., and was brought to a very pleasant close at 11.30 by the singing of the National Anthem, followed by three hearty cheers for Her Majesty the Queen.

NELSON.

In celebration of the Jubilee of the Uniform Penny Postage, the officials of the Nelson Post-Office were entertained to supper at the Railway Inn, by Mr. Whittam, the Postmaster. About thirty sat down to the excellent supper provided by Mrs. Riley. The company included the clerks, postmen, messengers, and sub-postmasters in the town, as well as Mr. Chadwick, the station-master, and representatives of the press. The after proceedings, which were of a convivial nature, were presided over by Mr. J. Hodgson, sub-postmaster of Leeds Road, who, after the usual loyal toasts, called upon Mr. Whittam to make a few remarks.

NEWCASTLE-ON-TYNE.

It is my pleasing duty to report that a large number of the Staff assembled in this Office last evening to join in the spontaneous token of dutiful respect of giving three cheers for Her Most Gracious Majesty the Queen. As the cathedral clock in this city chimed the advent of the hour of ten, three right hearty cheers for the Queen were given, and ere the volume of sound had died away the "Newcastle-on-Tyne Post-Office Hand-bell Ringers"—all postmen—rang out some merry peals, concluding with the National Anthem.

NEWMARKET.

This evening the officers performing special duty at Newmarket, together with the Post-Office officials, right royally responded to the invitation of Mr. T. Mason, the superintendent, and assembled in the instrument-room for the purpose of giving effect to the proposals contained in the official circular of the 24th June, 1890.

After a few appropriate words from Mr. Mason, at 9.57 all present joined in singing the National Anthem, and at ten P.M., prompt, three deafening cheers were given for Her Majesty the Queen.

During this interesting ceremony the Newmarket Drum and Fife Band played the National Anthem and other excellent music outside the Post-Office.

OXFORD.

All those present filed outside the office at two minutes to ten, and immediately upon receipt of the signal from London most hearty cheers were given, not only for Her Majesty, but also for the heads of the department, the Head-Postmaster of Oxford, and the service in general.

The National Anthem was then sung.

Although it was impossible, owing to the exigences of the service, to celebrate the occasion with any special festivities, yet, I am happy to say, the officers here were unanimous in doing all they could to show their dutiful respect.

RIPON.

Having a great wish to commemmorate the day, I invited all the Staff to supper at a temperance hotel, which I have every reason to believe was much appreciated.

At ten precisely they all assembled outside the Post-Office and gave three hearty cheers for the Queen, three for the Prince of Wales and all the Royal Family, and three as lusty for the Postmaster-General.

ROCHDALE.

In recognition of the Jubilee banners were displayed at the Post-Office, and about ten at night the members of the Staff of the office assembled and gave three cheers for the Queen, while their band played the National Anthem. Light refreshments, provided by the Postmaster, were afterwards partaken of; and a number of letters which went through the post before the introduction of the Penny Post, bearing different charges, and also some specimens of the earliest Rochdale postmarks, the property of Mr. R. Warrall, one of the Post-Office clerks, were exhibited during the evening. The office had on hand a number of Jubilee envelopes, and these were sold very quickly on Wednesday.

It may be mentioned that while prior to the introduction of the penny postage, fifty years ago, the town of Rochdale was served by only one postman, at the present time thirty-three are employed, and while there were then no clerks engaged here, there are now twenty-two.

SALTBURN-BY-THE-SEA.

By invitation of the Postmaster the whole of the staff assembled in Mr. Darley's drawing-room to celebrate the Jubilee of the Uniform Penny Postal System and the opening of the new Post-Office at Saltburn. After partaking of an excellent supper, led by the president, all united in lusty cheers in honour of Her Majesty. The evening was afterwards spent in an agreeable way, enlivened at intervals by vocal and instrumental music.

Sherborne.

The front of the Post-Office was decorated with flags of a national and patriotic character.

At nine P.M. the Staff, to the number of thirty, met in the sorting-room, where, through the kindness of Mrs. Stabler, the wife of the Postmaster, refreshments were partaken of.

At 9.55 P.M. the health of Her Majesty the Queen was proposed by Mr. G. P. Ellaway, the senior employé connected with the office, and on receipt of a telegram from South Kensington, at ten P.M., ringing cheers were given for Her Majesty which were again and again renewed.

Stockton-on-Tees.

I beg to report that the response to the invitation of your Committee for the Staff of this office to assemble and give three cheers for Her Majesty the Queen, upon the occasion of the celebration of the Post-Office Jubilee at South Kensington Museum was most loyally and enthusiastically met by the staff of the office.

The Postmaster addressed the men as to the object of the occasion, and the staff then retired and subsequently held a convivial meeting to celebrate the event.

Stoke Prior (Leominster).

We celebrated the Jubilee of the Penny Post in this small village by decorating our office very early on Wednesday morning with flowers and evergreens, and with suitable mottoes, one of which was a quotation from Edward Capern, the Postman Poet.

> "Oh, a happy lad is the Rural Post,
> And a right loyal servant I ween;
> For let a proud foe but threaten a blow,
> He shouteth, 'Hurrah for the Queen.'"

Without the stimulus of even the threats of a proud foe, or the stimulants so often needed by the British subject before he can express his loyal feelings, several of the inhabitants came at ten o'clock, and helped us to give three very hearty cheers for the Queen.

Stratford-on-Avon.

The whole staff assembled outside the office at ten P.M., and on receipt of the signal from South Kensington three ringing cheers were given for " Our Beloved Queen." The men then adjourned to an hostelry, opposite the place of Shakespeare's birth, and a social hour was spent.

A gentleman of the neighbourhood generously presented the entire Staff with a Jubilee envelope, which was much appreciated; a few songs were sung, and the proceedings terminated with the National Anthem, and " Auld Lang Syne."

The Union Jack was hoisted on the office in honour of the event.

Sudbury (Derby).

The fact of this being a small office prevented any great demonstration, but the invitation from the executive committee to unite with our brother and sister officers in giving three cheers for our Gracious Sovereign was reponded to most cordially. With the exception of one rural postman, who represented us at the conversazione, we all assembled outside the Post-Office at ten P.M. Greenwich time. We gave for her Gracious Majesty, our beloved Queen, not only three, but three times three cheers.

Swansea.

Early on the morning of Jubilee Day the Swansea Post-Office, beautiful in its Tudor architecture, was further decorated by streamers of gay bunting led across the thoroughfares from its windows, while the Royal Standard with worked letters, " G. P. O.," waved from the flagstaff on its lofty tower. Public attention was speedily aroused and furthered by a paragraph in the local daily paper.

At nine P.M. the public had assembled in thousands, and traffic in three thoroughfares was completely blocked. The Post-Office full military band under Bandmaster Courtney (late Sussex Regiment) playing appropriate selections of music to the great gratification of all assembled, while the whole building was illuminated by variegated coloured lights, the tower having four mammoth torches ablaze at its corners. A few minutes before ten P.M. the Chief Clerk, in a stentorian voice briefly explained the circumstances of the occasion, and conveying the Postmaster's invitation to the surging mass to join with him and his Staff in three hearty cheers for their beloved Queen when he received his signal by wire. Swansea's large time-gun boomed its message, three mighty cheers rent the air, while a Royal salute of twenty-one detonators and twenty-one signal rockets were fired from the office tower at intervals of thirty seconds; the band immediately playing the National Anthem.

The outside programme being ended, the joint Staffs (postal and telegraph) received refreshments in the retiring rooms of the office, and the invitation of the executive at South Kensington to join them in the Jubilee celebration was complied with in a most hearty and enthusiastic manner.

TENTERDEN (ASHFORD).

Such a day as the Jubilee of the Penny Postage, an institution that is the backbone of England's business success, is too important to be allowed to pass over without recognition. Tenterden, although a small place, came nobly to the fore on this day. Early in the morning a brilliant display of flags might have been seen proudly waving to and fro over the balcony in front of the Post-Office. This at first gave the inhabitants quite a shock, but on enquiries they were greatly disgusted at their own lack of knowledge respecting the great day, and at the same time eminently pleased at the loyal feeling displayed in their midst. The red notice referring to the Jubilee envelopes was conspicuously displayed outside the office, causing little knots of people to assemble to talk over and ventilate their opinions regarding the Rowland Hill Benevolent Fund. About twenty envelopes were sold and a general good feeling prevailed here all day.

As the office closes at 8.30 P.M. we made up a pleasant little party indoors and passed the festive cup to the strains of flute, violin, and piano, winding up the auspicious day by singing heartily, "God Save the Queen."

TEIGNMOUTH.

On Wednesday evening I entertained my indoor and outdoor Staff with refreshments previous to taking them out on the flat roof of the Post-Office. I explained to them the object of their being called together, and gave them a short history of the growth of the Post-Office. I then gave the health of the Queen, which, I need scarcely say, was received with much enthusiasm.

We then went out on the roof of the office, and each man was given a hand-coloured fire, and took up his appointed position around the building. The band of the 3rd V.B.D. Artillery was below, and was instructed to play the National Anthem immediately after I had called for three cheers for her Majesty the Queen.

Seeing an immense concourse of people around the band, I, at three minutes to ten o'clock called for silence, and in a few words explained the object of our meeting together, and begged the assembly to join with the Staff in giving three cheers for her Majesty at ten o'clock.

TIVERTON.

A meeting of Post-Office employés was held in the Tiverton Office, commencing at a quarter to ten. Mr. W. H. Snell, Postmaster, invited several gentlemen in the town to be present to give three hearty cheers for the Queen, among those who responded to the invitation being the Mayor (Mr. J. F. Ellerton).

Early in the evening the Town Band, under Mr. Barker, took up a position in front of the Post-Office and played a selection of music. By a quarter to ten a large crowd had assembled in Bampton Street, evidencing the interest of the public in the ceremony within.

Coffee and cake were distributed among the guests in the Post-Office. In general conversation it transpired that five of those present could remember the introduction of the Penny Post. Precisely at ten o'clock a message came by telegraph that those present at the conversazione in London were cheering the Queen; and at the call of Mr. Snell three hearty cheers were

CELEBRATIONS OF THE JUBILEE IN THE PROVINCES. 271

given amid waving of hats for her Majesty. The crowd outside took up the cheers, and the band started "God save the Queen," in which those in the Post-Office joined. Cheers were also given for the Rowland Hill Benevolent Fund, and for Mr. and Mrs. Snell.

Mr. Snell, mounting a Parcel Post basket, said that was the first time he ever remembered a meeting within the walls of a Post Office; he was old enough to remember when elevenpence had to be paid for a letter from London, and, he thought, when an old woman in pattens used to deliver all the letters in the town, at any rate, he could remember when Gould's father delivered all the letters, and filled up his time as a shoemaker.

The Mayor, who was received with loud cheers, began, "My Friends." When he could be again heard he exclaimed, "The man who does not feel the postman is his friend is not worthy the name of an Englishman." Proceeding he said one of the greatest commercial epochs in the history of the country was the introduction of the Penny Postage.

Mr. S. Osmond (postman) sang "God bless the Queen of England," the National Anthem was sung, and the gathering came to an end shortly after eleven o'clock.

TORQUAY.

The Postmaster has pleasure in reporting that the staff connected with this Office responded to the invitation to take part in the Post-Office Jubilee celebration. This was the more gratifying in view of the very early duty which some of the men had to take part in on the following day. The Post-Office band assembled on the occasion and played a selection of music, concluding with the National Anthem, after which, on a signal received by wire from South Kensington, three cheers for Her Majesty the Queen were given most heartily both by the Staff inside and outside the Head Office in Torwood Street.

TRURO.

The officers came on duty at an early hour before their duties commenced and decked the building with flags which they had been busy in obtaining and preparing the previous day. On the top of the office the Royal Standard was displayed, and in front a flag with the words "Jubilee of 1*d*. Postage," so that all the good citizens of Truro might know the reason for the gay appearance of the building.

At 9.45 P.M. all the officers assembled in the Postmaster's room, when he briefly explained the reason for the gathering, and precisely at ten o'clock the signal for cheering was received, when three ringing cheers, with one cheer more, were given for Her Most Gracious Majesty in a way that only loyal Cornishmen can give, and the National Anthem was sung. After this, at the invitation of the Postmaster, all repaired to another room and sat down to some refreshments, and a very pleasant time of about an hour and a half was spent in conversation, songs, &c.

WAKEFIELD.

The officials and employés mustered to the number of over fifty, and Mr. Pye (the Postmaster) thanked them for coming so readily and in such numbers, and asked them to join in wishing that Her Most Gracious Majesty might long live to reign over us, and to show this by three times three. The Post-Office band led the company in the singing of the National Anthem, and the cheers were given as only Yorkshire voices can give them.

The oldest man in this part of the service, John Crossley, caused much merriment by his "speech." Mr. Crossley joined the service in 1831. The Postmaster then read a short account showing the wonderful development of the Post-Office work under the system of uniform postage.

Mr. Milnes having proposed a vote of thanks to the Postmaster, this most interesting and enthusiastic gathering separated, the presence of the lady telegraphists having added a certain charm to the pleasing scene.

WARRINGTON.

On the night of July the 2nd all the officers connected with this office who were off duty—about seventy—assembled in the rooms in the basement, and, without interference with public business, passed a pleasant hour together, songs were sung, and light refreshment was provided without cost to the staff.

At 9.55 P.M. official work was, for a few minutes, suspended; the officers on duty joined the others, and all awaited the telegraphic signal from South Kensington at ten o'clock, when enthusiastic cheers were given for the Queen, and gratitude was expressed for the Jubilee holiday.

WEST HARTLEPOOL.

That portion of the office used by the public was tastefully decorated with bunting during the day of celebration, and the sorting-room was in the evening set apart for refreshments. Shortly before 10 P.M. over two-thirds of the staff assembled in the instrument room to wait for the promised signal from South Kensington, and after a few words explanatory of the occasion from the Chief Clerk (Mr. T. W. Lucas) the time gun clock announced the moment for cheering, and three loud expressions of loyalty were given for Her Majesty the Queen.

WOOLWICH.

At a few minutes to ten the officials, led by the Postmaster (Mr. Lockwood), his daughters, and some friends sang the National Anthem, and then gave three hearty and ringing cheers for the Queen.

Every window of the Post-Office building and along the parapet was illuminated with coloured fire by the staff.

A crowd in the street having by this time assembled cheered lustily.

YORK AND NEWCASTLE TRAVELLING POST-OFFICE.

All the officers assembled at the mail carriage at Newcastle-on-Tyne station, and at 10 P.M. three hearty cheers were accorded to Her Gracious Majesty the Queen. The National Anthem was also sung.

SCOTLAND

Aberdeen.

I beg to inform you that this night a unanimous meeting of the combined staffs, postal and telegraph, of both out and indoor, was held here.

Shortly before ten o'clock Mr. Mitchell, Postmaster, addressing the large company said: "A great number of our brothers and sisters are at present celebrating the Jubilee at Kensington. We would all likely have been there had it not been for the great distance, but we can all at least join with them in our loyalty to our beloved Queen, and accordingly when the signal arrives from Kensington we will all join in three cheers."

He had scarcely finished speaking when the signal from London was received. The Postmaster thereupon called for three cheers for the Queen, which were enthusiastically given, the company also joining in singing "God Save the Queen."

Cheers were afterwards given for Mr. Raikes, the Postmaster-General.

Ayr.

In harmony with a general movement throughout the country, the Post-Office officials at Ayr celebrated the Jubilee of the Penny Post by a social gathering in the King's Arms Hotel last night. They were joined by officials from Dalmellington, Monkton, Prestwick, and elsewhere, and by a few specially invited friends, and, including female relatives, the company altogether would number nearly 100. Mr. Ramsay, the Postmaster, occupied the chair, and Dr. Watt and Mr. R. W Stevenson officiated as croupiers.

During the day flags were floating on the roof and from the windows of the Ayr Post-Office in honour of the occasion.

Cupar (Fife).

In Cupar the officials of the Post-Office, to the number of twenty, assembled in the building to do honour to the event. Mr. Lang, Postmaster, presided. It had been arranged at headquarters that a telegram should be sent at ten o'clock to all the offices in the kingdom, at which time the officials were to give three cheers for Her Majesty. Accordingly, punctually at ten o'clock, Mr. Lang, having in a few sentences sketched the object of the meeting, proposed " The Queen." The toast was cordially drunk, and three hearty cheers were given for Her Majesty. Led by Mr. Brown, the company then sang a verse of " God Save the Queen," and at the call of Mr. Lang, the cheers were renewed. Mr. Ogilvie proposed the " Postal Service," and commented in flattering terms on the efficiency and courtesy displayed by the staff of Cupar Post-Office. Mr. Lang, in acknowledging the toast, said it was appropriate that that gathering should have met within the walls of the Post-Office, where the daily duty of those assembled was performed. " The Press " was proposed by Mr. Bruce and replied to by Mr. Ogilvie; and the " Ladies of the Postal Service " by Mr. Brown, and acknowledged by Mr. Nelson. A pleasant hour or two was afterwards spent in social intercourse.

DUNFERMLINE.

Mr. Macmaster, the Postmaster, was in London at the conversazione but under the direction of Mr. D. Scott, the head clerk, the officials made a full muster, and on the London signal arriving, a hearty cheer was given. The National Anthem was sung with great enthusiasm, and the following telegram was despatched: —" Postmaster-General, Conversazione, London. Dunfermline officials assembled, join in cheer; hip! hip! hurrah!" A beautiful display of coloured lights was made in the windows of the Post-Office facing High Street and Guildhall Street, and after this came a procession through the principal streets of the burgh. Parcel-post barrows and some articles of Post-Office furniture were utilized in the procession, and the ranks of the officials were strengthened by a considerable turn out of ordinary citizens. On returning to the Post-Office the officials held what was christened a " hastily-arranged conversazione." Mr. Hunter proposed " The Health of Her Majesty "; Mr. Melville " The Postmaster-General "; and Mr. Milne " The Postmaster of the

City of Dunfermline." During the evening songs were rendered by Messrs. Milne, Hutchison, Scott, Black, and others. In addition to the Postmaster, two of the Dunfermline postmen attended the London gathering.

Dundee.

The officials connected with Dundee Post-Office were not behind in celebrating the Jubilee of the Penny Postage. Shortly before ten o'clock nearly all the employés in the post office and telegraph departments assembled in the telegraph messengers' room. The apartment was uncomfortably crowded. The gathering was presided over by Mr. Geo. H. Gibb, Postmaster, who, after addressing them, announced that he was to send the following telegram to F. E. Baines, Esq., C.B., South Kensington, London:—

> " Her servants pray—God save the Queen,
>   With one united heart,
> From banks of Tay and Forth and Clyde,
>   Spey, Ness, Dee, Ayr, and Cart.
> Three cheers from Postmaster and Staff at Dundee."

(Loud and continued cheering.) The first stanza of the National Anthem was then sung, after which Mr. Gibb stated that he had received the following telegram (time, 10.1 P.M.) from Mr. Baines, South Kensington—"Three cheers for the Queen." (Loud and continued cheering.) The assembly afterwards gave three cheers for Mr. Gibb, and "three times three" were given for Mrs. Gibb.

Edinburgh.

Between two and three hundred members of the staff of the Edinburgh Post-Office and its city branches took part in the celebration of the Jubilee of the Penny Post last night. A few minutes before ten o'clock about forty of the lady telegraphists of the service and eighty-four boy messengers, along with a number of the departmental clerks and officials, assembled in the telegraph instrument room at the General Post-Office.

The chief officials, the Surveyor-General for Scotland (Mr.

A. M. Cunynghame), Mr. Marrable, Mr. Halliburton, Mr. Hyde, and Mr. Gray were present at the South Kensington ceremony Mr. Braid expressed his pleasure at seeing the company gathered around. He explained the absence of the chief officials, and he said he was sure the company all wished success to the proceedings in which they were taking part, &c., &c.

As Mr. Braid finished his speech the clock pointed to the hour of ten, and the test clerk blowing his whistle, three loud and hearty cheers were given by all assembled. The first verse of "God Save the Queen" was then sung, and before it was finished the message had been received at two minutes past ten :— "Three cheers for the Queen." The reply was sent :—" F. E. Baines, South Kensington Museum. Edinburgh staff assembled, cheers for the Queen and sings the National Anthem, 10.5 P.M.— BRAID." The message and reply having been announced, the members of the staff who were not on duty in the instrument room, dispersed with renewed cheers. The signal was given to the sorting department (where fifty-three persons were on duty) as soon as it had been received in the instrument room, and the same form of jubilation having been indulged in, a message and reply identical with those mentioned were received and sent away.

GATEHOUSE (KIRKCUDBRIGHTSHIRE).

The Jubilee was held here with all the honours befitting the occasion. The Postmaster, who is senior bailie of the burgh, obtained permission from the Provost to hoist the Royal Standard on the clock tower and ring the bell. All the officials met at the office and were suitably regaled by the Postmaster.

GLASGOW.

I enclose various reports as to the celebration of the Postal Jubilee on the 2nd inst. at this office. They are most satisfactory, and the whole spirit displayed by the force under my control was excellent. It was wholly spontaneous.

The Post-Office band, forty in number, first got together and suggested a short musical programme, which was carried out; and I think no further, or better, testimony is needed than the fact that over 350 sorting-clerks and postmen came down in their own time, and at a late hour, to do honour to the occasion. There were about seventy men in the telegraph room, and there, also, the proceedings were most hearty and the utmost good feeling displayed.

INVERGORDON (ROSS-SHIRE).

Circumstances unfortunately preventing the attendance of the Sub-Postmaster at the South Kensington Jubilee Conversazione, he, in accordance with the proposal of the Executive Committee, along with his assistants, Colin Macleod and Jessie Macgregor, also Duncan Munro, town postman, and Peter Munro, rural postman, assembled in the Post-Office here at 9.55 P.M. on the 2nd July, 1890, and at the hour of ten (Greenwich time) gave three hearty cheers for Her Gracious Majesty the Queen.

Thereafter the Sub-Postmaster entertained a few friends, who, on the proposal of the chief magistrate of the town, drank the health of the Queen with Highland honours, and on the proposal of the Sub-Postmaster heartily responded to the toast "The Postal Authorities," coupled with the name of Mr. Baines, Chairman of the Jubilee Executive Committee.

LOCHMADDY.

The staff met on the night of the 2nd July to drink to the Queen. This was done at 10 P.M., and a telegram was then despatched to South Kensington to show that the cheers there were taken up as heartily here in the outer Hebrides amongst "the dim shielings on the misty islands."

The toast "Slainte Banright" was received with Highland honours, and the Postmaster-General's health was also pledged.

PERTH.

In connection with the celebration of the Penny Postage Jubilee in the fair city, the officials of the Post-Office, who were obliged to be on duty, were mustered together at ten o'clock, and at the call of Mr. Taylor, the Postmaster, gave evidence of their loyalty, and appreciation of her kind interest in their concerns, by giving three hearty cheers for the Queen.

A number of the staff also celebrated the event by having supper in the King's Arms Hotel. Mr. Farquhar, Chief Clerk, presided over a company of about thirty gentlemen. Supper was commenced shortly after 9.30 P.M., in course of which, however, materialism had to give place to loyalty. At a minute to ten o'clock operations were suspended; a verse of the National Anthem was sung with great heartiness; and precisely at ten o'clock the company, as befitting obedient servants and loyal subjects, united in giving three hearty ringing cheers for Her Majesty the Queen. A telegram from the South Kensington Jubilee Conversazione was also read by the chairman, and received with applause. In proposing the toast of the evening —"The Penny Post"—the chairman gave a most interesting account of the advantages its establishment had conferred, upon the country. Other toasts followed, and an excellent musical and literary programme tended greatly to the enjoyment of a most harmonious meeting, which was fittingly concluded by the company joining in singing, "Auld Lang Syne."

STRANRAER.

A goodly number of the employés of the department assembled at the Post-Office here to unite in cheering for the Queen.

Before separating the company were entertained with light refreshments.

IRELAND.

BELFAST.

I beg to report the message from South Kensington was received in Belfast at 10.2 P.M., and was telegraphed almost simultaneously to Armagh, Newry, and Dundalk.

The following reply was immediately returned :—"South Kensington. Belfast, Armagh, Newry, and Dundalk also cheer."

And while the message was being sent there was hearty cheering by the staff in attendance, numbering over 100 persons, including myself, the telegraph superintendent, two assistant superintendents, and the officer in charge of the sorting office.

The sorting staff and postmen assembled in the instrument room, and by a signal sent to the delivery room, the telegraph messengers also joined in the cheering.

The whole proceedings were very unanimous.

Collinstown (Co. Westmeath).

I beg leave to inform you that I successfully performed the pleasing duty of cheering Her Most Gracious Majesty the Queen at 10 P.M. this Jubilee night, though entirely unaided, as my wife was unable to remain up later than 8.30 P.M.

Dungarvan.

I have pleasure to report that the Post-Office Jubilee was celebrated at this office by a supper given by me to all persons connected with this Post-Office.

At 9 30 P.M. supper was laid in a room which had been previously decorated with flowers, fairy lamps, &c., by my children. At the hour mentioned all sat down to supper, and at 10 P.M. (Greenwich time) I proposed the toast of the Queen, which was received with three hearty cheers.

In as few words as possible I gave a short history of the progress of the Post-Office. I then said a few words to all as to their faithful and loyal discharge of their duties, and promising my friendship to all such. This was followed by speeches by some of the men, and by music and songs by my children.

Letterfrack (Galway).

Myself and sister being in charge of this Post-Office in the far west of Ireland, she as assistant, myself as sub-Postmistress, felt very great pleasure in assembling in the office at 10 P.M., and with our old postman in uniting in giving three cheers in right hearty old style for our beloved Queen, and in wishing health, long life, and prosperity to Her Majesty.

Renvyle (Co. Galway).

I beg to inform the Executive Committee through you, their Chairman, that, being in charge alone of this sub-Post-Office—the most remote in this county—I felt very great pleasure at ten o'clock in uniting my voice in spirit with the multitude assembled at the Museum in giving three hearty cheers for the Queen, and wishing Her Most Gracious Majesty a long and prosperous reign.

Roslea (Clones).

The Jubilee of the Penny Post was celebrated here with great illuminations. The Post-Office was lit up from 9.30 to 10.30 p.m., also the street lamp opposite the door; and a few of the spectators joined with the officials in giving three hearty cheers for Her Most Gracious Majesty.

Tulla (Limerick).

At 8.15 p.m. the employés connected with the above office sat down to tea and cake specially prepared by my wife and daughters for the occasion.

The room, which looks into the office, had been previously decorated with some artistic designs, the principal one being a crown composed of beautiful and select flowers, red, white, and blue; at each side being placed the rose, shamrock, and thistle entwined, all being surmounted with an arch bearing the words "God Save the Queen." Singing, with piano accompaniment, was kept up until 9.45 p.m. Precisely at ten o'clock (Greenwich time) I gave the word "Three cheers for the Queen." The order was heartily responded to with three ringing cheers. Before separating, all, ten in number, including family, joined in singing "God Save the Queen."

Tullamore.

I have the honour to report that my entire staff—telegraphists, postmen, telegraph messengers, rural postmen on the establishment stationed at sub-offices, and others in the service—attended at Tullamore Head-office at 9.30 p.m. (Irish), ranging themselves in order under the Royal Standard, which had been hoisted over the entrance early in the day.

I informed them that Her Majesty was graciously pleased to become Patron of the Rowland Hill Fund, and the invitation of the Executive Committee I also communicated. On receiving the signal at 9.35 P.M. (10 o'clock Greenwich time) three cheers for the Queen were given most loyally and with enthusiasm, and joined in by the large crowd which had assembled. The liberation of some fire balloons and a discharge of fireworks then followed, after which I entertained the staff at my house.

WATERFORD.

In common with the Post-Offices throughout the United Kingdom, the Jubilee of the Penny Postage was celebrated on Wednesday night in Waterford. At 9.30 P.M. the telegraphists and Post-Office officials assembled in the instrument room, and at ten o'clock (Greenwich time) precisely, on receiving a signal from London, three cheers were given for the Queen. Mr. P. Hand, Acting-Postmaster, afterwards hospitably entertained the staff at supper in the Waterford Arms Hotel, where the toasts of the Queen, of Mr. Hand, and of the newly-appointed Postmaster, Mr. Walsh, of Queenstown, were duly honoured.

POSTMASTERS' BREAKFAST.

JULY 3, 1890.

POSTMASTERS' BREAKFAST

(From the *Times*, July 4, 1890.)

IN connection with the celebration of the Jubilee of the Uniform Penny Postage, Mr. Raikes, M.P., the Postmaster-General, was entertained at breakfast yesterday morning at Exeter Hall by a large number of Postmasters, assembled from various parts of the United Kingdom. Mr. Raikes, who occupied the chair, was supported by Sir A. Blackwood, secretary of the General Post-Office, and a number of the leading postal officials. It was the first assembly of the kind ever held.

After the toast of "Her Majesty the Queen" had been duly honoured by the entire audience rising and singing the National Anthem,

Mr. RAIKES, after thanking those present for the honour conferred upon him in inviting him there as their guest, said that he ventured to avail himself of that opportunity to congratulate them upon what he believed was the first gathering of the Postmasters of the United Kingdom. He did not know with whom the idea originated, but he could not imagine a more proper sequel to the festivities of the previous night, when the postal service of the country was so strongly represented at the gathering at South Kensington, than that the Postmasters should have the opportunity of seeing and meeting each other, and that the superior officers of the department, who had been so kindly asked to be the guests, should have an opportunity of seeing face to face so many gentlemen with whom they were in constant correspondence, and of improving the acquaintance which even in the epistolary form was generally so agreeable on both sides.

He would hesitate to abuse their kindness by venturing to dwell upon any of those burning questions which recently had occupied the attention not only of the service, but also of the public; but he should be very ungrateful if he did not take that opportunity of saying how greatly he, and those on whose experience and counsel he had principally to rely, were beholden to the Postmasters of the United Kingdom for the admirable and loyal co-operation which they constantly received from the members of the postal service. That gathering represented not only Postmasters from the metropolis and the provincial towns of England, but from the sister kingdom also; some of their visitors having come from as far north as Inverness and as far west as Mullingar. It was therefore a truly representative gathering.

He knew well that the duties of Postmasters were most exacting, and that they occupied a most responsible position. The public generally appreciated that to a certain extent; but any one who had filled the office that he had had the honour to occupy during the last four years must know much better than the public how great was the strain upon the Postmasters in the ordinary discharge of their daily duties, and how greatly the strain had been intensified by recent events, which had called for all the energy and all the discretion which could at any time animate any official in the public service.

He must say that, without exception, the Postmasters of the United Kingdom had by their cordial assistance and loyal support made it possible for those who, in times of considerable stress and difficulty, had to conduct the affairs of that great department, to carry them on in a manner advantageous to the public and worthy of the State. Such was the patriotism, the *esprit de corps*, which distinguished the Postmasters of the United Kingdom, that even if too active science or too urgent democracy should cast upon the Post-Office additional burdens, they would still be willing to do what they could to give effect to the demands, and even to add to that work, which he believed would now overtax the energies of almost any other class of the public service.

So long as the postal servants felt that they could render important service to the State and their country, and so long as the performance of that service was recognized and appreciated, as he was sure it was, not only by those who were primarily responsible for the duties of the department, but also by that large public to whom their work was indispensable—so long would they get a brilliant example of all that went to make a man in the highest sense worthy of the title of a citizen of this great Empire.

After a few remarks from Mr. T. W. Angell (South-Western District of London), Sir A. Blackwood, Mr. Baines, and others, the company separated.

FREDERIC HILL, ESQ.

THE ROWLAND HILL MEMORIAL AND BENEVOLENT FUND.

SPECIAL JUBILEE EFFORT.

MEETING AT THE MANSION HOUSE,

NOVEMBER 11, 1890.

ROWLAND HILL MEMORIAL AND BENEVOLENT FUND.

MEETING AT THE MANSION HOUSE,
NOVEMBER 11, 1891.

Patron.
HER MAJESTY THE QUEEN.

Trustees.
R. KNIGHT CAUSTON, Esq., M.P., 9 Eastcheap, E.C.
WALTER GILBEY, Esq., Pantheon, Oxford Street, W.
DANIEL R. HARVEST, Esq., Dowgate Dock, E.C.
S. HOPE MORLEY, Esq., 18 Wood Street, E.C.
Sir HENRY W. PEEK, Bart., 20 Eastcheap, E.C.
H. ROKEBY PRICE, Esq., 1 Cowper's Court, Cornhill, E.C.
Rev. R. J. SIMPSON, M.A., 12 Downe Terrace, Richmond Hill.
Sir F. WYATT TRUSCOTT, Alderman, 103 Victoria Street, S.W.
Sir JAMES WHITEHEAD, Bart., Highfield House, Catford Bridge, Kent.

Bankers.
BANK OF ENGLAND.

Honorary Auditors.
G. N. READ, SON & CO., Chartered Accountants, 49 Queen Victoria Street, E.C.
R. RABBIDGE, Esq., Chartered Accountant, 32 Poultry, E.C.

Honorary Solicitors.
Messrs. WYNNE-BAXTER & KEEBLE, 9 Laurence Pountney Hill, E.C.

Committee of Recommendation.
HERBERT JOYCE, Esq., Third Secretary, General Post-Office.
J. J. CARDIN, Esq., Receiver and Accountant-General, General Post-Office.
G. C. STEET, Esq., Medical-Officer-in-Chief, General Post-Office.
R. C. TOMBS, Esq., Controller, London Postal Service.
H. C. FISCHER, Esq., Controller, Central Telegraph Office.
LEWIN HILL, Esq., Principal Clerk, Secretary's Office, General Post-Office.
F. J. LAWRENCE, Esq., Principal Clerk, Secretary's Office, General Post-Office.
A. BELCHER, Esq., Post-Office Savings Bank.

Secretary to the Committee of Recommendation.
S. WILSON, Esq.

The Report, which was very concise, contained the following paragraphs:—

The year 1890, as being the year in which has been commemorated the Jubilee of Penny Postage, will long be remembered as one of exceptional interest in the history of the Rowland Hill Benevolent Fund, particularly on account of the special efforts which the Trustees have reason to know are being made by the Jubilee Celebration Committee on behalf of the Fund. But it is not of the Jubilee year that the Trustees have now to speak. The accounts of the Fund are made up each year to the 30th of June; and, as the Committee referred to will not be in a position to make a definite statement of their proceedings until the meeting takes place at which this report is presented, the trustees have not felt themselves able to include in their present report any reference to events which, however interesting in themselves, do not properly belong to the period which the report embraces.

The trustees have much pleasure in announcing that Her Majesty the Queen has graciously condescended to become Patron of the Fund.

The Lord Mayor (Mr. Alderman Savory) was in the chair. There was a large gathering, and the following is a full report of the proceedings.

THE LORD MAYOR.—Ladies and Gentlemen,—It is a great pleasure to me that the first charitable meeting at which I am called upon to preside in this Mansion House should be the meeting of the Rowland Hill Benevolent Fund, a Fund which I feel confident, and am quite persuaded, is doing most excellent and valuable work; an Institution of which one of my valued predecessors in office, Sir James Whitehead, was not only, I believe, one of the founders, but in which he has taken a most valuable and personal interest. It is not for me to dwell at any length this afternoon upon the advantages of this Fund, but I shall call upon those gentlemen who are familiar with the work of the Fund to give you their experience of it. I will now call upon Sir Henry Peek to move the first resolution.

Sir Henry Peek, Bart.—My Lord, Ladies and Gentlemen,—With your permission I will read the Report, which is very short. [Report read.]

Shortly put, the receipts have been, from every source, £2,710. The grants are £1,027, and the secretary's salary £52 10s.; advertising, printing, and stationery, £27; invested in Nottingham Corporation Stock, £674.

Now, ladies and gentlemen, I hope you will agree with me that this is a very satisfactory Report, and I move that it be received and adopted. As one of the Trustees, I have been present at the meetings during the year, and I am sure that every shilling has been well spent. The object of this Fund is to do as much good as we possibly can with as little expense, and I hope you notice in the administration of this Fund how very small these expenses are. The secretary—and a very good secretary too—is very cheap at £50 for a whole year. Those who subscribe to this Fund have the satisfaction of knowing that nearly the whole of their subscriptions and donations will go to the objects of the Fund. It has given the Committee great satisfaction to know that now that a few of these Reports have been circulated, a great many Post-Offices have for the first time helped us this year. I dare say that whilst I was reading some of you saw a hint of what was coming this afternoon. It is the scheme of some of the gentlemen, whose names appear in this Report, and the Memorial Fund will be put in such a position that we shall be able to do much more good. We have received sums from the extreme parts of Ireland, from the extreme north of Scotland, and from the west of England. The applications for grants have come from every part of the United Kingdom, and I can assure you that every minutia is most carefully considered and acted upon to the fullest extent we think it right to go at present, but I hope that next year we shall be able to go a very great deal further. I should like to finish up by telling one little anecdote. A poor man applied to us for assistance, and of course we required to know all about him. This postman was going his rounds, and was about to deliver a newspaper, when a half-sovereign dropped out of it. Some one had wanted to send a half-sovereign in this way. The postman took the newspaper safely back to the office, and the half-sovereign with it too. I hope all in this room will do our duty in that station of life to which it has pleased the Almighty to call us.

Mr. CAUSTON, M.P.—As one of the Trustees, I have very much pleasure in seconding the adoption of this Report. I am sure you will agree with me that it is an interesting Report. I do not intend to make a speech, but I think that we must draw attention to the unfavourable side of matters. I should like to draw the attention of those who ought to subscribe to the fact that whereas the provinces contribute a larger sum of money than is made in grants, in London this is not the case. With regard to the provinces the amount received was

     £535 and the grants £445.
  Scotland £65 ,, ,, ,, £45.
  Ireland £165 ,, ,, ,, £117.

Whereas in London, including all the subscriptions and donations and the calls that are made, the total income was £340, while the amount of the grants made was £444. I think that is not satisfactory to the citizens of London, and it only requires that their attention should be called to the fact for it to be remedied. Although the grants made are comparatively small, it is not because assistance is not required, but because the authorities have thought it wise to set aside a portion of the receipts for investment so as to increase the income. Only thirty-five firms or individuals in the City contribute to the Fund. I hope after this meeting a great improvement will take place.

The resolution, "That the Report and Balance Sheet be received and adopted," was then put to the meeting, and carried unanimously.

Mr. BAINES, C.B.—My Lord Mayor,—The duty which falls to me to perform is very simple. It is to prefer a humble request to your Lordship that you will be pleased to receive, for transfer to the Trustees of the Rowland Hill Memorial and Benevolent Fund, a modest sum of money which a small body with a very long name, the Executive Committee of the Uniform Inland Penny Postage Jubilee Celebration, have in hand for the purposes of the Fund.

In receiving the money, your Lordship may desire to know something of the circumstances under which it happens that the Executive Committee, whose functions are but temporary, stands possessed of funds for the purpose indicated, and I believe that a short statement on this head will also be interesting to the meeting and those who are directly connected with the Benevolent Fund.

For about a year a Committee of Post-Office servants have been actively engaged, with the full consent and approval of the Postmaster-General, Mr. Raikes, and with the active sympathy and co-operation of the Secretary of the Post-Office, Sir Arthur Blackwood, in organizing, or assisting to organize, a variety of entertainments in honour of the memory of Sir Rowland Hill, and of his great work of cheapening and rendering uniform the Inland rates of postage, the Jubilee of which occurs this year.

It struck the Committee while labouring with that object that they might perhaps at the same time do some good in another way. The Trustees of the Benevolent Fund have in previous Reports, as in the present Report, lamented, if that be not too strong a word to use, the inadequacy of the Fund at their disposal to meet the numerous cases in which they would have been glad to give substantial relief. Their total invested property, as appeared from the accounts, amounts to only £17,000, and when regard is had to the very large number (approaching a hundred thousand persons) who are engaged in various ways in the Post-Office, it will be readily understood that there are many cases in which, from no fault of their own, serious distress overtakes them, or their widows and children, and which no Superannuation Act, however liberally framed, can provide against. Accordingly, it was an agreeable task for the Committee to contemplate that, while labouring for the entertainment of the well-to-do, they should attempt what might be in their power for the benefit of the more humbly placed. They thought, too, that this year of the Jubilee of Penny Postage men's hearts opening perhaps to the memory of Sir Rowland Hill, they might be disposed, seeing how the Post-Office has been regarded with kindness and consideration for many years by the public, to open their purses for the benefit of those faithful servants of the State, who, in all weathers and under all circumstances, convey, with exactness and fidelity, the correspondence entrusted to their charge. So, my Lord, the idea occurred to the Committee that they should try to raise £3,000 and round up the £17,000 to £20,000.

I dare say your Lordship, accustomed to the vast sums which are handled in the City for benevolent purposes, will smile at the limited ambition of the Committee: but they bore in mind that the purses of the benevolent are nowadays subject to innumerable attacks, and that, moreover, the public had in past years liberally contributed to the foundation of this Fund. However, with the object of getting £3,000 together, they set to work. The first windfall which came to them was the result of the action of that generous and enlightened Corporation of which your Lordship is the head—the Corporation of the City of London.

They gave, I need not remind those assembled here, a conversazione in honour of the Jubilee of Penny Postage at the Guildhall. It was organized by a Committee of the Corporation, under the leadership of that tried friend of the Post-Office, Alderman Sir James Whitehead, and it was conducted with splendour and great success. The co-operation of the Postmaster-General had been invited; and, accordingly, a Post-Office was established in the Guildhall, at which, to mark the special nature of the gathering, a Guildhall Penny Postcard was produced. This, though of a face value of a penny, was sold for sixpence, the public amiably concurring. The whole supply was bought up in about an hour, and the comfortable sum of £220 profit resulted to the Benevolent Fund. Your Lordship may be interested in knowing that these penny postcards have since been sold for a guinea apiece.

Then a most munificent gift was made to the Committee. The eminent firm of De la Rue and Co., Postage Stamp Printers,

Bunhill Row, in the most handsome and graceful way, gave us, altogether unsolicited, the very large sum of £200. We at the Post-Office are very sensible, not only of this act of munificence on the part of Messrs. De la Rue, but of much kindly co-operation extended to the Executive Committee during their various Jubilee celebrations. I am happy to be able to state, as will have been seen by the Report, that at this stage her Majesty the Queen, on proper representation being made, was graciously pleased, with her accustomed goodness, to become the patron of the Benevolent Fund. Then all went on merrily.

The Lord Rothschild, who had already been a most liberal donor, gave, on the application to his lordship personally of Sir James Whitehead, the further substantial sum of £100. Messrs. Thomas Cook & Sons, of Ludgate Circus, also most liberally gave the like sum, and I am sure the meeting will go with me in the hope that the personally conducted tours under that liberal firm may continue to flourish like a green bay tree.

The well-known firm of Lea & Perrin, of Worcester, also followed this lead of brilliant liberality. Mr. Lea gave £50 for himself, and £50 for his firm—£100 in all.

Then a further stroke of good fortune happened to us. That noble and beneficent lady, the Baroness Burdett-Coutts, united in an appeal to the public with Mr. William Lidderdale, Governor of the Bank of England, and our honoured friend, Sir James Whitehead. That appeal met with a liberal response. At the same time our colleagues throughout the country zealously co-operated with the committee in putting the merits of the Fund before the merchants and others. The banks gave us liberal and substantial help—many of the principal banks in London and the country opening their books for the receipt of donations, and in some cases themselves giving liberal aids to the Fund.

The first to lead the way were Messrs. Cox & Co., of Charing Cross, who opened their books and gave us £50. Messrs. Coutts & Co. gave us £50, and the London and Westminster Bank fifty guineas; the London and Brazilian Bank £25, and eighteen other banks in town and country substantial sums.

The firm of Rathbone Brothers, by the hands of Mr. Lidderdale, gave us £50. The Philatelic Society gave us £50. One of those munificent people who do good by stealth, blushing to find it fame, viz., "A friend," at Ayr in Scotland, gave us £50. Messrs. Bass, Radcliffe & Co., the great brewers at Burton-on-Trent, gave £50; Sir John Burns, the chairman of the Cunard Company, £50; Messrs. Findlay & Co., by the Lord-Provost of Glasgow, gave £50. Messrs. John and James White, merchants of that city, gave £50. The famous steamship firm of Hull—Messrs. Wilson & Sons—gave £50. Sir James Kitson, of Leeds, gave £50. The White Star Steamship Company, per Messrs. Ismay, Imry & Co., of Liverpool, gave us £50. In short, without wearying your Lordship with a too lengthy recapitulation of these benevolences, I would bring my remarks to a point by stating that the result was such that we have not only succeeded in getting the £3,000 necessary to round up from £17,000 to £20,000, but we have received from the public in cash, or in promises as good as cash, a total sum of fully £7,000.

Here, my Lord, as regards public liberality, I might bring my remarks to a close, but I entreat that you will permit me to pay a tribute of gratitude, thus publicly, first to those who have made those liberal donations, secondly to the Baroness Burdett-Coutts, Mr. Lidderdale, and Sir James Whitehead, who have so largely assisted us with the appeal, and, thirdly, to my valued colleagues throughout the country who have so ably supported us.

Where all have done so well, it is invidious, perhaps, to mention names; but I cannot forbear from saying that from Liverpool, thanks to the liberality of the merchants and others, the popularity of the able and justly esteemed Postmaster, Mr. J. D. Rich, and last, perhaps, to the goodness of our cause, more than £1,100 [1] has been remitted by the Postmaster (a sum which at one time threatened wholly to eclipse the amount deliverable

---

[1] Subsequent donations have raised the sums contributed to the following amounts:—Liverpool, £1,655; Glasgow, £667; Leeds, £521; Manchester, £205; Birmingham, £132; and Ayr, £128.

from the metropolitan city and is now only a few pounds short of it).

At Glasgow a scarcely less brilliant result has been obtained. Mr. Richard Hobson, being in touch with the leading merchants and others in that city, has been entrusted by them with more than £600 [1] for the benefit of the Fund; while, third amongst prominent towns, is the good borough of Leeds, where the energetic and much respected Postmaster, Mr. Leal, has received from the merchants upwards of £320.[1] Sheffield comes next, presenting by the hands of Mr. Mawson £174 to the Fund; while the great centre of provincial industry—Manchester—has also contributed considerably to the Fund, the Postmaster, Mr. Johnston, having remitted upwards of £150 [1] for this purpose, and Birmingham, £118.[1] I ought to add that there are many other towns which, in proportion to their population and industrial activity, have sent up very liberal contributions; for instance, the little town of Ayr in Scotland has given us £121.[1]

And now, my Lord, after this long story I might sit down were it not that there yet remains a word to be said on a point scarcely less interesting than that which has already been dealt with, and which must be my excuse for speaking for a minute or two more. I said in my opening remarks that the Executive Committee had been engaged in organizing entertainments. The chief of these, I dare say the meeting will bear in mind, was a conversazione on a large scale in succession to, and indeed the complement of, the Guildhall conversazione. This was held on the 2nd July, and I take the opportunity of respectfully tendering the warm thanks of the Executive Committee to the Lords of the Committee of the Privy Council for Education for their kindness in placing at our disposal the beautiful Museum at South Kensington. About four thousand persons were present. As in the case of the Guildhall conversazione, which His Royal Highness the Prince of Wales honoured with his presence, so at South Kensington His Royal Highness the Duke of Edinburgh accepted the office of President, and Her Royal and Imperial Highness the Duchess of Edinburgh was

[1] See note on previous page.

also kind enough to come amongst us and take an active interest in the proceedings. To our great pleasure several members of the Corporation accepted our invitation to be present, but civic engagements deprived us of the honour of the presence of the Lord Mayor and Sheriffs. Following the precedent of the Guildhall conversazione, the Committee, with much care and thought, produced a Penny Jubilee Envelope enclosing a correspondence card. The envelope aimed at recording both a centenary and a Jubilee of postal progress. The card bore a medallion of Sir Rowland Hill, with the legend, contributed by the happy thought of Sir James Whitehead, and embodied in the words—"He gave us Penny Postage." The public took so kindly to this envelope, and our colleagues throughout the country threw themselves so heartily into the scheme of distribution, that I am happy to be able to state that the result has been somewhat to add to that £7,000 already mentioned. That will be paid over intact without the deduction of a penny for expenses. We have—in the shape of the penny postage stamp—paid a royalty to the Crown of £1,000, and after defraying other expenses, amounting to about £2,000 more, there is yet a residue of profit which enables us to add to the amount just named no less a sum than £10,000. In the aggregate, therefore, the result of the Jubilee effort so far has been to double the capital of the Trustees. It stood at £17,000 when we were last in this hall —it is now upwards of £34,000.

My Lord Mayor, our books are not finally closed. The Committee will continue its operations until the end of the Jubilee year, and then, after audit, hand over its final balance, having reason to believe that some other donations will yet reach us. We have not yet called in all the promised donations, but we have so far approximated to that end as to be in a position to hand to your Lordship a cheque on account on the London and Westminster Bank for £16,000.[1] This will, of course, be at the absolute disposal of the Trustees. All that we ask is that the capital sum may be ear-marked

---

[1] A further payment of £5,000 was made to the Trustees in March, 1891.

under a name which our Honorary Solicitor, Mr. Breton Osborne, and the Honorary Solicitors, Messrs. Wynne Baxter and Keeble, will arrange between them.

SIR JAMES WHITEHEAD, BART.—The resolution which I have to submit to the meeting is as follows:—

> "That this meeting acknowledges with pleasure the liberal donations which have been received from the public, and whilst regarding with satisfaction the large and permanent increase which has already been made to the Fund, looks hopefully to a still further augmentation of its resources."

The speech, the admirable speech, and the very business-like manner in which that speech has been delivered by Mr. Baines has taken from me very much of the responsibility attached to this resolution, and while I am going to ask you to give the thanks of this meeting to those who have contributed and to those who are going to do so, I think we ought to recognize all that has been done by the officials of the Post-Office.

I have had something to do with the Fund from its very initiation, and in the first place we had very great difficulties to get it launched, but to-day it assumes very considerable proportions, and will enable us to do a very great deal more good. I cannot help feeling, my Lord, that this meeting to-day is a very good augury for your mayoralty. You have commenced under very good circumstances, and I trust this will be the first of a series of meetings of benevolent, charitable work. The public have come forward and subscribed very handsomely indeed, because they now begin to recognize that this Fund is doing a great amount of good amongst a very worthy class of public servants.

The subscription-list has been very largely augmented, and I am satisfied that when the objects of this Fund are well known we shall get a great deal more than we have done. Frequently, I am sure, we ought to give five times the amount we have been able to give to applicants. Some people have unfortunately got the impression that the object of this Fund is to supplement the small incomes which those who serve the Post-Office derive from the service, but a perusal of the Report will entirely remove the fallacy.

It will be seen that we do not augment the incomes of those already connected with the Post-Office, but that we render help where we believe help is needed, and where there is a disposition on the part of the applicants to help themselves. In some cases we put them into small establishments; in some cases we assist them to get a horse and trap, or a mangle; but chiefly we assist them by granting sums of money to those in poverty through no fault of their own. It seems to me that this is the very best system of help, because while it assists persons it allows them to retain their independence. Of course we know that there are cases, even amongst those who are in the employ of the Post-Office—who are recognized as being on the staff of that Department—where their means do not enable them to cope with difficulties which arise. In some cases we find men have a long illness, and that long illness is productive of poverty.

In some cases a man dies and leaves a heavy doctor's bill behind him. A thousand and one contingencies will arise, even in the lives of those whose incomes under ordinary circumstances are sufficient for their needs, and in many of these instances, while the applicant is living and is in the service of the Post-Office, it may happen that his wages, although adequate for him while in health, are totally inadequate when in sickness.

There is one feature in this Fund which will commend it to the public. It is carried on in a quiet, unobtrusive kind of way. We aid those only who are in real want. We do not publish any names. We spare the feelings of those who are in distress, and we take care that their distress is not in any way known. Sir Henry Peek has already remarked that this Fund is carried on with hardly any expense. When I appeal to you on behalf of this Fund, and while I thank those who have already subscribed to it, let us, looking, as we hope, for an increase to the Fund, not forget that there is an enormous correspondence carried on in this country, and that it is all passed through the hands of our postmen. Let us remember how very seldom it is that a letter is lost, or that there is any tampering. We must then think that we have a very worthy body of public servants, who are deserving of the approval and support in time of need of the benevolent public.

In the work of this Fund and in the extension of its usefulness we desire to do honour to the name of the great postal reformer to whom we owe so much, and we desire to honour his name all the more because while he lived he was a good friend to those connected with the Post-Office, and because we believe that this Fund would have his hearty and cordial approval.

Mr. GRAVATT briefly seconded the motion, which was carried.

Mr. J. C. LAMB.—I have the very pleasant duty of moving

"That the best thanks of the meeting be accorded to the Trustees for their services."

Perhaps I may be allowed to say a few words in making this motion. We have seen in the papers a few attacks upon the Post-Office, and have heard that a great Department ought to be able to make arrangements for its own distressed servants. Now, no shopkeeper is able to supply himself with what will keep him for the rest of his life if he falls into misfortune, and it seems to me that it is a ridiculous assumption that the State should provide for the misfortunes of its servants. Other friends think that even some of the small privileges which Civil Servants now have should be taken away from them.

Fortunately for this Fund, the Trustees belong neither to one class nor to the other. They are men of benevolence and of judgment and of wisdom. They see that it is not the part of the Post-Office, as a business concern, to look after the widow of the mail-cart driver. These men read public opinion, and they find that although the servants of the Post-Office are not rich, at least they take an interest in the Fund and help us to produce the splendid result which Mr. Baines has put before you to-day. The Post-Office thanks these Trustees because they help to bind the bonds between us and the public. They help us to put ourselves in touch with the public. They put us alongside the public and show them that we are not fossils, bound with red tape, but that we are only too glad to learn from the public what they want from us and to do it. I think you must feel confidence when you look at the names of these Trustees, who are such eminently trustworthy men.

The motion was seconded by Mr. Cardin, and carried.

SIR S. A. BLACKWOOD, K.C.B.—I ask your Lordship's permission to introduce to the meeting a resolution of an exceptional character. This has been an exceptional year. Probably we shall never see the like of it again, and, as Mr. Baines, my excellent colleague, has already mentioned, it has given rise to a body which can never be called into existence again for at least fifty years. The exceptional thing of the year which we are now concluding is the labours of that body, which are a justification for the introduction of the resolution upon this occasion.

It was a very happy idea of Mr. Baines, I think, to utilize the Jubilee year not only for commemorating Sir Rowland Hill's great work, but also for adding largely to the resources of the Rowland Hill Fund. But before anything could be done in that direction it was necessary to enlist other help. We could not undertake this task alone, and I wish to mention the deep debt of gratitude which the Post-Office is under to the Corporation.

The moment that I approached your Lordship's predecessor he readily promised us his aid and gave us all the assistance that lay in his power. That assistance was very great and very valuable. The Court of Common Council rose to the emergency and with great liberality placed at our disposal your ancient Hall. We were seconded by Sir James Whitehead. Sir John Monckton was especially obliging.

The fact that we had secured the co-operation of the first municipal body of the world pledged us to success, and I need not say that that success has been obtained. Before that could be done it was needful to create the machinery in the Post-Office itself, and accordingly the Executive Committee of the Celebration was called into existence. It was necessary that that Committee should be a representative one, and one composed of the most able officers in our service, and if any credit is due to me, it is only this, that I was able to select the most able and energetic officers.

We wanted for one thing financial skill. Where could I turn to a better possessor of that quality than my friend Mr. Cardin? We wanted military ardour, and that was found in the Colonel of the 24th Middlesex Rifle Volunteers, Colonel Thompson. We wanted administrative ability, and you will readily understand that in Mr. Tombs, the Postmaster of London, we had abundance of that quality. To represent scientific skill we had Mr. Preece.

Great as were the resources of these gentlemen they wanted a guide, and in my friend Mr. Baines I found the man.

I think therefore that we had in that Committee exactly what the circumstances of the case demanded; we could not have had a better one; and, as the proof of the pudding is in the eating, the cheque for £16,000 which Mr. Baines has handed to your Lordship is evidence of the truth of my contention.

I was amazed that every day Mr. Baines should come into my room with some fresh idea, to bring this personage or other into the ceremonial. Day after day his labours, and those of the Committee who assisted him, were extremely arduous. They went on from victory to victory.

The thing was launched by the Guildhall Celebration, honoured, as it was, by the presence of the Prince of Wales. We felt after that was over that the battle was half won. At South Kensington we had a night that will never be forgotten. That was a proof of the remarkable skill and ability with which the Committee carried on their work.

The Committee have done good work. They have succeeded in placing this Fund upon a permanent and established basis. It has received a start in this year which will be the prelude to far greater advances in the future. The interest shown in it is a proof that it has taken hold of the public mind, and that the excellence of this benevolent body is recognized as one that entitles it to public support.

I therefore desire, in the name of this meeting, to move that a very hearty vote of thanks should be given to this Committee, to whom the proceedings of this afternoon must be very gratifying. But the truest thanks to them will come from those who are the recipients of the bounty which the public has contributed mainly through the members of the Committee.

They will have been the means of bringing comfort and consolation, good cheer and encouragement to many a broken and aching heart, not only in the present but also for the future, so that in years to come there will be those who shall rise up and call them blessed. I think they have deserved well of the public, well of the Department, and well of their country, and I envy them the pride and the pleasure with which they will receive the thanks of this meeting under your Lordship's presidency.

The motion was seconded by Mr. Harvest, who proposed a vote of thanks to the Lord Mayor for presiding and for giving the use of the Mansion House. This was seconded by Mr. H. R. Price.

MR. BAINES.—I desire to express the extreme gratification of my colleagues on the Executive Committee and myself at the gracious words which have fallen from you. Our work has been throughout a labour of love, and I may say that our service has been most cheerfully and willingly rendered.

Allow me of your kindness to mention one other name. We, too, have an honorary secretary, and of that honorary secretary I cannot speak too highly. We have received very valuable assistance from others—from Mr. Beckley, Mr. Aitken, and Mr. Wilson; but I am sure that those gentlemen will be the first to admit that the heat and burden of the day have fallen upon my friend and colleague, Mr. Gates. When I tell you that in addition to the punctual and faithful discharge of heavy and responsible official duties he has dealt with 30,000 letters and a quarter of a million of printed communications, I will venture to say that in Mr. Gates there is not one of the State's "bad bargains."

SIR A. BLACKWOOD.—This meeting has been already slightly irregular. I venture to commit another irregularity by asking you to signify your approval of the resolution [the vote of thanks to the Lord Mayor] in the ordinary way.

The Lord Mayor.—I have to thank the meeting for passing this resolution. My only feeling is that no thanks are really due to me for presiding on this occasion. I feel it to be my duty to open the doors of this Mansion House to any charitable movement, and it has been a great pleasure and happy augury that on the first opportunity I have had of doing so during my mayoralty I have received a cheque for £16,000 for charitable purposes. I hope however that this will not be the only result of the Committee's labours, but that before the Committee is dissolved the Rowland Hill Benevolent Fund may amount to £100,000, according to the wish that has been expressed; and I trust that this meeting may be in every way satisfactory to the Fund.

THE ROWLAND HILL MEMORIAL AND BENEVOLENT FUND.

SPECIAL EFFORT TO INCREASE THE INVESTMENTS OF THE TRUSTEES.

STATEMENT showing the Total Sums remitted by Postmasters, Sub-Postmasters, and Letter Receivers throughout the United Kingdom; including the Subscriptions sent to the Jubilee Celebration Committee direct.

	£	s.	d.		£	s.	d.
HER MAJESTY THE QUEEN	25	0	0	Brought forward	2,396	16	2
London	2,121	2	10	Barnsley	43	7	3
				Barnstaple	10	0	6
HEAD OFFICES—				Barrow-in-Furness	3	2	6
ENGLAND AND WALES.				Bath	6	2	6
				Batley	7	8	1
Abergavenny	4	4	6	Bawtry	5	1	0
Abingdon	2	7	0	Beccles	11	3	6
Acklington	1	1	6	Beckenham	32	14	6
Aldershot		10	0	Bedale	30	4	0
Altrincham	30	6	0	Bedford	12	9	3
Ambleside	10	0	0	Berkeley		5	0
Amersham	1	6	0	Berkhamsted	1	17	6
Ampthill	3	0	0	Berwick	41	19	1
Andover	2	17	6	Beverley	1	1	0
Arundel	2	10	6	Bicester	1	14	0
Ascot	15	15	0	Bideford	8	11	0
Ashbourne	36	6	0	Biggleswade	1	1	0
Ashby de la Zouch	1	7	6	Bilston	1	1	0
Ashton under Lyne	1	1	0	Bingley	11	0	0
Atherstone	13	5	0	Birkenhead	13	2	0
Aylesbury	1	0	0	Birmingham	132	4	0
Aylsham		16	6	Bishop Auckland	3	8	0
Banbury	27	2	7	Bishop's Stortford	1	0	0
Bangor	43	2	0	Blackpool	1	1	0
Barnet	52	14	9	Blaenau Festiniog		15	6
Carried forward	£2,396	16	2	Carried forward	£2,778	9	4

	£	s.	d.
Brought forward	2,778	9	4
Blandford	43	0	6
Bletchley Station		5	0
Bodmin	1	11	9
Bognor	1	1	0
Bolton	88	6	0
Boston	6	19	6
Bourne		17	6
Bournemouth	56	2	0
Brackley		5	0
Bracknell	2	2	0
Braintree	1	13	6
Brecon	1	2	0
Brentford	6	6	0
Brentwood	10	1	6
Bridgend	5	5	0
Bridgnorth	9	17	3
Bridgwater	77	6	0
Bridlington Quay	3	3	0
Bridport	4	3	0
Brigg	1	0	0
Brighouse	3	3	0
Brighton	2	0	0
Bristol	72	14	6
Briton Ferry	6	7	6
Broadway	1	8	4
Bromley		10	0
Bromsgrove	1	0	0
Brough	7	9	6
Buckingham	8	19	4
Bungay	13	6	0
Burnley	130	18	6
Burton-on-Trent	109	10	3
Bury St. Edmunds	22	8	6
Calne		5	0
Camberley	20	12	6
Camborne	1	0	0
Cambridge	33	0	6
Canterbury	2	2	0
Cardiff	108	0	6
Cardigan	1	0	0
Carlisle	35	13	1
Carnarvon	7	15	7
Carnforth	16	13	6
Chatham	30	17	3
Cheltenham	26	15	0
Chepstow	2	9	3
Chertsey	15	12	0
Chester	1	0	0
Chesterfield	1	1	0
Chester-le-Street		10	6
Chichester	25	0	0
Chippenham	8	18	3
Chipping Norton	5	10	0
Chislehurst	17	4	6
Chorley	6	15	0
Carried forward	£3,846	7	8

	£	s.	d.
Brought forward	3,846	7	8
Chulmleigh	1	1	0
Cirencester	4	18	0
Clevedon	5	3	0
Clitheroe	5	17	6
Cobham	18	10	0
Cockermouth		10	0
Colne	30	4	0
Congleton	1	11	0
Corwen		10	6
Coventry	67	6	0
Cowes	10	10	0
Crawley	1	1	0
Crediton	5	6	0
Crewe	6	1	0
Crewkerne	8	14	3
Cricklade	1	1	0
Cromer		10	6
Croydon	1	1	0
Cullompton		5	0
Darlington	81	12	9
Dartford	6	14	6
Darwen		6	0
Denbigh	1	19	0
Derby	3	3	0
Dereham	6	15	0
Devonport	1	1	0
Dewsbury	17	9	0
Diss	14	3	6
Dolgelly	1	1	0
Doncaster	3	2	0
Dorchester	13	13	0
Dorking		5	0
Douglas	17	4	0
Dover		10	0
Dowlais	1	4	0
Driffield	8	12	0
Droitwich	5	0	0
Dunmow	2	2	6
Dunstable	3	8	7
Durham	12	2	7
Dursley	2	2	0
East Grinstead	1	0	0
Eccleshall	13	9	9
Edenbridge	1	0	0
Elland		10	6
Enfield	1	1	0
Epsom	3	3	0
Evesham	3	3	6
Exmouth	1	15	0
Eye	3	3	0
Fakenham	3	5	0
Falmouth	2	2	0
Fareham	3	0	0
Faringdon	6	1	0
Farnborough	3	13	6
Carried forward	£4,266	6	7

310   JUBILEE OF PENNY POSTAGE.

	£	s.	d.
Brought forward	4,266	6	7
Farnham		5	0
Ferry Hill	3	6	0
Flint	2	18	3
Folkingham		10	0
Frome	2	13	0
Gainsborough	6	0	0
Gateshead	1	1	0
Gloucester		8	6
Godalming	12	11	6
Gosport	23	0	6
Grantham	32	0	6
Gravesend	26	11	6
Grays	2	9	0
Great Yarmouth	33	7	0
Guernsey	10	17	9
Guildford	9	17	9
Guisborough	11	18	6
Halesworth	12	5	11
Halifax	1	3	0
Harrogate	2	2	0
Harrow	12	3	6
Hartlepool		12	0
Hastings	2	0	0
Havant	28	8	6
Haverfordwest	7	14	0
Hawkhurst	13	0	6
Haywards Heath		6	6
Helston	1	1	0
Hemel Hempstead	11	0	0
Hereford	10	12	0
Hertford	1	0	0
Hexham	13	12	7
Hinckley		15	6
Hitchin	28	4	9
Hoddesdon	2	5	6
Holbeach	1	4	4
Holyhead		18	6
Holywell	22	15	9
Horncastle	15	7	6
Horsham	7	0	9
Hounslow	5	13	0
Howden	2	1	6
Huddersfield	7	6	0
Hull	135	19	6
Huntingdon	10	14	6
Ilford	2	7	6
Ilkley	1	11	0
Ingatestone		5	0
Ipswich	59	15	0
Isleworth	19	13	6
Ivybridge		10	0
Jarrow	5	0	0
Jersey	8	12	6
Keighley	52	8	0
Kelvedon		10	0
Carried forward	£4,954	3	5

	£	s.	d.
Brought forward	4,954	3	5
Kendal	50	12	6
Keswick	6	0	0
Kidderminster	4	12	0
King's Lynn	7	14	0
Kington	1	11	0
Kirkby Lonsdale	2	1	0
Kirkby Stephen		5	0
Knutsford	8	0	0
Lancaster	15	17	0
Launceston	2	2	0
Leamington Spa	1	11	6
Leatherhead	5	6	0
Ledbury	1	1	0
Leeds	521	7	4
Leek	11	6	0
Leicester	2	4	6
Leominster		7	6
Lewes	14	17	6
Lichfield	2	2	0
Lincoln	62	0	9
Liverpool	1,655	9	2
Llandudno	3	18	0
Llandyssil		16	6
Llanelly	12	5	0
Long Stratton	1	1	0
Loughborough	14	2	10
Louth		13	0
Lowestoft	2	2	0
Ludlow	1	0	0
Luton	2	0	0
Lutterworth	1	0	0
Lydney		10	0
Machynlleth		5	0
Maidenhead	1	13	0
Maidstone	8	7	0
Maldon	3	8	3
Malton	3	8	0
Malvern	55	6	3
Manchester	204	19	0
Manningtree		18	0
Margate	1	0	0
Maryport	4	16	6
Matlock Bath	10	6	6
Micheldever Station		6	6
Middlebrough	6	6	0
Midhurst	3	2	0
Monmouth	23	7	0
Morpeth	16	4	9
Mountain Ash	6	15	0
Nantwich	7	10	0
Needham Market	2	13	0
Nelson	24	0	0
Newark	23	12	8
New Barnet	2	10	6
Newbury	3	0	0
Carried forward	£7,783	14	5

ROWLAND HILL MEMORIAL AND BENEVOLENT FUND.

	£	s.	d.		£	s.	d.
Brought forward	7,783	14	5	Brought forward	8,463	3	8
Newcastle, Staff.		7	4	Ruabon	2	15	0
Newcastle-on-Tyne	24	3	6	Rugby	16	16	6
Newmarket	1	1	0	Runcorn	7	11	0
Newport, Isle of Wight	1	8	8	Ryde	28	18	6
Newport, Mon.	19	12	0	Saffron Walden	18	18	0
Newport Pagnel	1	2	0	St. Albans	3	0	0
Newton Abbot	51	1	0	St. Clear's	9	4	6
Newton le Willows	1	0	0	St. Helen's	3	3	0
Newtown, Mont.	14	18	0	St. Ives	1	1	0
Normanton	1	0	9	St. Neots		7	4
Northallerton		10	0	Sandbach		10	0
Northampton	46	13	0	Sandwich		10	0
North Walsham		16	0	Sandy	9	11	0
Norwich	53	8	1	Saxmundham	10	13	6
Nottingham	47	4	7	Scarborough	8	2	0
Nuneaton	5	12	6	Scole		14	0
Oldham	10	6	6	Seven Oaks	7	2	0
Ormskirk	5	0	0	Shaftesbury	15	5	3
Oswestry	6	6	0	Sheerness	4	6	0
Ottery St. Mary	2	11	0	Sheffield	173	7	6
Oxford	10	14	0	Shepton Mallet	3	2	0
Pembroke		7	0	Sherborne	15	0	0
Pembroke Dock	2	2	0	Shipley	6	0	0
Penrith	36	3	6	Shoreham	2	14	6
Penryn	4	0	0	Shrewsbury	17	14	0
Penzance	25	9	0	Sidmouth	2	15	0
Pershore	5	10	0	Slough	1	0	0
Peterborough	2	2	9	Soham	2	0	0
Petersfield	2	2	4	Southall	1	10	0
Plymouth	20	0	0	Southampton	8	19	0
Ponder's End	2	0	0	Southport	1	1	0
Pontefract	28	17	0	South Shields	24	15	6
Pontypool	15	12	0	Sowerby Bridge	6	7	6
Pontypridd	10	2	10	Spalding	2	1	6
Poole	2	0	0	Spilsby		10	0
Portsmouth	2	10	0	Stafford	102	5	0
Prescot	21	11	0	Staines	53	14	8
Preston	24	5	3	Stalybridge	1	1	0
Pwllheli	1	10	0	Stevenage	9	4	0
Ramsgate	12	7	6	Stockport	27	12	9
Reading	4	5	0	Stoke-on-Trent	6	9	7
Redcar	4	12	0	Stonham	2	6	6
Redditch	10	4	0	Stony Stratford	10	9	6
Red Hill	2	13	0	Stourbridge	1	1	0
Redruth	1	5	0	Stourport	2	2	0
Reigate	2	2	0	Stowmarket	8	10	6
Rhayader		15	0	Stratford-on-Avon	2	0	0
Richmond, Surrey	13	9	0	Stroud	1	1	0
Richmond, Yorks		5	0	Sunderland	78	11	0
Ringwood	6	14	6	Swaffham		10	6
Ripon	4	8	0	Swansea	11	19	6
Rochdale	6	19	6	Tamworth	2	4	0
Rochester	56	10	2	Tarporley		5	0
Romsey	3	3	0	Taunton	2	0	0
Rotherham	38	16	0	Tavistock	2	14	0
Carried forward	£8,463	3	8	Carried forward	£9,206	11	3

JUBILEE OF PENNY POSTAGE.

	£	s.	d.
Brought forward	9,206	11	3
Teignmouth	6	15	0
Tenbury	16	9	0
Tenby	5	0	0
Tetbury	5	0	0
Tetsworth	3	15	0
Tewkesbury	5	4	6
Thame	1	0	0
Thetford		10	6
Thirsk	3	18	6
Tiverton		19	0
Todmorden		10	0
Torquay	5	5	0
Torrington	4	13	0
Totnes	18	9	1
Tring	41	2	2
Trowbridge	2	10	6
Truro	2	6	0
Tunbridge Wells	18	0	0
Twickenham		10	0
Ulceby	1	13	6
Ulverston	6	0	0
Uxbridge	55	14	3
Ventnor	3	0	0
Wakefield	50	13	4
Wallingford	1	1	0
Walsall	8	9	0
Waltham Cross	10	12	6
Wangford	1	0	0
Ware	3	3	0
Warminster	1	0	0
Warrington	11	3	0
Warwick	1	14	9
Watford	22	7	6
Wednesbury	2	11	0
Wellingborough	15	8	0
Wellington, Salop	4	13	6
Wellington, Som.	1	6	0
Wells, Som.	6	1	7
Welshpool	13	2	6
Welwyn	10	0	0
West Bromwich	2	2	0
Westbury, Wilts.		15	6
West Hartlepool	50	6	6
Weybridge	21	16	2
Weymouth	35	3	0
Whitby	1	1	0
Wimborne	23	1	0
Winchfield	2	0	0
Windermere	13	14	0
Windsor	3	3	0
Witham	1	18	0
Wolverhampton	17	18	5
Woodford Green	2	10	6
Woodstock	1	10	0
Woolwich	6	5	6
Carried forward	£9,762	7	6

	£	s.	d.
Brought forward	9,762	7	6
Worcester	100	0	0
Workington	8	15	0
Worksop		5	0
Worthing	55	12	0
Wragby	4	6	2
Wrexham	5	0	0
Yeovil	1	0	0
York	20	14	0

SCOTLAND.

	£	s.	d.
Aberdeen	11	11	0
Aberfeldy		15	0
Alloa	6	10	0
Anstruther	6	1	6
Arbroath	22	19	6
Ardgay	1	9	0
Auchterarder	10	0	0
Ayr	128	9	0
Beith		14	6
Biggar	2	17	6
Campbeltown	13	18	6
Castle Douglas	10	15	0
Coatbridge	41	4	0
Coldstream		6	6
Crieff	4	8	6
Cumnock	1	0	0
Cupar, Fife	32	2	6
Denny		10	0
Drem		6	0
Dumbarton	25	11	0
Dumfries	9	7	0
Dunbar	1	10	6
Dundee	78	11	6
Dunfermline	27	1	0
Dunkeld		10	6
Dunoon	1	1	0
Ecclefechan	1	0	0
Edinburgh	95	6	0
Forfar	25	18	6
Fort George Station		16	0
Galashiels	5	0	0
Glasgow	667	8	6
Greenock	54	11	0
Haddington	3	13	6
Hawick	3	1	6
Helensburgh	6	13	5
Inverness	2	0	0
Jedburgh		12	0
Kelso	19	13	6
Kilmarnock	2	5	0
Kingussie	1	3	6
Kirkcaldy	24	18	0
Kirkcudbright	2	4	6
Kirriemuir	7	15	0
Carried forward	£11,321	10	1

ROWLAND HILL MEMORIAL AND BENEVOLENT FUND.

	£	s.	d.		£	s.	d.
Brought forward	11,321	10	1	Brought forward	11,594	7	2
Lanark		12	6	Enfield	2	6	0
Langholm	2	0	0	Ennis	5	7	6
Larbert	1	1	0	Galway	8	13	2
Lerwick	9	12	6	Kells		18	6
Linlithgow		12	6	Kilkenny	1	5	0
Lochalsh	1	17	0	Killarney	1	2	0
Lochmaddy		7	0	Killucan		17	0
Lockerbie	1	5	0	Kingstown	1	3	0
Macduff	1	3	0	Letterkenny		10	0
Markinch	1	1	0	Londonderry	31	15	6
Melrose	3	1	6	Monaghan	1	1	0
Midcalder		10	0	Mullingar	3	10	6
Mintlaw Station	4	5	6	Naas	1	6	0
Moffat	1	0	0	New Ross		8	6
Montrose	18	1	0	Newry	3	11	6
Nairn	2	16	0	Newtownards		5	0
Newtown St. Boswell's		5	0	Ovoca	1	0	0
Paisley	10	18	3	Piltown	1	16	0
Peebles	3	0	0	Queenstown	1	17	0
Penicuik	1	1	0	Thomastown	4	18	0
Perth	9	5	6	Tullamore	2	2	0
Pitlochry	11	0	0	Waterford	2	11	6
Port Ellen		5	0	Youghal	1	1	0
Port Glasgow	2	0	0				
Portobello		10	0				
Portree	2	17	5	**SUB AND RECEIVING OFFICES**			
Rothesay		5	0	**IN THE UNITED KINGDOM.**			
Saltcoats	1	5	0				
Selkirk	3	0	0	Aberlour, Craigellachie		13	0
South Queensferry	1	2	6	Acock's Green, Birming-			
Stranraer	10	0	0	ham	2	0	0
Thornhill	3	19	0	Allington, Grantham		6	6
Thurso		5	3	Ammanford, Llanelly	1	2	0
Trancnt	1	3	6	Aspley Guise, Bletchley			
Troon	2	5	0	Station		10	0
Wishaw	6	18	6	Aston-Clinton, Tring	2	0	0
				Auchtermuchty, Lady-			
IRELAND.				bank	1	1	0
				Avon Dassett, Leaming-			
Abbeyleix	3	12	6	ton Spa		8	8
Armagh	1	0	0	Badminton, Chippenham		8	0
Athy	1	0	6	Ballycommon, Tulla-			
Ballymote	1	1	0	more	1	0	0
Bandon	5	9	0	Bannockburn, Stirling	1	3	0
Belfast	13	18	6	Barford, Warwick	1	1	0
Cahir	5	15	0	Bickley Station, Bromley	13	7	0
Carrickfergus	7	7	8	Bignall End, Newcastle,			
Cookstown	2	0	0	Staff	2	10	0
Cork	3	14	6	Bletchingley, Red Hill		10	0
Curragh Camp		15	0	Bonnybridge, Denny		5	0
Drogheda	1	10	0	Bowdon, Altrincham	5	0	0
Dublin	98	14	0	Bridge of Urr, Dalbeattie	2	10	0
Dundalk	4	10	0	Bruton, Bath		7	6
Dungannon	1	1	0	Budleigh Salterton, Ex-			
Dungarvan		17	0	mouth	3	18	3
Carried forward	£11,594	7	2	Carried forward	£11,713	13	9

JUBILEE OF PENNY POSTAGE.

	£	s.	d.
Brought forward	11,713	13	9
Cassop Colliery, Ferry Hill		11	9
Charlbury, Enstone	1	0	0
Cheam, Sutton	1	1	0
Cheshunt, Waltham Cross		10	6
Chirk, Ruabon	1	2	6
Clarecastle, Limerick		5	0
Combe Down, Bath		8	6
Condover, Shrewsbury		10	6
Crantock, Grampound Road		5	0
Crowcombe, Taunton		5	0
Culworth, Banbury	2	5	10
Deerhurst, Tewkesbury		18	5
Deganwy, Llandudno		5	0
Dishforth, Thirsk	1	17	0
Dovercourt, Harwich	1	6	0
Dromahair, Sligo		10	0
Dublin, Flint		5	0
Earlswood, Red Hill		7	0
East Ayton, York	1	15	0
Elstree, Watford	1	1	0
Elvington, York		7	6
Evershot, Dorchester		10	0
Felton, Acklington	3	0	0
Forgandenny, Perth	1	0	0
Fownhope, Hereford	2	10	0
Fyvie, Aberdeen	1	1	0
Garstang, Preston	1	12	9
Glenealy, Wicklow		12	0
Gorebridge, Dalkeith	10	10	0
Great Somerford, Chippenham	2	16	0
Haileybury College		10	0
Hampton Court, Kingston-on-Thames	10	8	0
Harmer Hill, Shrewsbury		14	0
Harringworth, Kettering		10	0
Hatfield Woodhouse, Doncaster		5	0
Heckington, Sleaford	1	6	0
Hele, Cullompton	1	11	6
Henbury, Bristol		5	0
Hendford, Yeovil	2	2	0
Hillingdon Heath, Uxbridge	1	8	6
Hopton, Thetford		5	0
Invergarry, Inverness	2	12	6
Isle Ornsay, Broadford	1	1	0
Kennoway, Leven		5	0
Kildysart, Ennis		5	0
Kilgerran, Cardigan	1	5	6
Kiltegan, Athy	3	2	6
Kimbolton, St. Neots		5	0
Kingskettle	2	0	0
Carried forward	£11,784	4	6

	£	s.	d.
Brought forward	11,784	4	6
Kippax, Leeds	4	10	0
Knapp Hill, Woking	3	10	0
Knockin, Oswestry		10	0
Knocklong, Kilmallock	1	0	0
Langham, Oakham	1	12	0
Lemsford, Hatfield	1	6	0
Lesmahagow, Lanark		5	6
Little Torrington, Torrington		18	0
Llauelltyd, Dolgelly		8	0
Maesycwmmer, Cardiff	1	0	0
Marham, Downham		5	0
Meole Brace, Shrewsbury		6	6
Mildenhall, Soham		9	0
Milnthorpe, Carnforth	3	3	0
Milverton, Taunton	6	1	0
Minchinhampton, Stroud	5	0	0
Morebath, Tiverton	2	2	6
Moreton	1	1	6
Murthly, Perth	10	10	0
Narborough, Leicester		10	0
Newhall Street, Birmingham	1	1	0
New Malden, Kingston-on-Thames	1	0	0
New Quay, Llandyssil	1	0	0
New Street, Barnsley		13	6
Neyland, Pembroke Dock	1	1	0
Norbiton, Kingston-on-Thames		7	6
Northop, Flint	2	8	6
Ockbrook, Derby	5	5	0
Peasenhall, Saxmundham	1	1	0
Penn, Amersham	3	5	0
Penshurst, Tunbridge	1	1	0
Philipstown, Tullamore		5	0
Pirbright, Woking		5	0
Pitcaple, Aberdeen	1	1	0
Pittenween, Anstruther	3	3	0
Porthleven, Helston	1	1	0
Portlaw, Piltown	1	1	0
Portsoy, Banff		5	0
Queensbury, Bradford	1	1	0
Rannoch, Pitlochry	1	1	0
Ratho Station, Linlithgow		5	6
Rockferry, Birkenhead		10	0
Roslea, Clones	1	10	0
Ruspidge, Newnham		7	0
Ruthin, Flint	7	10	0
St. Agnes, Penzance		10	0
Seaford, Lewes	1	0	0
Seaton, Axminster	1	6	10
Sedgwick, Kendal	1	2	0
Sessay, Thirsk	4	7	6
Shanklin, Ryde	1	1	0
Carried forward	£11,875	8	10

ROWLAND HILL MEMORIAL AND BENEVOLENT FUND.

	£	s.	d.
Brought forward	11,875	8	10
Shoeburyness, Southend		10	0
Shortlands, Bromley, Kent	1	1	0
Silsoe, Ampthill	1	1	0
Silverton, Cullompton		7	0
Somerton, Taunton	1	6	6
South Darenth, Dartford		16	6
Sowerby, Thirsk	10	3	0
Sparkford, Bath	2	5	6
Spondon, Derby		10	0
Stanwick, Higham Ferrers		5	0
Stoke-by-Neyland, Colchester		5	0
Sutterton, Boston		13	0
Swallow Nest, Rotherham		5	0
Swinefleet, Goole		5	0
Swinton, Rotherham		5	0
Taverham, Norwich		5	0
Tayinloan, Tarbert	5	0	0
The Wrythe, Sutton, Surrey	2	11	9
Thurlby, Bourne	1	3	3
Timperley, Altrincham	6	19	0
Trefnant, Rhyl	2	2	0
Tulla, Limerick	2	1	6
Uffculme, Cullompton		5	0
Valley, Bangor	2	10	0
Victoria Road, Dukinfield		5	0
Waldringfield, Woodbridge		7	0
Watton, Thetford		17	6
Weeley, Colchester		16	0
Wellington College Station, Wokingham	7	0	0
Carried forward	£11,927	10	4

	£	s.	d.
Brought forward	11,927	10	4
Westbourne, Bournemouth	1	5	6
Westgate-on-Sea, Margate		7	4
West Hoathly, East Grinstead	8	4	6
Wheatley, Oxford		5	0
Whithorn, Newton Stewart	2	13	0
Whyteleaf, Croydon		5	0
Winforton, Hereford	4	16	0
Winscombe, Axbridge	1	1	0
Winster, Derby		10	0
Witham, Hull		7	0
Woodbury Salterton, Exeter		8	0
Yatton Keynell, Chippenham		5	0
Sums under 5s. from other Head, Sub, and Receiving Offices	8	7	0
Donation of the Borough of Hampstead	66	3	0
Donation of the Legal Profession	172	3	2
Donation of the Guarantors of the South Kensington Conversazione	65	10	0
	£12,260	0	10

APPENDIX.

APPENDIX.

CHRISTMAS, 1890.

MR. R. C. TOMBS, the Controller of the London Postal Service, thus graphically describes the operations of the Post-Office in London at the Christmas season in the Jubilee year of the Inland Uniform Penny Postage :—

It may fairly be asserted that one of the minor wonders of the century is the diffusion, through the agency of Her Majesty's Post-Office, of social greetings, cards, and presents at the Christmas season, numbering—with the ordinary correspondence—more, in a few days, than the missives in postal circulation throughout the whole of the first year after the introduction of the marvellous penny postage system, the Jubilee of which has, during the last few months, been so gloriously celebrated. What has been accomplished this year once more demonstrates that as the postal service is one of the most powerful levers in the nation's progress at ordinary times, it can add vast enjoyment to the classes and masses by its quick and wide-spreading circulation on exceptional occasions such as that just over. The busy and impressive scenes witnessed at the last Christmas season in the old General Post-Office building in St. Martin's-le-Grand, and its rapidly developing Parcel Post sister office at Mount Pleasant, at the 200 district, branch and sub-offices dotted over the Metropolis, and in the travelling post-offices running through the length and breadth of the country, were such that they could not well be dismissed, even temporarily, from the minds of those who, in probable course, would have to shape the arrangements for the season of 1890 ; and it may be said that the echoes of the previous Christmas had scarcely died away ere preparations were commenced, and were going on all the year, to put the Department in a position to undertake its great annual task and to overcome all the difficulties inherent to it.

Primarily, attention had to be paid to the question of

ADDITIONAL SPACE

in which to do the work. The Valentine has had its day, the number dealt with in London having dwindled from 4,000,000 in 1876 to 320,000 in 1890. The Christmas card is still as popular as ever, but that, too, may in the near future cease to be a fashionable medium of conveying an expression of kindly feeling. Neither one nor the other, however, affected the question of space so much as the Christmas parcels. It must be expected that the parcel traffic will bring in its train year by year a greater task for the post-office to accomplish, and for this work to be satisfactorily and expeditiously got through, ample room in buildings and yards is a *sine quâ non*. To meet the requirements of the season just over, the following premises were hired for parcel post work. In the Paddington District: temporary depots in the South Wharf Road and at the Horse Repository, 407 Edgware Road; ground for the erection of a temporary shed in Glenthorne Road, Hammersmith; and a room at Upper Westbourne Park Receiving House. In the South-Eastern District: The Rink, Blackheath; School Room, New Road, Camberwell; Ravensbourne Club, Lewisham; and a room at Dulwich Receiving House. In the South-Western District: the London Scottish Rifle Brigade Drill Hall, James Street, Westminster; St. Peter's Hall, Chelsea; Bedford Hall, Clapham; and the Exhibition Buildings, West Brompton. Rooms, &c., were also obtained in other districts.

Forecasts of Business.

A few weeks before Christmas, in a short leader in one of the daily newspapers, it was stated that there was a serious falling off in the Christmas card wholesale trade; but this was speedily contradicted in the same newspaper by a large manufacturer, who stated that the demand for cards was equal to, if not greater than, that in any former year. That statement accorded with information previously supplied by the principal wholesale vendors of Christmas cards in London, and was borne out by the large increase in the number of Christmas and New Year's cards despatched to places abroad, which was a clear indication of what might be expected as regards the inland postings later on.

Extra Staff.

Irrespective of these signs, however, with the previous Christmas season in mind, when the stress of both letter and parcel work was so great as to be quite beyond the utmost efforts of the regular and extra force to deal with it in a satisfactory manner, it was deemed prudent to prepare for the strain this year by the engagement of a much larger supernumerary staff than on the last occasion. The total number of extra officers employed was 4,050, or 410 more than in the preceding year. These, added to the officers regularly employed in or on behalf of the London Postal Service, made up a total of about 20,000. The men required for sorting duties had to be placed in training several weeks beforehand to fit them for the work.

It will readily be conceived what a boon to the casuals temporary employment must have been in the bitter weather which prevailed during the time they received pay from the Post-Office. The supernumerary force got together was of a superior kind to that of former years. At the General Post-Office 450 men were engaged who could give their whole time to the Department, and these men were kept going, during the pressure, from 9 A.M. to 9 P.M. daily. Their assistance between the time of the regular staff going off duty in the morning and its re-attendance in the evening was productive of the best results, and tended in no small degree to the letters being turned over and got rid of with regularity and rapidity.

Mail Services for Abroad.

Of late years public opinion has directed itself to anomalies existing in regard to the charges for postal communication between this country and other parts of the empire, with the result that on the 1st January, 1891, the postage on letters for nearly all the British Colonies was reduced to $2\frac{1}{2}d.$ the half-ounce. It will perhaps be in place therefore for especial prominence to be given in this report to the particulars incidental to the foreign letter mail intercommunications at the Christmas season. The following table will perhaps be interesting as showing the length of time occupied in the conveyance of greetings from the United Kingdom to foreign countries and our Colonies.

APPENDIX.

Name of Country, &c.	Date of Despatch from London.	
	TO ARRIVE ABOUT	
	Christmas Day.	New Year's Day.
New Zealand	30 Oct.	7 Nov.
Queensland, Tasmania	7 Nov.	13 Nov.
New South Wales, South Australia, Victoria, and Western Australia	13 Nov.	21 Nov.
Borneo, Japan, Queensland (*viâ* Italy), Tasmania (*viâ* Italy)	14 Nov.	,,
Penang	21 Nov.	5 Dec.
Hong Kong, Java	,,	28 Nov.
New South Wales (*viâ* Italy), South Australia (*viâ* Italy), Victoria (*viâ* Italy), Western Australia (*viâ* Italy)	,,	,,
Venezuela	26 Nov.	10 Dec.
Gold Coast, Natal, Singapore, Transvaal	28 Nov.	5 Dec.
Argentine Republic	29 Nov.	4 Dec.
Brazil	4 Dec.	,,
Cape Colony, Ceylon, India (Bombay), Sierra Leone	5 Dec.	12 Dec.
Zanzibar	,,	5 Dec.
Bermudas, British Columbia, Cuba, United States (San Francisco)	6 Dec.	13 Dec.
Mexico	10 Dec.	17 Dec.
St. Helena, West Indies	,,	10 Dec.
Aden, Beyrout, Cyprus	12 Dec.	19 Dec.
Canary Islands	,,	23 Dec.
Gambia		12 Dec.
Canada, United States (New York)	13 Dec.	20 Dec.
Egypt	19 Dec.	25 Dec.
Madeira, Malta	,,	26 Dec.
Gibraltar	20 Dec.	27 Dec.

The notices directing the public when to post for the foreign and colonial Christmas and New Year's letter and parcel mails were exhibited and widely distributed early in October, and, judging from comments in the newspapers, these notices, acting as reminders not to forget kith and kin beyond the seas at the festive season, were much appreciated. The notices probably prompted tradesmen not to be behindhand in meeting the demand for cards to be sent abroad, for soon after they were issued the inscription "Christmas Cards for Foreign Mails" appeared in stationers' windows.

POST EARLY NOTICES.

Notwithstanding that large posters were exhibited early in October on the mail vans and carts and at the principal Post-Offices in London warning the public as to foreign posting dates, it was observed that a great many letters and parcels, evidently intended for delivery either at Christmas or the New Year, were posted too late to catch the proper mails, causing no doubt much disappointment both to the senders and to the addressees, and it is desirable that another year notices should be issued week by week, as more striking reminders than a general list issued in October. Very many puddings, pies, and other goodly fare of the kind would reach their destination too late for consumption on Christmas Day. Scarcely had Christmas Day dawned before the "Post Early" notices, then no longer necessary, were removed from the mail vans and carts, and those relating to "Reduction in Postage" on letters for India and the Colonies substituted, thus dismissing Christmas and directing the public mind to the important change about to take place.

Australasian Colonies.

The first outgoing Christmas letter mails were those for the colony of New Zealand. The two fortnightly mails affected took nine per cent. more letters, &c., between them than were despatched by the corresponding mails in the previous year. The increase over two ordinary mails was thirty-five per cent. The next principal mails to be despatched were those for the Australian colonies. Those sent by the all-sea route were not appreciably affected by the Christmas cards, but by the overland route, viâ Brindisi, there was a considerable increase. The postal articles sent by the four weekly Australian mails which took the Christmas and New Year's cards rose by ten per cent. over the previous year's figures, and the increase over an ordinary period was thirty-six per cent. The heaviest mail was carried by the Peninsular and Oriental Company's steamer *Massilia*, which took 622 mail bags, containing about double the usual number of letters, &c.

India and China.

The Christmas and New Year's correspondence caused a very considerable addition to the mails for India, China, and the East. The four mails affected thereby consisted of 2,633 bags as against 2,060 by four ordinary mails, and 2,395 by the four corresponding mails of last year.

Cape of Good Hope.

The letters, &c., sent by the three Cape mails which carried the bulk of the Christmas and New Year's cards were fifty per cent. in excess of the letters, &c., sent by three ordinary mails. One mail alone consisted of 280 bags, whereas 257 was the largest number sent by a single mail at the previous Christmas season.

West Indies.

Nearly 100 additional bags were despatched by the Christmas mails to the West Indies as against about seventy at the previous Christmas season.

Canada and United States.

The splendid steamers of the Cunard, White Star, and Allan lines, which are constantly crossing the waters which divide the old from the new world, carried heavier mails than usual. The posting of Christmas and New Year's cards for the United States and Canada was spread over three weeks, and the mail bags despatched to the United States during that period were 2,739, and to Canada 797. This exceeds the number of bags despatched during three ordinary weeks by 1,164 and 317 respectively. During the week ended the 13th December 1,455 bags in all were sent from London to the North American continent, being an increase of 259 on any previous record. The Christmas mail for

British Columbia

was despatched from London on the 6th December, and took nearly twice as many letters, &c., as an ordinary mail. Since the extension of the Canadian Pacific Railway to Vancouver in June, 1886, the transmission of the mails for

British Columbia has been greatly accelerated. The journey of 6,000 miles by sea and land is accomplished at the rate of 430 miles a day, so that the Christmas cards posted in London on the 6th December would be at their destination four or five days before the Christmas festival.

THE BERMUDAS.

It may be worthy of remark that the Christmas mail for the Bermudas carried 1,000 more letters than in the previous year, the comparatively large increase being no doubt attributable to a regiment of Her Majesty's Guards being stationed there.

MADEIRA, WEST AFRICA, &c.

The Island of Madeira, the celebrated winter resort, received nearly 2,000 additional letters by the Christmas mail, a striking contrast to the very few missives of the kind which were sent to the fever-stricken British Possessions on the West Coast of Africa. About 8,000 more letters than usual were sent to the British Military and Naval Stations—Gibraltar and Malta—in the Mediterranean. As much public attention is now directed to the CONGO FREE STATE, the fact that to this vast region only about 260 letters are sent per mail, and that the Christmas mail took 329, and the New Year's Mail 340, may be interesting. Attention was recently called in the daily newspapers to the entry of the East African Company into the Universal Postal Union, and public curiosity was aroused by the fact being mentioned that new postage stamps had been specially prepared for sale by the Company, to prepay correspondence from East Africa to other parts of the world. The letters from this country are sent to Mombassa and Lamoo. By an ordinary mail the letters, &c., for Mombassa number 240, but by the mail of the 5th December, which fitted into the Christmas delivery, 550 letters, &c., were forwarded, and to Lamoo 120 letters, &c., instead of the usual number of about fifty by an ordinary mail. The inward Christmas mails received from these places contained comparatively few letters, about 130 coming from Mombassa, and twelve only from Lamoo. The Christmas cards despatched this year to the Colonies and foreign countries were rather smaller in size than those sent in previous years.

INWARD MAILS.

The mails from India, China, and the East, which arrived on the 15th December, consisted of fifty-six bags more than usual. The excess letters were 23,000, and the newspapers 12,250, whilst the registered letters rose from 2,800, the normal number, to 4,200. The succeeding mail which arrived four days before Christmas was correspondingly heavy. By the mail from Australia, which arrived on the 23rd December, ninety extra bags, and 40,000 additional letters, &c., came to hand ; about 600 extra mail bags containing 176,000 letters, &c., were received from the United States during the week ended the 27th December. The heaviest mail ever received from that country arrived by the North German ss. *Trave* on the 26th December. It consisted of 718 bags as against 716 received by the same vessel on the same date in the previous year.

CONTINENTAL LETTER MAILS.

During the season 600 extra bags, and nearly 400,000 additional letters, &c., were despatched from this country to the Continent. The inward mails showed an increase of 900 bags, and over 600,000 letters.

FOREIGN PARCEL MAILS.

The five mails for NEW ZEALAND which were more or less affected by Christmas postings took out 3,839 parcels, being an increase of 1,424 over an ordinary period, but only twenty-four over the corresponding season in the previous year. The heaviest mail consisted of 1,106 parcels, or nearly three times as many as the usual number. As regards the parcels for the AUSTRALIAN COLONIES, the results are very satisfactory. The number of mails taken into account was eight, and the total number of parcels despatched by them was 9,532, as against 7,815 at the previous Christmas season, and 5,232 at ordinary times, being an increase of 22 per cent. and 82 per cent. respectively. The heaviest mail of the eight left the Tilbury Docks by the Orient steamer *Cuzco*, on the 20th November, and consisted of fifty-eight boxes containing nearly 2,000 parcels, or over three times the normal number. This is the largest parcel mail to the Australian Colonies yet on record. It must be remarked, however, that it was too late for the Christmas and New Year's deliveries in most cases. The parcel mails for the ARGENTINE REPUBLIC are despatched to Buenos Ayres fortnightly, and are usually contained in two boxes, the average number of parcels being about fifty. The Christmas mail which went out on the 20th November by the Royal Mail steamer *Magdalena* from Southampton, consisted of five boxes containing 107 parcels, and the New Year's mail, which left by the *La Plata* a fortnight later, of five boxes and 105 parcels, or more than double the normal numbers in each case. The parcels for CAPE COLONY, NATAL, the ORANGE FREE STATE, and other places in SOUTH AFRICA usually number 580 per mail. The four mails which were affected by the Christmas and New Year's season took out in the aggregate 6,047 parcels, against 5,041 sent by the corresponding mails in the previous year. This gives an increase of over 1,000 parcels, or 20 per cent. The largest mail of the four—which was also the heaviest mail ever despatched to the Cape—was that made up on the 38th November for conveyance by the Union Company's steamer *Tartar* from Southampton. It consisted of 1,592 parcels. The parcel mails for some of the smaller British Possessions also showed a large increase. For instance, ninety-six parcels were sent to MAURITIUS, thirty-seven to ASCENSION, and sixty-nine to ST. HELENA, for delivery at Christmas, as against forty-two, twenty-nine, and forty-five respectively at an ordinary period. The Christmas mail for ZANZIBAR was twice as heavy as an ordinary mail. The aggregate number of parcels sent to CHINA and the STRAITS SETTLEMENTS by the three fortnightly mails, which included the Christmas and New Year parcels, was 2,852, as against 1,554 by three ordinary mails, and 2,224 by the corresponding mails of the previous year, being an increase of 83 per cent. and 28 per cent. respectively. The mail despatched on the 26th November was the heaviest, the number of parcels being 150 per cent. in excess of the ordinary numbers. The sailors on board Her Majesty's ships on the CHINA STATION were not forgotten, as seventy-five parcels for the fleet were sent out by the mail of the 26th November, as against about thirty at ordinary times. The most important parcel mail despatched from this country is that for INDIA. The Foreign and Colonial Parcel Post system was inaugurated with this post, and it has always retained the first place in point of numbers. The parcels forwarded by the weekly mail to Bombay number 1,261. The Christmas mail which went out on the 26th November by the P. & O. steamer *Carthage* took 2,882 parcels, and the New Year's mail despatched the following week 2,899 parcels. There was a still greater increase as regards the mail despatched on the 10th December, which consisted of no less than 3,361 parcels, being nearly three times the normal number. It was the heaviest mail to India yet on record. Of the parcels included in the mail, 444 contained Christmas cards, 588 Christmas books, and fifty-nine Christmas puddings, &c. All other outward foreign parcel mails were far heavier than usual.

HOMEWARD MAILS.

There was a marked difference in the contents of the outward and inward colonial parcels. Those going out contained a great many Christmas cards, puddings, and other articles incidental to the season; but very few parcels of the kind were imported. Out of 1,142 parcels received from Bombay for the Christmas delivery in this country only twenty-nine contained Christmas cards. The incoming parcels, however, consisted for the most part of miscellaneous articles suitable for Christmas presents.

APPENDIX. 325

INSURED FOREIGN PARCELS.

The system of insurance of parcels for places abroad obtains with India and Aden only. The ordinary parcels despatched to India are more numerous than those received; but in the case of insured parcels the proportions are reversed, the average number of such parcels exported at ordinary times being forty-five, and those imported 177. This is no doubt owing to the fact that insurance of parcels was established in India long before it was commenced in this country, and the system is more familiar there than it is here. The insured parcels sent by the Christmas mails in both directions showed a very considerable increase. The average number despatched by four mails in November and December was 122, or nearly three times as many as usual. The greatest number sent by any one mail was 137. The homeward mail arriving on the 16th December brought 270 insured parcels, and that arriving on the 24th December 359, being an increase of ninety-three and 182 respectively on the ordinary mails. Of the 359 insured parcels received on the 24th December 165 contained jewellery.

Very marked indeed was the increase in the continental parcel traffic. During the Christmas week the parcels despatched from London numbered 20,230, that being an increase of 11,713 on a like number of days at an ordinary period. The inward continental parcels rose from the usual weekly number of 4,970 to 11,800 for the Christmas week. The greatest number despatched was on Sunday the 21st December, when 3,585 parcels were forwarded, as against 1,420 on an average day. On Saturday the 27th instant 2,816 parcels were received from the continent, or 2,000 in excess of an ordinary day's arrival. Of this number 1,800 were imported from Germany *vid* Hamburg.

The excess number of parcels forwarded from London to places abroad during the whole season was not far short of 60,000, and about 28,000 extra parcels were imported.

CONTRABAND FOREIGN PARCELS.

Only thirteen parcels were seized by the Customs Officers for false declaration of contents in order to avoid payment of duty. In former years very many more parcels, the contents of which were declared by the senders as sweetmeats, toys, fancy articles, &c., and found to be contraband goods, such as cigars, cigarettes, tobacco, and silver plate, were confiscated.

This fact speaks well for the vigilance displayed by the Custom House Officers on former occasions, which has no doubt taught smugglers a salutary lesson, and they have now become honest people as evidenced by the fact that 175 more parcels declared to contain tobacco, &c., were received on this Christmas than at the previous season. The parcels detained under the Merchandise Marks Act numbered only eleven, as against fifty at the preceding Christmas.

INLAND LETTER SERVICES.

In the week preceding the Christmas season the fog, frost, and snow gave rise to the gloomiest apprehensions. The mail trains arrived from one to three hours behind time, and the services throughout London were dislocated in consequence. The drivers of the mail vans and carts were in a benumbed condition. The horses were jaded and worn out, owing to the slippery state of the streets, and to the great strain caused by the heavy fall of snow. Altogether it was difficult to look forward to the Christmas week with any degree of equanimity. The usual difficulties of the season were intensified from the fact that Monday the 22nd December, when it was expected there would be considerable activity in the posting, was the blackest day of all the year, and private, and indeed business, posting was only carried on where absolutely unavoidable. Truly that day will be marked in Post-Office annals as "darkest Monday."

The fog, the frost, and the snow combined had the effect of putting all the mail-van arrangements out of gear. The horses, not recovered from the fatigue of the previous week, were not up to the mark to encounter the Christmas heavy work, and the contractors were at their wits' ends. So slippery were the roads that in the hilly districts of Highgate and Hampstead the postmen had to meet the carts and carry the bags to the sub-district sorting-office on their backs. The officers were indeed tried by the fog. Indeed one poor fellow suffering from bronchitis was so much affected by it that, after being seen by the medical officer, he was obliged to be taken home in a cab. The night mail trains from the several London termini were despatched very late, some of them starting nearly two hours behind the proper time.

Brighter Outlook and Heavy Mailing.

Matters considerably brightened on Tuesday morning, the 23rd December, when the fog lifted; the thoroughfares became passable, and by about three o'clock in the day something like a restoration of ordinary working was achieved. The Christmas correspondence now poured into the chief office in St. Martin's-le-Grand, there seeming no limit to the postings, and from that time it was a continuous struggle for the mastery. The work went on therefrom by night and day without intermission, and it was not until seven o'clock in the morning of Christmas Day that the primary sorting of the letters, &c., was finished.

"Clear-up" at St. Martin's.

The large accumulation of letters which had taken place in the Railway Division Rooms began to be overcome at about eight o'clock, and soon after that time some of the supernumeraries, who had been on for a very lengthened spell, were permitted to leave. A general clear-up was made at about 9 A.M., when the bulk of the staff was allowed to go home. The despatching officers had, however, to stop till noon to make up the bags for despatch by the night mails. The letters, although not more numerous than last year, were received equally late, but on the whole very satisfactory despatches were effected. The letters, which were included in the bags for the night mails, bore no earlier date of provincial posting than the 24th December. It was noticeable that about nine out of every ten letters in circulation on the 24th December contained Christmas cards. The cards on the whole were considered to be rather smaller in size than in previous years.

At the General Post-Office the brunt of the battle has always to be encountered, as, being the large forwarding office of the world, it becomes, at times, congested with its "through" work. This year was no exception to the rule; but it can safely be said that the circulation branches were never more than about six hours behind the work, and that is borne out by the fact of the absence of complaints of delay. Vast as the preparations have been, and large as was the extra force employed throughout London, not a single penny was expended unnecessarily. In order to keep important letters from bankers, merchants, &c., unmixed with the mass of Christmas correspondence, and thus ensure their due despatch, arrangements were made for such letters to be specially collected or handed in over the counter at the General Post-Office or at Lombard Street Branch Office. Altogether 80,000 important letters were thus saved the risk of delay, and satisfaction was given to City bankers and merchants.

This year's record of numbers does not exceed that of last year, and it may be assumed, therefore, that the excess cards, letters, circulars, &c., dealt with in London during the season amounted to about 50,000,000,—that is about treble the normal numbers for one week, or nearly four letters at Christmas for one at an ordinary period. That through the channel of the General Post-Office in St. Martin's-le-Grand alone close upon 25,000,000 more letters than usual passed during the Christmas week, shows the vast capabilities of Post-Office head-quarters. Heavy as the correspondence was, no difficulty was experienced in rapidly transmitting it from one point of London to another, or from railway station to station, as about 1,000 vehicles and drivers, 1,500 horses, and 300 hand-carts were available for the purpose.

The Electric Light,

only recently installed at the General Post-Office, was used on the first and second floors, with excellent results, the atmosphere in the sorting-offices having been much purer than on previous occasions, and the large staff massed in the several offices were enabled to work in far greater comfort than heretofore. The superintending officers and men were alike loud in its praises. The men certainly performed their duty far better this year than they have ever done before, and that is attributed to the improved atmosphere. There was an absence of that languor which has been so perceptible amongst the officers at the close of the duty in previous years. The duty was completed an hour earlier than it would have been if the men had been compelled to work again in a vitiated air. The benefit of the electric light was especially felt on the outside platforms and in the yards at the General Post-Office where the mail vans are loaded and unloaded. The brilliant light shed by the large arc lamps admitted of the labelling of the bags being easily read. It also materially assisted the work of marshalling vans and in preventing congestion of traffic. As a consequence the mails were placed in and taken out of the vans—even at the busiest times—without confusion, and with great celerity.

The letter duties in all the main line

TRAVELLING POST-OFFICES,

which are affiliated to the London Postal Service, were successfully completed throughout the recent Christmas season. On Christmas Eve the quantity of season work sent into the respective mails was enormous, but, aided by the special arrangements in force, under which direct bags had been established between all points where the amount of correspondence was sufficient to justify such a step, it was found possible to complete each duty. In the up night mails the failures at junctions, and the additional time for sortation which was secured through the slow running of the trains, admitted of the letters being all sorted and duly disposed of. The mails from the General Post-Office were forwarded to the trains with great promptitude. This was specially so as regards the night mail despatches from Euston. On Christmas Eve the last bag for the special mail was actually in the train half a minute before the appointed time of departure. Reference must be made to the apparatus for despatching and receiving letter bags from the mail trains when in motion, as this is tried to its utmost capacity at the Christmas season. The number of exchanges of mails daily from the station standards into the carriage nets is 516, and from the carriages to the stationary nets it is 530. The total number of mail bags included in these exchanges is about 2,000. On an average about 110,000 letters, &c., a day are exchanged by the apparatus at a normal period, of which about 85,000 or nearly four-fifths are sorted in the Travelling Post-Offices, the remainder being sent direct in bags from one town to another through the Travelling Post-Offices unopened. At the Christmas season the number of letters, &c., exchanged by the apparatus was increased by about 60 per cent.

INLAND PARCEL DUTY.

From the busy duties at the General Post-Office and District Letter Offices thoughts had to be turned from time to time towards the parcel offices. It might be supposed that, from the bold display of "post early" notices, people would take care to post their parcels sufficiently early to admit of delivery at latest on the morning of Christmas Day, but they have yet to become alive to the fact that bulky parcels cannot be handled so easily and with such rapidity as letters; and while such is the case it is out of the question for them to expect that the one should be dealt with in as little time as the other at the Christmas season. It is evident that the public now place great confidence in the parcel arrangements of the Post-Office, for although there is free-trade in parcel-carrying, yet the increase in the parcel traffic of the Christmas season shows nearly as great an expansion as the letter service.

The troubles caused by the

ADVERSE ELEMENTS

to the letter service affected the parcel service even in a more marked degree.

The fog in the East End was so dense that the mail cart drivers could not see their horses' heads. And the guard who accompanied the Indian and Australian parcel mails to the docks had the utmost difficulty in finding the ship. The mail van arrangements were entirely upset by the late arrival of trains, the vehicles being kept waiting at stations for hours, and having in many cases to be driven off to perform other services. The same thing happened with the force. Men were up all night at the stations with little to do, and when they had gone home to rest and the trains arrived, the platforms were crowded with baskets for a time with scarcely any one to touch them, and with few vans to carry them away. Then a jaded force had quickly to be got together again. Reserve vans had been placed at each station, but even these were drawn away.

At the Mount Pleasant Parcel Office, which is the chief depôt in London, from the 23rd December was

A Most Remarkable Scene.

The very large premises and the temporary sheds erected for the occasion were literally choked with parcels of all shapes and sizes. The baskets, bag protectors, barrels, and other receptacles were opened as rapidly as possible, but, notwithstanding this, there was scarcely room to move in any part of the building. The vans were unloaded immediately they arrived, so that there was no detention of them, and consequently no dislocation of the vehicular service. Inside the building the receptacles were opened and the parcels carefully packed in heaps against the walls, in order to confine the bulk within the narrowest possible limits. At 5 P.M. on the 24th December, so numerous were the parcels, that it seemed as though it would be a matter of impossibility to clear the office for many days. As parcels disappeared others came in. Never before had so many parcels under 11 lbs. in weight been aggregated in one depôt.

On Christmas morning it was evident that the

Vast Accumulation of Parcels

could not be cleared off by the tired and jaded men who had been on duty for about twenty-four hours, and there was nothing for it but to disperse the staff, which was done at noon. When the order was given for all the men to break off and to resume their labours at midnight there was a cheer, showing that the men were animated with British pluck, and would be ready and willing to recommence the struggle after a little rest. By noon on the 26th December (Boxing Day) the accumulation was disposed of, but there were heavy and late arrivals from the provinces on that morning, and on the following morning also.

The business transacted at

The Public Counters

was far in excess of any previous year. Taking the three days immediately preceding Christmas Day the number of transactions, excluding the sale of stamps, was 18 per cent. more than last year, and about 66 per cent. more than in ordinary. A similar comparison shows an increase of 60 per cent. over the usual sale of stamps. But even this large increase in transactions and sales does not fully indicate the extra work involved. The stamp sales were largely made up of very small purchases, and these involve as much work individually as large ones. Thousands of demands were made for single stamps, and the number of inquiries and requests to weigh letters was much higher proportionately than at ordinary times. At many offices on the busiest days the parcels handed in were seven or eight times, and postal orders and registered letters from four to five times more numerous than usual. There was a constant stream of people at the counters from early morning till late at night, and many offices were crowded to the doors for hours together. At many of the more important of these offices the business is conducted by a female staff, which coped with the extra work in a most satisfactory and creditable manner.

Posting of Parcels.

At the chief office on the 23rd December, 6,000 parcels were handed in over the counter, the ordinary daily number being about 2,500. The largest number handed in on any one day last year was 4,600.

At the Putney Branch Post-Office the average day's posting of parcels is about 100. On the 23rd December this number rose to 800. At the High Street, Hampstead Branch Office, the number of parcels posted on the same date were twelve times as many as on an ordinary day.

A considerable increase took place even in

Telegraph Business.

There were 27,000 more messages handed in, and 29,000 more sent out for delivery from the telegraph offices in London than ordinary. Fortunately this very important branch of the service was not affected by adverse elements, and the other services, crippled as they were, derived much assistance from its powerful agency.

Death of a Superintendent.

Sad to relate, Mr. G. W. Martin, who for the many years the Christmas card has been in vogue, ever took a prominent part as assistant superintendent, or superintendent, in the annual struggle at the Chief Office, died at 6 p.m. on Christmas Eve, usually his busiest hour in the whole year.

Notwithstanding the slippery state of the roads, yards, slopes, &c., very few men met with

Accidents.

At midnight, when the work was at its height in St. Martin's-le-Grand, there was an accident to one of the three lifts which are used in carrying the bags and correspondence from floor to floor. A man carrying bags dropped a small bundle on one of the trays of the lift, and this bundle became firmly jammed into the ironwork, the effect being that one of the chains snapped. Fortunately no one was injured, but the loss of the use of the lift at such a time was seriously felt.

The first unpleasant incident of the Christmas period was the loss of four insured parcels from a box forming part of a homeward Indian parcel mail. The robbery was discovered immediately the mail was opened and occasioned much anxiety, which however was allayed by a letter received from the Commander who was in charge of the mail steamer, from which it transpired that the theft was found out on board, and is said to have been committed by the Arabs, who were discharging cargo day and night from the hold when the ship was aground in the Suez Canal.

Another incident of the season was that the Finsbury Park Branch Office was in imminent danger of being burnt down on the morning of the 24th instant. The adjoining shop took fire and was soon burnt out. It was feared that the Branch Office would suffer the same fate, but happily this was averted by the efforts of the Fire Brigade.

On the morning of Boxing Day at the Mount Pleasant Refreshment Room the bread supply was exhausted, and the neighbourhood was scoured to find a baker's shop open in order to get bread for breakfast. After a long search a baker was discovered in the act of drawing his bread from the oven, and his whole stock was secured.

The work of the Post-Office was splendidly accomplished throughout the season of pressure by

The Willing Efforts of the Whole Staff,

notwithstanding that the men had to battle not only with Christmas cards and parcels, but with adverse elements. Great as was the strain upon the staff dealing with letters, it was still greater and more trying as regards the men engaged upon parcel work, as the latter is performed under more adverse circumstances. The men going off duty on the 24th December could not be allowed their previously allotted twelve hours' rest, and had to resume duty at 7 P.M.

Three of these persons, mere lads, who lived at long distances from the Office, were found to have improvised beds for themselves in the booths erected for refreshment purposes. They had no soft couches, but had made cribs of large parcel-baskets, which they had filled with straw from the floor, and mail-bags had to serve as sheets, blankets, and counterpanes. Their Controller was sorry that his entrance deprived them for a few minutes of the sleep which they so much needed and had so well earned.

THE OUTPOST DUTY

was probably the most unpleasant, viz., that performed by officers who were at the railway stations throughout the night attending to the arrivals and despatches. The platform of a large railway station is not the most pleasant place in the world to spend a night on, and they always appear to be colder places than are to be found anywhere else.

The Postmasters, upon whom devolve the responsibility of carrying on the Post-Office administration in the districts of London, were most energetic, from senior to junior, in leading their forces on to meet the vast influx of work. Their frequent telegrams were indicative of the business being carried on with spirit throughout, and the Department is much indebted to them for their great exertions, and for their methodical organization. The staff officers at Head-Quarters greatly distinguished themselves, and each one has added another to the many obligations already received by the Department at their hands. The Controller can give them no better guerdon than a good word, but that good word he heartily accords to all, from the highest to the lowest, in the London postal service. In order that an idea may be gained of what took place

AWAY FROM HEAD QUARTERS,

a report made by the Postmaster who presides over the district embracing Paddington, Notting Hill, Kensington, Hammersmith and adjoining suburbs is here given :—

"It is safe to say that there never was a Christmas season when the postal service was thrown into such disorganization by the weather as it has been this year. Trains were delayed by the fogs, and carts by the snow. The regular flow of work was prevented all through the week. The staff thus had to do their work under great disadvantages, and the outdoor work was rendered exceptionally fatiguing. In spite of all hindrances, however, the pressure was met satisfactorily in all branches of the duty, especially in the letter department. The collections and deliveries of letters went on promptly and without interruption. There was not the slightest hitch or accumulation of work from the beginning of the pressure, on Sunday the 21st December, to the close on Christmas morning. The parcel duty was less satisfactory, as it is bound to be at all times of pressure. The one great difficulty is its bulk, which causes a block to be inevitable, unless there are great facilities for storing the baskets, and an unstinted van service. The temporary depôt in Edgware Road, used for collecting purposes, was not pressed on Monday the 22nd December, as the fog and snow prevented local posting. On the 23rd, and for a great part of the 24th December, the collections into that depot were enormous, and the work was done at high pressure. From the afternoon of the 24th to that of the 25th—Christmas Day—it rendered invaluable help in despatching duties to the Paddington Station depôt. The South Wharf Road temporary depôt dealt satisfactorily with the town and some of the suburban deliveries. The Hammersmith "booth" for parcel duty was threatened with failure, as the weather was so inclement, and the Gas Company could not lay on the gas (which was relied upon for both light and warmth), because the pipes could not be interfered with during the frost. The Office of Works, however, promptly supplied oil lamps and coal stoves, with which the staff made shift.

"It was at the Paddington Station depôt where most of the difficulty of the season pressure lay. All went well till the 24th, when the little depôt was overwhelmed with railway and inter-depôt work. The state of affairs would have been most embarrassing if baskets had not been stacked on the vacant site at Francis Street. The small triangular space in front of the depôt was piled up to its fullest extent with hundreds of baskets which there was no possibility of arranging suitably. Under these trying circumstances it redounds to the credit of the inspector and his staff that early on the morning of Christmas Day the depôt was absolutely clear—though abundance of work came in afterwards from Mount Pleasant and other districts, which necessitated the staff remaining on duty till 1 P.M., and resuming work at 11 P.M. on Christmas Day.

"All the casuals have worked admirably, the policemen having again given valuable help; and the commissionaires have behaved satisfactorily. In telegraph work the pressure was exceptionally great this Christmas."

www.ingramcontent.com/pod-product-compliance
Lightning Source LLC
Chambersburg PA
CBHW031419230426
43668CB00007B/360